LIPPINCOTT

EDUCATIONAL SERIES

EDITED BY

MARTIN G. BRUMBAUGH, Ph.D., LL.D.

PROFESSOR OF PEDAGOGY, UNIVERSITY OF PENNSYLVANIA, AND EX-COMMISSIONER
OF EDUCATION FOR PUERTO RICO

AMS PRESS
NEW YORK

LIPPINCOTT EDUCATIONAL SERIES

THE

Educational Theory

OF

IMMANUEL KANT

Translated and Edited

WITH AN INTRODUCTION

By

EDWARD FRANKLIN BUCHNER, Ph.D. (Yale)

Professor of Philosophy and Education in the University of Alabama

PHILADELPHIA

J. B. LIPPINCOTT COMPANY

1904

Reprinted from the edition of 1904, Philadelphia

First AMS edition published 1971
Manufactured in the United States of America

International Standard Book Number:0-404-03628-7

Library of Congress Number:71-137251

AMS PRESS INC.
NEW YORK,N.Y. 10003

TRANSLATOR'S PREFACE

KANT continues to be such an important figure in both the educational and the cultural tendencies of the present day that it is not sufficient for one to know the scant outlines of some of his views on educational problems, as they may be given place in the usual summaries in the manuals on the history of education. These views should be set forth in their entirety, which has not been done hitherto in English. Again, the renewed interest in Kant as a great pedagogical *Klassiker*, displayed in the recent decades by the appearance of several editions of his *Ueber Pädagogik* in Germany and of a translation of it in France, and the increasing study of educational history by direct appeal to the views of those who have moulded that history, offer ample justification for the appearance of the present translation. And, finally, the contributions which philosophy and philosophers have made to the systematic developments of pedagogy should be given a larger exploitation than has been done hitherto by the students of educational foundations.

The translation on which the present volume is based was made a decade ago as a portion of larger historical studies, and without any thought of having it get beyond the form of manuscript. In the course of time it repeatedly gave service to students in the fields of the history of the Kantian philosophy and of modern educational theory. It is hoped that the scope of this

double service may now be enlarged by the additions
and interpretations which have brought the volume to
its present form.

It has not been an easy task to put Kant's *Ueber Pädagogik* into smooth, readable English.   Many of the
sentences in the original are imperfect, being mere notes,
brief reminders to a lecturer, as it were.   Some of the
free renderings adopted were made necessary by reason
of the general character of the material.   The reader
can also be profited if he regards many of the *Notes* as
literal " texts," which can be made to yield their ripest
meanings by reflecting upon them as such.

To the translation of *Ueber Pädagogik* I have added,
in the foot-notes and the appended Selections,—all the
translations being newly made,—passages from Kant's
other technical and popular writings.   By this means I
have endeavored to bring together all of the material
Kant has to offer on the general theme of education.
From these it will be seen that, after the awakening of
his educational interest, his views continued to be very
much in accord with the general scheme laid down in
the lectures.

Most of the editions (not including Rink's) of the
Ueber Pädagogik have been consulted in the preparation of the present edition, most assistance, probably, being
derived from Dr. Vogt's.   His editorial novelty of num-
bering the Sections gives a good articulation to the contents, and is therefore retained in the present translation.
The marginations are additions of the present editor.
The Selections have been taken uniformly, except in the
few instances otherwise indicated, from Hartenstein's

Immanuel Kant's Sämmtliche Werke, eight volumes, Leipzig, 1867–1868. The preparation of this volume had been completed before Miss Churton's translation in *Kant on Education* came to my hand.

It is a great pleasure to acknowledge the aid of my wife, whose interest and skill have been of special service in the revision of the translations. I am also indebted to my friends and former colleagues, Professor George M. Duncan, of Yale University, for the use of his list of the English translations of Kant's writings, which he has brought down to date for this volume, and President G. Stanley Hall, of Clark University, for access to special monographs in his private library.

EDWARD FRANKLIN BUCHNER.

TUSCALOOSA, ALABAMA, October 16, 1903.

EDITOR'S PREFACE

IMMANUEL KANT has profoundly influenced the modern world. His system of thought has been discipline and inspiration to the culture-aspiring minds of the last century. His influence will continue. It is not generally known that he applied his philosophical speculations to the problems of public education. That he should do so is not strange. He recognized that education is the source of progress among individuals and nations. That he should feel it incumbent to aid concretely and specifically the great work of education is in harmony with his life activities and his philosophic theory.

Two types of pedagogical literature are to be deplored : those produced by enthusiasts who lack insight, and those produced by theorists who lack sympathy or touch with actual educational agencies. The former are usually in poor taste and lack due proportion ; they make much ado about the "nothings" of education and fail to see the broad fundamental principles that condition and control true pedagogic progress. The latter are usually so far removed from the experience of teachers and so attenuated in analysis as to lose all vitalizing guidance. Clearly we have constant need of treatises with a basis in philosophic insight and with a recognition of the fundamentals in the simple phases of practical experience.

Such a contribution Kant here makes. These *Lecture-Notes* are of great practical value because they consistently unfold in outline a rational pedagogical system. The vital matter is not wholly what system they unfold, but rather that they do unfold a system. The discerning student will be able to supply such details on the concrete side as experience affords, and such as Kant no doubt supplied in his expositions before his class.

In a sense it is to be regretted that the fuller treatment by the masterful thinker is not available. In another sense this is matter for congratulation. It leaves the student free to think, and it compels analysis and verification. A mastery of the treatise will lead to original inquiry and amplification. Such a mastery will eventuate in the true formulation of a system of educational theory in which the essential guidance is supplied and the detailed verification is left to the student. Such a study will necessarily carry conviction and foster thought.

The educational doctrines of Hegel and of Herbart have been fairly well reported to American educators. The educational doctrines of Immanuel Kant are practically unknown to the great teaching body of the United States. It is unfortunate that one should become acquainted with only a part of the German theory of education, and as a result attach himself as disciple to this or that leader, assuming his name and accepting his doctrines as if the whole of educational wisdom were found in the works of one man. It is still more unfortunate for American teachers to follow blindly in detail any foreign system of education. The fundamental quality of the

American school system, especially in its organization and administrative aspects, is unique. A study of any system of educational thought produces its best results by stimulating inquiry and by providing a systematic theoretic outline into which experience and reflection may cast themselves and by which old and accepted theories may mould themselves into new forms. In this plan of study current activities may be put to rational tests. It is one thing to be a blind and adoring follower; it is quite another thing to have an insight broad enough to promote rational inquiry and to arrive at true conclusions. A study such as this text affords is of the most specific value in furthering the loftiest ideals of professional inquiry.

We have no national system of education, nor have we as yet a national theory of education. Our varied practices, due to local and State control, have given us widely divergent views of educational theory. We are a great national laboratory, in which, with no uniform preparatory training, we have thousands of pedagogic experimenters, evolving bit by bit educational ideas of varying values.

If it were possible to train our teachers in fundamental educational law, this diversified study, in its many-sided aspects, would eventuate in a system of educational doctrine indigenous to our own social and civic life; whence arises the need of wider agitation for thorough professional study for our teachers. In achieving such a result it is unquestionably wise to know all that has been thought by great minds and all that has been done by great teachers in the past. To

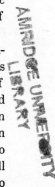

master any educational system is to give the student power to master his own experience and to organize it into law and set it forth in principles.

If, as Kant conceives, education signifies training up the mind to an ideal, the first problem of the teacher is to determine this ideal, and, having once conceived clearly what it is, present this conception in clear language. Important as this is as a primary condition of all study of educational doctrine, it is usually not seriously attempted. All that is frequently attempted is to seek a definition of this ideal or end in some treatise and to memorize it for examination purposes. It might be well to consider to what extent such a group of memorized words can condition practice. What teacher ever consciously and deliberately set to work to realize in each pupil such an ideal? Is it not true that most are content to follow the day's routine without ever dreaming unto what all this activity tends? Will it not mightily modify the burden of routine if into daily duties a live ideal is made to fit? The teleologic aspects of educational theory are as yet " more honored in the breach than the observance," if, indeed, they are not wholly overlooked.

To fix upon some end, to determine some purpose, and then to harmonize all practices therewith are elements of primary significance. Such an end will by common consent be conceived as an ethical end, and no other is worthy of serious thought or attention from teachers. The end must be expressed in terms of conduct,—in altruistic service to mankind and in abiding faith in the divine order at work in the universe.

Dogmatic teaching and pedantry abound in books for teachers. Attempts to create a scientific spirit are not infrequently rendered abortive by the complacent arrogance of superficial training in ready-made methods. The literature that creates unrest by arousing inquiry is all too rare. It is believed that this volume will do much to quicken an interest in fundamental educational principles. Dr. Buchner has furnished a carefully rendered text and wisely guarded guidance. He has succeeded in making the author's own views transparent to English readers, and in supplying only such addenda as a discriminating and devoted teacher finds necessary to connect at every essential point the thought of the author with the experience and insight of the teacher.

M. G. B.

PHILADELPHIA, December 22, 1903.

CONTENTS

I

II

III

SELECTIONS ON EDUCATION FROM KANT'S OTHER WRITINGS.

IV

INTRODUCTION

THE CHRONOLOGY OF KANT'S LIFE AND IMPORTANT WRITINGS

FROM 1724 to 1804 there was lived in Königsberg, Prussia, the northern frontier post of German civilization, one of the few lives really important for *Kant's Life* the culture of modern times. Every person *and Writings.* who is struggling in individual efforts to get a substantial view of the world and of human life, and, especially, every teacher who is seeking the *rationale* of his art and ideals, should know something of the unique and forceful life lived and wrought by Immanuel Kant. That life is devoid of those events which usually make biography so interesting. No life could be more simple than his; yet it had a charm which has held the attention of the century intervening, and a charm which still captivates us. His life was, indeed, unique, being expressed in four great interests,—namely, those of *a university teacher, an author, a philosopher,* and *a man with a character.* To use a striking modern phrase, he made a brilliant "success" in each of these points.[1]

---

[1] It would go too far beyond our present needs to prepare anew a memoir of this life. The chronology will be adequate for immediate reference. The reader will find the following books to con-

11

1724. April 22. Birth of Immanuel Kant at Königsberg. His parents were poor but pious people.

1732. Kant enters the *Collegium Friedericianum.*

1737. Death of Kant's mother.

1740. Kant completes the course at the school and enters the university in his native city. The institution was rather belated in its equipment and teaching.

1746. Death of Kant's father. Kant's first book : *Thoughts on the True Valuation of Living Forces.*

1746–1755. The uncertain nine years during which Kant served as private tutor in a few families of culture, not far distant from his native city.

1755. Kant admitted to the degree of Doctor of Philosophy. Kant qualifies as a Docent in mathematics, physics, and philosophy at the university in Königsberg, presenting his *New Exposition of the First Principles of Metaphysical Knowledge,* and giving his first lectures during the winter semester of 1755–56.

It is interesting to note the academic regularity and the wide scope of Kant's professional activity. His lectures covered, as was not altogether uncommon in the work of some members of the philosophical faculties of one and two centuries ago, the entire range of the theoretical sciences of his time, excluding the historical sciences. The following data regarding his lectures, not including his private and critical seminaries and exercises, have been compiled from original sources by

---

tain more or less full and clear accounts of his life and works : Stuckenburg, *Life of Immanuel Kant,* London, 1882. Wallace, *Kant,* Blackwood's Philosophical Classics, Edinburgh, 1886. Paulsen, *Immanuel Kant, His Life and Doctrine.* Translated by J. E. Creighton and A. Lefevre, Scribner's. New York, 1902.

Dr. E. Arnoldt.[1]   Although somewhat incomplete, they set forth Kant's scholastic right to entertain an educational theory.   This table gives the number of times he lectured on the subjects named, giving the first and the last semesters respectively.   (The double years mean winter semesters, the single years summer semesters.)

Logic, between 1755–56 and 1796, 54 times.
Theoretical Physics, between 1755–56 and 1787–88, 20 times.
Mathematics, between 1755–56 and 1763, 16 times.
Metaphysics, between 1756 and 1795–96, 49 times.
Physical Geography, between 1756 and 1796, 46 times.
Moral Philosophy, between 1756–57 and 1788–89, 28 times.
Mechanical Sciences, between 1759–60 and 1761, 2 times.
Natural Right, between 1767 and 1788, 12 times.
Encyclopædia of Philosophy, between 1767–68 and 1787, 11 times.
Mineralogy, 1770–71.
Anthropology, between 1772–73 and 1795–96, 24 times.
Pedagogy, between 1776–77 and 1786–87, 4 times.
Natural Theology, 1785–86.

1755. *A General Natural History and Theory of the Heavens.*
It contained the first presentation of the "nebular hypothesis," restated independently many years later by Laplace, by whose name it is usually known.   Kant's book remained practically unknown through the failure of its publisher.

1762. Rousseau's *Émile* appeared, which Kant read, and by which he was greatly influenced.

1764. *Observations on the Feeling of the Beautiful and the Sublime.*
Kant declined the suggested appointment to the professorship of poetry.

---

[1] *Kritische Exkurse im Gebiet der Kantforschung,* 1894.

1766. *Dreams of a Spirit-seer explained by the Dreams of Metaphysics.* Kant appointed assistant librarian in the royal palace.

1770. Kant promoted to the professorship of logic and metaphysics. His Latin dissertation was *On the Forms and Principles of the Sensuous and the Intellectual Worlds.*

1776. *On the Philanthropinum at Dessau.*

1781. *Critique of Pure Reason.*

1783. *Prolegomena to every Future Metaphysics,* etc.

1784. *Idea of a Universal History from a Cosmopolitan Point of View.*

1785. *Fundamental Principles of the Metaphysics of Morals.*

1786. *The Probable Beginnings of Human History.*
Metaphysical Foundations of the Natural Sciences.

1788. *Critique of Practical Reason.*

1790. *Critique of Judgment.*

1792. *On Radical Evil.*

1793. *Religion within the Limits of Mere Reason.*

1796. Kant ceased to lecture because of old age.

1797. *The Metaphysics of Ethics,* Pt. I.   *The Doctrine of Right,* Pt. II.   *The Doctrine of Virtue.*
On a Supposed Right to Lie from Humanitarian Motives.

1798. *Anthropology with Reference to Pragmatic Ends.*

1800. *Logic* (edited by Jäsche).

1802. *Physical Geography* (edited by Rink).

1803. *On Pedagogy* (edited by Rink).

1804. February 12.   The death of Kant in Königsberg.

HISTORY OF THE "LECTURE-NOTES ON PEDAGOGY"

THE educational theory entertained by Kant, considered from one point of view, is rather an indefinite quantity. It stands as the sum-total of his labors in the interest of science and of human destiny. The dependence of man upon the formative influences of experience constituted for Kant the chief reason for giving attention to the structure of that experience. It was thus that the careful elaboration of his theoretical views on the nature of science, philosophy, morality, and art represents the great overflow of his interest in education into the basic channels of human speculation. The author of the Critical Philosophy herein becomes one of the few great men of history who have affirmed that there is a philosophical basis to a true pedagogy.

The educational theory vindicated by Kant's systematic and technical scientific efforts represents the larger setting of his views on education. These, fortunately, received their definite expression in the lectures on pedagogy which he gave to the university students in Königsberg during four semesters between the winters of 1776–1777 and 1786–1787, according to the dates established by the researches of Dr. Arnoldt. The *external* origin of these lectures is to be found in an old rule at the university, which required one of the professors of

15

the philosophical faculty to give lectures *publice* on pedagogy, two hours a week, to the students.[1] This requirement was met by Kant four different times. The arrangement of rotation was given up when Herbart, as Kant's successor to the chair of philosophy, gave all the lectures on pedagogy himself.

Kant began to lecture on pedagogy to thirty auditors on October 23, 1776, and continued until March 19, 1777. The title of his course was *Pädagogik über Basedow's Methodenbuch.*[2] After 1780 he used a book by his former colleague, Dr. F. S. Bock, *Lehrbuch der Erziehungskunst.* We know practically little or nothing in detail about the actual lectures given on the general theme of pedagogy, beyond the fact that they were repeated three times, and beyond the contents of the literary remains translated below under the title *Lecture-Notes on Pedagogy.* Kant's method of lecturing was to use an acceptable text-book, and to expand it, without necessarily accepting its principles, by the aid of his own notes inserted on the margins and between the lines. He was also in the habit of jotting down much of his lecture material on loose pieces of paper, which served him in his lectures. These "sketches," as Hartenstein calls them, were published at Easter, 1803, —like his treatise on *Logic,*—because of the desire

The Origin of Ueber Päda- gogik.

---

[1] It is not improbable that the government order establishing this rule had its constraining example in the pedagogical seminary which Gesner instituted at Göttingen (about 1735 ff.).

[2] Arnoldt, *Ibid.*, pp. 572, 573.

of some of his later pupils, who were very anxious that none of Kant's teachings should be lost. This loose pedagogical material was given to Theodor Rink,[1] who alone seems responsible in his editing for the arrangement given to the notes, which were published under the title *Immanuel Kant, Ueber Pädagogik*. Rink's arrangement cannot be looked upon as perfect, nor can it be held that it represents the order in which Kant gave his lectures. At the same time, Kant cannot be excused from his share of the responsibility for the logical imperfections in his *Notes*. It can well be believed, however, that the attention given by the more recent editors to these *Notes* has resulted in giving them as complete an order as they really contain.[2]

It has been a question as to when Kant put his hand last to these *Notes* and gave them their "finishing touch," if they can be said to possess one. In his preface, Rink remarks that the book would be "more interesting" and "more exhaustive" if Kant's time for lecturing on the subject had not been as limited as it actually was, and if he had only found opportunity to develop the

Relation of the Lecture-Notes to his Mental Development.

---

[1] Rink was a university student at Königsberg from 1786 to 1789. In 1792–93 he was frequently a guest at Kant's table. He was again in Königsberg, holding the university posts of *privat-docent* and extraordinary professor of philosophy and theology from 1795 to 1801. From his earliest residence there he continued a close student of Kant's philosophy. From 1801 to 1811 he was a preacher in Danzig, where he died.

[2] See the separate editions mentioned in the literature at the end of the Introduction, p. 96.

subject of education.[1] The repeated divisions of educational activity, which were left standing without any
marked attempt at solidifying them into one broad,
sweeping view of education with which they were to be
coördinated, may, perhaps, be taken as an indication
that Kant took a new departure as he approached the
problem of education at successive times. Willmann
suggests that he did not revise his notes on pedagogy at
any time after the middle of the eighties, which would
be after the last course of lectures on pedagogy given by
him.[2] The chief ground on which this suggestion rests
is the fact that not one of the many divisions of the factors in education mentions the table of the twelve categories, first published in 1781, which Kant was in the
habit of applying to all sorts of scientific material.

On the other hand, there seems to be several suggestions within these *Notes* tending to show that Kant did
not neglect this product of his earlier academic interests.
His own foot-note—note 2, Section 69 (p. 173)—refers
to works dated 1801 and 1802. His theory of the mental faculties, so far as contained in these *Notes*, is the
psychology which grew apace in his later years rather
than that fully accredited in the seventies and the
early eighties. And, finally, the towering conception of
morality on which he makes education rest, both theoretically and practically, is the morality which he expounded late rather than early in the critical stage of

---

[1] This preface is reprinted in Hartenstein's edition of *Ueber
Pädagogik*, viii. pp. 455, 456.

[2] *Immanuel Kant, Ueber Pädagogik*, p. 118, note 19.

his own development. I have endeavored to scatter throughout my foot-notes the dates of the composition of those passages from his other writings selected for comparison with the views expressed in the text. These dates will also aid the reader in framing his own conclusions on this general question.

The much more interesting and vital point is this: What is the *internal* origin of Kant's educational theory? When did Kant develop an interest in pedagogy? Mere external necessity—that is, academic obedience to an old rule—will not alone account for these *Lecture-Notes*. Further than this we have scarcely any data for definite assertions. It is true that his earliest writings show that he had at least a current interest in education as one of the proper topics with which human understanding should engage itself. There is also his own experience of nine years as a private tutor in several families near his native city, which put him into possession of much practical knowledge of the need and possibilities of instruction and training. It may even safely be affirmed that his interest in education definitely antedated the lectures; for during those earlier years of the sixties, often called his "empirical" stage by his biographers, he was familiar with Montaigne and Rousseau, the latter effecting a great change in his mind, if one can judge by some of the fragments he left. More unquestionable still, as an index of the inner growth of his educational interest, is the announcement of his lectures for the winter of 1765–66, which is a veritable profession, and confession, of pedagogical faith. As may be seen from the translated passages in Selections VII. and IX., he set forth a high ideal for his own teaching in demanding that youth should be taught, not mere information, but how to think. Here is where education was regarded as that definite, formative experience which makes man to be what he can in reality be. Kant, as it were, having been awakened by various influences to the problem of education, one is left to wonder why this interest did not survive with its first enthusiasm, and lead him to develop the question systematically and exhaustively.

Finally, and much more suggestive than all the foregoing indications, is the fact that Kant had a perennial interest in education and the relation of its practices to the philosophical doctrines which he was slowly working out in the eighties. The scope of this interest can easily be gathered from the fact that numerous passages in his technical writings have direct reference to education, from his many (undated) fragments, and from his frequent allusions to the office of the teacher. And one should not fail to take account of the pedagogical value to him of his active academic career which stretched out over forty years. Regarded from these points of view, educational theory is an essential item in Kant's views on man, and not a mere accident of his office. It is in this sense, and with this full justification, that Davidson [1] has set him forth as the most important historical individual in the whole of modern education.

---

[1] *A History of Education*, New York, 1900, pp. 220–224.

THE SOURCES OF KANT'S EDUCATIONAL THEORY

WHENCE did Kant derive his theory of education? From one point of view, his contribution to the philosophical phases of educational problems has been so characteristically his own that such a question can receive its only answer by a direct appeal to the concourse of ideas which constitutes the system of philosophy created in his later years. On the other hand, it is true that there were definite outside influences operating upon him which display themselves in some of the different features of his conception of the foundation, method, and goal of education. If one sweeps his glances over the *Lecture-Notes* and the Selections, he will readily see that those great features whose sources are in question are these. The Introduction exploits a new contrast between the natural origin of man and his possession of a characterizing reason as the foundation of pedagogy, and critically points out the limitations of the then current theories and practices. In physical education, the naturalism of Rousseau is unquestionably reproduced. Mind training is set apart on the basis of his own psychology, and moral and religious education are discussed in accordance with the scientific principles of his own discovery. From beginning to end, there is a continuous emphasis placed upon the education of the individual, not in his solitude, but

The Origin of Kant's Educational Ideas.

21

as a man, as a citizen, and as a member of a kingdom of ethical ends.

An attempt to enumerate the sources of these views must include both men and Kant's own experience as a

The Influence of Men and his Experience.

teacher. Of the men most likely to have had an influence upon him in this connection, we must name Montaigne, Rousseau, and Basedow and his associates. There were other men whose conceptions bore in upon Kant, but they are not of prime importance here. The second group of sources includes his years of experience as a private tutor and as a public university teacher, his keen powers of observation and analysis, out of which grew his *Anthropology*,—a great repository for pedagogical material, —and the conclusions of his philosophical reflections. The effects of some of these influences are more or less clearly traceable in his educational discussions, while others necessarily lie buried far beneath the surface.

With Montaigne Kant was very familiar. For a time this advocate of definite educational ends was one of his

His Relations to Three "Reformers."

favorite authors. Kant was probably the most illustrious "disciple" of Rousseau, as he is not infrequently called. The *Émile* produced a great impression upon him ; so great that he gave up his daily afternoon walks while reading it,—so the story runs. (See Selection I., Fragments Nos. 25, 28, 42, 43, 55.) The Philanthropinists received his enthusiastic support in calling for public subscriptions, and confirmed his belief in the necessity of making scientific experiments in the whole field of education. (See Selection III.) His adoption of the *orbis pictus* idea in language instruction may also have been derived from the experiments at the Institute of Dessau.

Kant's own activity gave him the right of first-hand experience to entertain an educational theory. How much his theory may be an outcome of his His Experience reflections upon his own experiences it is and his Theory. not easy to state definitely.[1] Section 34 very probably is a direct recollection of his nine years spent as a private tutor. We know little or nothing of these years, passed, it is said, in at least three families of culture, which opened to his view the life of the world in a larger way than he had ever experienced before. He said of himself later, that there could never have been a worse tutor in the world than himself, because he could not even apply those pedagogical rules which he knew. Nevertheless, he may well be regarded as knowing both educational virtues and vices at first hand. His pedagogical reaction against Pietism also stands out rather clearly in Sections 106 and following.

Kant was also aware of some of the special problems connected with the higher training of the adolescent. In the *Lecture-Notes* this latest stage of education is not touched upon beyond mention of its earlier begin-

---

[1] It would be fair to ask how far the home and school training of Kant may have influenced his educational theory ; but the data to answer such a question are not ascertainable, except, perhaps, in the tribute he paid late in his life to the memory of his " honest, morally exemplary and estimable" parents, who, he said, "gave me an education, which on its moral side could not possibly have been better, and for which I am profoundly thankful every time I think of it."—Hartenstein, viii. p. 805.

nings at puberty.   In Selections VII. and IX. especially, Kant's early recognition of the great duty of a university to the youth within its walls is clearly set forth. Kant himself was a most interesting teacher, making lasting impressions upon his students. The glowing testimony of Herder to his marked pedagogic powers, even before his advancement to the professorship, is supported in the tributes paid by later students. This influence can hardly be regarded as solely due to pedagogic instincts which he might have possessed, for he consciously strove towards the great aim of awakening his students to ripe individual thinking. The extent of Kant's insight into the prime need for educational reforms, particularly in the universities, is easily to be gathered from the fact that he strove to bring about a complete change in both the aim and the spirit of that instruction. Although he was trained in early youth under the strong influences of Pietism, he now came to be the vibrant voice which called most loudly in the eighteenth century for an education which should be inspired by, and organized under, the new ideal of *the worth and beauty of a free humanity.* The *Aufklärung* of the century, which struggled against the concepts of "the useful," either in religion or in industry, thus found its champion and "its victor," as Paulsen calls Kant, in the new humanism which has inspired the education, both elementary and higher, of the nineteenth century. The source of this view is not to be found in any particular psychological spring, nor did it break forth at a particular moment whose date can be fixed. But that Kant became its civilizing oracle is the fact of historical importance in education. Indeed, the very construction and the influence of the Critical Philosophy itself are supremely questions of a true and a higher pedagogy.

It remains to speak a little more fully of the influence of Rousseau, the fiery apostle of nature, upon Kant, the pedagogue. The not uncommon habit of historians is to regard Kant as merely working out the impressions made upon him by the author of *Émile*.[1] But to set this down as *the* source of his educational theory goes far beyond the historical warrant, as the following scheme of the agreements and disagreements on points in educational theory of the two thinkers amply shows.

Kant and Rousseau.

Kant and Rousseau agree in regarding pedagogy as a form of human interest whose foundations must lie as

---

[1] Compayré is given to regarding Kant in this light in his *Histoire Critique des Doctrines de l'Éducation en France depuis le seizième Siècle*, cinquième éd., tome ii., Paris, 1885, pp. 94–100, and also in his *The History of Pedagogy*, Eng. trans., Boston, 1889, pp. 333 ff.

Duproix also represents Kant's extreme dependence upon Rousseau in his *Kant et Fichte et le problème de l'Éducation*, Geneva, 1895, Chapter iii.

No less a writer than Davidson, for example, entertains this opinion in its extreme form. After Kant was aroused by Hume, "He drew his chief inspiration from Rousseau." Specifying a few features of the Kantian system of ideas, he adds, "It is hardly an exaggeration, therefore, to say that Kant, in his three *Critiques*, does little more than present in philosophical garb the leading doctrines of Rousseau."—*Rousseau*, etc., New York, 1898, pp. 224, 225.

deep as the human nature it attempts to modify, rather than as comprising a set of voluntary quibblings and Their Points of carpings about the way of doing this or that Agreement. particular task of school routine. They also agree on the necessity for a fresh start in establishing the principles of education. Kant follows Rousseau in starting with the very beginnings of infancy (an almost pre-scientific child-study). Both are partial to a restricted and "negative" education during the early years of the child's life. When education can at all appeal positively to the child, the methods sketched and rules laid down spring from a rather common belief in the promise and potency of "self-activity." Each seems to approach the other in the idea of the "physical culture" of the mind, and they unite in the interdiction of romances. In moral and religious education there appears a certain approximation of Kant's views to those of Rousseau ; but he soon departs from his "master" in both items. To Kant, morality requires its pedagogical beginnings in discipline, the first true step in education, and religious instruction is necessary even as an expedient for social respect. He not only accepts Rousseau's idea of natural punishments, but adds to these both positive and artificial modes of discipline, as being necessary, if education is to fit man for life. We may add, finally, that Kant does at times make use of Rousseau's thoughts, even of his words and phrases.

Not only do we find Kant making additions to some of those points on which he is in agreement with Rousseau ; but, if we look to the other side of their relations, we shall discover Kant to be one of the sharpest critics the paradoxical naturalist in pedagogy ever had. With Rousseau, the end of education was the production and the perfection of the man known to naturalism; with Kant, moral idealism alone *Their Points of Disagreement.* enclosed the secret goal of man's pedagogical development. Both writers used the *word* "liberty" as descriptive of man's essence. Yet how differently each applied it, both to the culture of his age and to the norms of logic and psychology! Rousseau starts with society, and works back to nature; Kant first examines nature and savagery, and constructively feels his way upward to an ethically constituted social whole. The reformer esteemed all nature "good" as it comes from the hand of its Author. The philosopher declares man to be neither good nor bad at birth, and traces the origin of the bad to a lack of rules in formative training. One praises barbarity, and attempts to usher in the time when nature shall be allowed to work out her own potencies unhindered by human ideas and the conventionalities of a social education. Instinct and inclination are key-words in this process. The other, while starting with nature, shows how weak are instincts and how rude is savagery, and thus invokes the intelligence of which man is in need in order properly to direct those instincts in him, which are less trustworthy than they are in animal nature. For him reason and duty are to triumph over both instinct and inclination. Hence, Kant shows how education is a positive constructive force in human character, in the formation of which it is more prominent in his theory than it is in Rousseau's. In morals, and in the education for morality, they differ even more widely:

Rousseau's pedagogical ethics is all sympathy, as the tap-root, which Kant rejects as unbefitting a truly ethical character. And, finally, in the details of educational routine, the Swiss banishes books and studies and closes schools, whereas the German sees in instruction and in intellectual organization the great pedagogical promise of character, and hopes for the early day when true schools shall be.a welcoming shelter for a youthful humanity growing into its highest values and beauty.

Such, indeed, within the narrower field of educational theory, not to go into the wider range of philosophical doctrine, is the alleged Rousseaulian discipleship of Kant!

THE PHILOSOPHICAL BASIS OF KANT'S EDUCATIONAL THEORY

THE Kant known to the history of the development of modern thought and science is Kant the author of the Critical Philosophy, and not Kant the educational theorist. His services to meta- *The Educa-tional Influ-ence of Kant's Philosophy.* physics in general have been the contribu- tion to our modern intellectual heritage which has received chief attention. These have, both in direct and in devious ways, irradiated over almost all forms of modern culture and achievement, and it is incumbent upon us to see how Kant's profounder in-quiries may have been contributive to the foundations of an educational theory.

Davidson's enthusiasm is strong when he declares, " The presiding genius of the spiritual life of the nine-teenth century is Kant, the modern Socrates. . . . He gathered up in himself, and did his best to harmonize, all the forward movements of the three preceding cen-turies. . . . It was no longer (the question of old), How does the world get into the mind? but, How does it get out of the mind?—no longer, How does the mind appropriate a world already existing? but, How does it build up any world of which it can predicate existence? Kant saw that this was as great a change in the spiritual world as the Copernican astronomy had been in the material. According to this new view, education is no

29

longer world-appropriation, but world-building. Each
man, by his own mental processes, builds up his own
world. The question is, How is this done? and Kant
undertakes to reply." [1]

Kant's reply was given in the three chief instalments
of Transcendentalism : the *Critique of Pure Reason*,
Outlines of his Philosophy. the *Critique of Practical Reason*, and the
Critique of Judgment. The author of these
epoch-making books exploited a new method in
philosophizing,—namely, criticism,—and applied a new
touch-stone of truth,—namely, reason. In the results of
an interpenetrating combination of these two guides are
to be found, if at all, the philosophical basis of his educational theory. He raised three fundamental and
searching questions. How is it that man can have
knowledge ? or, How are his various sciences of nature
and of himself possible ? How is human conduct to be
understood in the light of the nature of knowledge ? or,
How must man act, possessing the sciences he has ?
And, finally, How are the two realms of knowledge and
action, of nature and conduct, related in the unitary
experience of the living individual ?

To answer each question, Kant took a whole, single
Critique. The first question led him to an epistemo-
logical view of the world ; the second, to an ethical
view ; and the third, to an æsthetical and teleological
view. His answers spring from a subjective analysis of
the knower, the actor, and the feeler, and not from an
objective observational tour of the world of nature as

---

[1] *A History of Education*, pp. 220 ff.

the object of our science, the condition of our behaviors, and the source of our typical satisfactions.

The first *Critique* defended human science by declaring it to be but a mirror of that nature which is a creature of man's understanding. Finite *Critique of Pure Reason.* reason is discovered to be a beehive of knowing activities. It comes upon the dawning confines of experience with a definite equipment for making the world. Our perception by the senses is a compound of sensations, imagination, and understanding. Space and time are but forms of our inner experience. The intellect has twelve ways of making rules for telling what a given object shall prove to be, which are the twelve categories. Reason here comes in with its over-ruling and unifying activities, making our " knowledge" a composite of particular sciences of natural objects, and of ideals of those supposed realities lying beyond the visible, known world.

The second *Critique* goes even further, and, declaring man to have a double character, one lying completely above the region of sense, science, and time, *Critique of Practical Reason.* defends the laws of the will, or the reason in conduct, as being truthful. Human actions are not the mere corollaries of the principles of the different sciences ; but they are the absolute requirements of the supreme law of duty, or conscience. Indeed, it is a " categorical imperative" which presides over the inner self and its relations of will to other selves. Here we have transcendental freedom and true character ; whereas in intellect we have incessant and necessary conditions which must be fulfilled before knowledge is gained. Thus it happens that duty and the moral law are more truly representative of man's nature and the destiny of his earthly career than the intellect and the acquisition of knowledge. Man's soul is will, not intellect, chiefly. But this rational will must be determined and arranged before the individual has any experience. The "purity" of the categories of the intellect is far exceeded by the transcendental "purity" of the moral law and its persistent call to duty. "Experience" is thus defined in terms of certain factors which lie outside of, and are known previous to, experience.

The second *Critique* carried out the spirit and the method introduced by the first, and thus constitutes an integral portion of Kantian philosophy. Reason as knowing, and reason as willing, however, stood at variance in the system. The latter brought back in affirmation what the former set forth in negation,—at least in limitation,—but failed to bridge the chasm thus created.

The third *Critique* appeared as an attempt to harmonize man's rational and practical (*i.e.*, moral) natures. *Critique of Judgment.* This was accomplished by a special treatment of those peculiar forms of feeling satisfactions which are involved in the highest exercise of "judgment," and especially by a declaration of the double relation of feeling—namely, to intellect, on the one hand, and to will, on the other—as a definite psychological truth. Beauty and purpose, art and teleology, thus become the crowning feature of the critical exploitation of human nature. The philosophy thus developed is, as Ziegler well puts it, "no philosophy for children, and yet it is the corner-stone and foundation of our entire modern philosophizing." [1]

The reader of Kant's educational theory is doubtless struck by the apparent absence in it of almost all his peculiar philosophical tenets.   At the same time, one is ready to ask, How is a pedagogy possible in his philosophical system? This search for universal principles hardly seems germane to the labors of the educationist, who must deal concretely with individuals.   How can there be any connection whatsoever between the *a priori* categories of the intellect and the transcendental freedom of the will, on the one hand, and the conditions of the development under which alone education can take place, on the other?   Would not those two doctrines make forever impossible—in fact, simply preclude—all education and training?

His Pedagogy apparently Independent of his Philosophy.

In the first place, and negatively, we must not confound the Kant of the *Lecture-Notes* with the Kant of the *Critiques;* nor does a recognition of a philosophical basis to the former necessarily involve an immediate acceptance of the latter.   Moreover, one should not

---

[1] *Geschichte der Pädagogik*, Erster Bd., 1st Abth. of Baumeister's *Handbuch der Erziehungs- und Unterrichtslehre für höhere Schulen*, München, 1895, p. 246.

For a detailed statement of how Kant answered his three great questions, the reader is referred to the biographies mentioned and to the various histories of philosophy accessible in English, such as Ueberweg, Falkenberg, Weber, etc.   Paulsen has brought together the latest results of the numerous investigations and discussions relating to Kant's system.

make the great blunder of supposing that Kant first
worked out his philosophy, and then, proceeding on this
as a basis, deliberately elaborated his rules as to how
man should be handled in order to become educated
as a mere corollary thereto. This is largely untrue
historically ; and the internal evidence presented in the
Lecture-Notes makes it somewhat improbable that he
completely reworked them into adaptation to the conclusions of both speculative and practical philosophy.
Furthermore, it is true that the place and function which
were given in the Critical Philosophy to education, as an
object of metaphysical inquiry, are practically nil. It has
also repeatedly been held that there is a violent contradiction between affirming the need of education for man,
and discovering man to have a mechanically operative
reason, which would resist all attempts at instruction,
and a transcendental freedom, which would forever
make impossible the training of will and the acquisition
of character.   Transcendental freedom, indeed, has been
stormed and battered again and again in educational
literature, particularly the Herbartian. As a final consideration to support the position that it is erroneous to
speak of a philosophical basis to his pedagogy, one could
point out the fact that Kant himself has apparently
denied any philosophical virtue in education.   Among
the various modes of determining conduct recognized in
the *Critique of Practical Reason*,[1] Kant mentions Montaigne's view, which took education—an " external, subjective, practical, material principle of determination"

---

[1] Hartenstein, v. p. 43.

—as the foundation of morality. This he rejected, on the ground that it is "empirical," and therefore cannot furnish "the universal principle of morality."

On the other hand, and affirmatively, Kant was a pedagogue in the fullest and best sense of the term, and is another brilliant instance of the double But they are closely related. truth that the true teacher must be philo- sophical, and that the true philosopher finds a perennial theme in the problems of education. That there is a close relation between his creed of transcendentalism and his deep interest in a worthy education is indicated in a forceful manner by the not infrequent efforts of numerous later pedagogical writers to set aside, or at least to revise, many of his principles of philosophy. The Herbartian era was well saturated with this *Kant-phobia*, which persists in our present-day method of working out the scope and needs of human education from the "scientific" point of view.

The suspicion in favor of Kant, thus apt to be aroused, grows into positive conviction when one reviews the many indications which show him Kant's Interests fundamentally Pedagogical. to have been true to the aims of pedagogy. Kant was a pedagogue both by the necessity of law and particularly by taste, the latter appearing a decade earlier than the former. He did not belong to the type of the musty, dry-as-dust professor, who might have spun out his pedagogical cobwebs with the indifference of mere abstraction. He was a pedagogue both by precept and by practice. He wanted to teach students "to think," and to develop their personalities into independence of school mechanism. He taught no fixed and closed system of philosophy, but strove to awaken the impulse to, and to develop the capacity for, philosophical investigation. He was Socratic in his practice, but he did not exploit his own theories at the expense of his pupils and other academic opportunities. His great books likewise attest his pedagogical instincts and insights. They each had a part on "method," and, as an author, he did not fail to address himself to the problem of how the doctrines he developed so abstractly could be fitted to the practical needs of man.[1] Indeed, Kant was a pedagogue throughout the whole Critical Philosophy, which was chiefly an affair of method. In this achievement he became a true teacher, not of single individuals in a class-room, but of an age, a nation, and, in truth, of the occidental race of men. By closing up certain blind alleys of speculation, he turned intellectual impulses into the great channels of productivity marking the nineteenth century. Can we not thus say, with full biographical, professional, and scientific reason, that Kant, even as the author of the philosophy of critical idealism, would have been a pedagogue without having ever thought about, or lectured upon, pedagogics? Yes. For every important system of philosophy inevitably contains the germs of a pedagogy, which manifest their influences sooner or later.

---

[1] This is most clearly a feature of the second *Critique* (see Selection XI. i.). Also, in the *Prolegomena to Every Future Metaphysics* (1783), it is the pedagogical conception and interest which spring first into mind. The book was prepared, not for the use of students, but for future teachers, to help them to discover the science.—Hartenstein, iv. p. 3.

No philosopher can thus escape being of the greatest interest in the history of education. Besides this, the Critical Philosophy and its accessory writings are well filled with pedagogical material, both by way of direct reference to the work of teaching and by way of an exhibition of certain postulates of education.

It is no real accident in academic culture which brings philosophy and education together. The pedagogical reasons for doing so in particular eras and institutions speedily give way, upon reflection, to more solid reasons for this union. The determination of man's being and becoming, and of the destiny it is for him to actualize in his own life and in the life of his species, is thin and abstract if it has no reference whatever to the art of training him. On the contrary, any effort made to facilitate and promote man's adaptation to his environment and approximation to this destiny is *pre*-human if it forgets to link and to subordinate itself to an intelligent description of the conditions under which the potencies in him can alone become dynamic, moving outward and upward. From this point of view, one is enabled to see why the philosophy projected by Kant, which is so often thought to be formal, schematic, is, in truth, contentful for the great task of stirring the higher pedagogic life of the race. The education that at all touches human nature can no longer, since his time, be even conceived of as a mere exchange, or as making merchandise, of routine information. On the contrary, the basis of his educational theory, which must be regarded as larger than his lectures on pedagogy, resides in his philosophical interpretation of man and his life as demanding an ever-increasing pedagogical aspiration for the ideals of experience thereby justified. Only a few features of the educational postulates defended by his philosophy can receive summary notice here.

1. Kant's philosophical *subjectivism*, both in its method and in its immediate results, is the corner-stone of his educational theory. The possibility and the limits of human education were by him first determined in an exploitation of this last advance upon man's inner citadel. If we say, with some historians, that Socrates was the founder of pedagogy because of his treatment of its relations to ethics, we must add that Kant completed the foundations thus begun by carrying to a finish the momentum of an analysis of the inner life.

Educational Postulates contributed by his Philosophy.

2. The first *Critique*, in undertaking a special study of the structure of human knowledge, resulted in a discovery of epistemology, and thus necessarily dealt with methods of thought (conditions of instruction), knowledge, science, and nature, and their relations, both real and ideal, to human efforts. Out of this work the following principles and influences became accredited to educational theory:

(*a*) The *great creative power* of the activity of pure reason was declared. Its productivity is the basis of all science and the true problem of philosophy. If nature is made by reason, education must deal, in principle, with the latter and not with the former. Instruction is seen to be more and more an affair of inner experience and less and less an affair of objects and so-called "content." Hence pedagogics can become "genetic" only in the light of a knowledge of the order of reason's activities. "Self-activity" has never received a greater vindication than in this *Critique*. From this resulted

(*b*) The *centralization of the individual mind* in the worlds of both nature and human society. Here education comes into the possession of a new, determining ideal. A "master" pedagogy of the spirit, to use the terms of Nietzsche, must replace the "slave" pedagogy of things.

(*c*) *Nature, or science, becomes educative only because of its constructive appeal to reason,* and not because an encyclopedic acquaintance with its facts is ever a bare possibility. Or, *vice versa*, knowledge of principles, and not of objective facts, is alone educative. Inductive criticism, which begins with the environmental data, and moves upward even to the ideals involved in every generalization, thus becomes an educational requirement, which is only now being fully met with in the widening application of "scientific" instruction. It should not be forgotten that these foundations of his theory manifested themselves most effectively through his larger influence upon later philosophy and science, and through them percolated down to educational practices.

In one particular, at least, this *Critique* had direct effect upon education. School instruction in mathematics, both in theory and in practice, became modified in accordance with the influence exercised by its first part, the Transcendental Æsthetics, which presented the theory of the intra-mental, non-empirical origin of space and time, and thus of geometry and arithmetic.

3. *Reason*, although it is the titular phrase of transcendentalism, declaring the epoch in which it originated, is no less a contributor to the foundations of education. Here "pure reason" becomes rational capacity at human birth, and "harmonious development" and "perfection" the process and the goal which inspire instruction. With Kant, reason is primarily something *functional*, and hence not an empirical content or enumeration, which is so frequently the criticism brought against it, along with the mistaken interpretation of it as "innate," and mere "form." Reason is a necessary pedagogical factor in psychological integration, which is, or ought to be, the growing ideal of every true teacher. Kant's philosophy, so uniformly regarded as merely based on a mechanically operative reason, is, in truth, a philosophy of *will*, which is the only fitting psychological term for the "transcendental apperception" of the first *Critique*. And a will philosophy alone can adequately underlie and support a pedagogy that shall be consistent with itself and secure "results" in human life. Productive individuality can thus become a true educational motto, and real schooling becomes a relation between souls. ("Reason," as a substantive term, has perhaps disappeared in the nomenclature of our biological era; but, does it not linger significantly in the "sound, healthy mind," "rational plan of studies," science *versus* superstition, and other such touchstones of current pedagogics?)

4. The empirical aspects of this subjectivism as wrought out in his psychology are reserved for the following section.

5. *Freedom and Morality* are the chief complementary determinations of the second *Critique*, which are declared to be the ultimate characteristics of personality, however that personality may theoretically be described and explained. Freedom is the condition, duty is the inescapable demand, and morally approvable conduct is the result. This freedom appears in two directions : (*a*) no being outside myself can determine me—absolute possibility is given within me ; (*b*) the individual is not left the prey of impulses and inclinations, but the "law" —will—gives an elevating mastery over them. Morality becomes herein the highest aim of life, and *another creative ideal* is accredited to educational theory. Will is the function and duty is the aim which are to become *regulative* in the whole process of education from its beginning to its end. Here philosophical theory and pedagogical theory link hands in giving experience its tendencies towards perfection; and the *Lecture-Notes* are filled with declarations of this final aim of all culture and education. (See Sections 5, 11, 12, 16, 18*d*, 19, 27, 29–33, 42, 44, 47–49, 51, 54, 55, 58, 59, 63, 72, 75–84, 86–88, 91–99, 103, 105, 106, 108. Cf. also Selections II., XI., and XII.) This principle of freedom demands of education that it shall erect a specific story of soul structure above the wide foundation of nature, impulse, instinct, and the acquired mechanisms of man's development. The unique value of this ethical cast to pedagogy is to be found in Kant's constant recognition of the antithesis between animal and human nature, between instinct and reason, between mechanism and freedom, and in his persistent declaration that true edu-

cation tends to lead the latter of each pair to triumph over the former. This philosophical basis makes possible *a pedagogy of the will,* re-emphasizes individualism, and again displays the virtues of subjectivism.

Mention should, finally, be made of the fact that Kant is *the great modern example of self-education.* He belongs

Philosophy and Life. pre-eminently to the heroölogy of pedagogy. It is appropriate to mention this, inasmuch as philosophy and personality, thought and character, are so intimately related. His philosophy and his pedagogy found their first application and continuous practice in his own life. From an obscure origin, he brought himself to the foremost place in modern culture. By control he extended the precarious strength of a weakly body to fourscore years. His health was a matter of will. By his punctuality, precision, and personal independence, he organized his own life on the lines of ethical freedom. By his firm adherence to his vocation,— a seeker after truth,—personal pedagogics became an exemplary life.[1]

That Kant himself regarded philosophy as having a basic relation to the practical pursuits of life, among which education is to be included, may be gathered from the following passage :

" All technical-practical rules (that is, those of art and of skill in general, or also of prudence, as the skill of having influence upon men and their wills), in so far as

---

[1] We may note here the absence of any marked contribution to his *own* educational theory derived from the third *Critique,* a point to receive mention later.

their principles rest upon concepts, must be counted only as corollaries of theoretical philosophy. For they concern only the possibility of things according to nature concepts, to which not only the means, which are to be found in nature, but even the will itself (as the faculty of desire, consequently, as a natural faculty) belongs, so far as it can be determined by impulses of nature in accordance with those rules. Yet those same practical rules are not to be called laws (such as physical), but only precepts; because the will comes not only under the concept of nature, but also under the concept of freedom, in reference to which its principles are called laws; and it alone comprises, with its implications, the second part of philosophy,—namely, the practical part."[1]

---

[1] *Critique of Judgment.*—Hartenstein, v. p. 178.

KANT'S PSYCHOLOGY AND HIS EDUCATIONAL THEORY

EVERY teacher trained in a normal school at the beginning of the twentieth century is apt to grow into an unquestioned acceptance of the "axiom":
My profession is based, in its scientific aspects, upon psychology; if I educate, I must first have a knowledge of the individual whose formation I am to direct. It is not easy for him to remember that there was a time when this axiom was a new and a theoretical doctrine; and for this forgetfulness the history of education is responsible. That this time was comparatively recent can be seen from the fact that Kant's generation saw only the dawning twilight of this belief of modern pedagogy. Its distinct beginnings may be traced as far back as Comenius; but it was Herbart who broke away the mists which ushered in our noonday sun. In attempting to appreciate the relative amount of reference to psychology in his educational theory, we should give Kant the benefit of the state of psychology at *his* time, and not insist that *our* psychology shall determine the scope of the historical perspective.

Psychology and Education: a Modern Idea.

Kant found psychology in the doctrinaire, classificatory stage. The former feature he submitted to a most searching and negative criticism and a final rejection. The latter trait he gradually extended, and, setting the seal of his authority upon it, made it the acceptable mode

44

of approaching the problems of the science for a century
or more.   At the time of the discovery of America by
Columbus, and the spreading of the spirit   The State of
of free inquiry, men began to record their   Psychology be-
psychological observations. These were usu-   fore Kant.
ally grouped under the term "anthropology."   Soon
after books appeared bearing the title "anthropology,
or psychology."   These observations made upon the
soul of man grew from age to age, and were thickened
with strong infusions of the scholastic dogma about
the soul.   Under the schematizing intellect of Christian
Wolff, this inchoate mass of material was divided into
two branches, *Psychologia Empirica* (1732) and *Psychologia Rationalis* (1734), and by him more. or less
thoroughly systematized.   The latter division of psychology sought to derive as much knowledge about the
nature, being, and destiny of the soul as might be possible through the processes of reasoning.   The former
division was the repository of the characteristic facts of
mind, to be derived from experience, and which were
explained in terms of "faculties," which the soul was
believed to possess, such as perception, memory, understanding, etc.   In the history of psychology, this step
taken by Wolff stands next in importance to the founding
of the science by Aristotle.   It also brought forth significant fruit in the labors of Kant himself, a presentation of the details of which we have attempted elsewhere.[1]   The inspiration of this suggestive division

---

[1] In my *Study of Kant's Psychology with Reference to the Critical
Philosophy*. Monograph Supplement No. 4.   *The Psychological*

resided in the questions, whether an independent science of mind is possible, and how closely that science is related to metaphysics. The Leibnitzo-Wolffian philosophy was dominant in the German universities during Kant's student days. It answered both questions affirmatively. As Kant reached his maturity in philosophical reflection, he rejected this affirmative position.

The most important detail in the classificatory trait of the empirical psychology of the days of the younger Kant is, perhaps, its possession of the two rubrics under which all the data of mental experience were placed. These rubrics, while always two, were variously designated: such as, "the intellectual powers" and "the active powers" of the mind, "understanding" and "appetition" or "desire," etc. Such facts as those of perception, or memory, or judgment were assigned to the first group; and those of feeling, sentiment, desire, effort, motive, will, etc., to the second group. Thus Kant himself writes in 1763, "the properties of a mind are understanding and will."[1] These rubrics, however, served a wider and deeper purpose. By an appeal to these "faculties," the psychologist thought himself to be dealing with *explanatory* necessities. Mind behaviors were to be made intelligible by pointing out these faculties as mental forces, which projected themselves specifically into the performances which might be observed. Kant at first continued to accept this growing tradition

Review, 1897.   New York, The Macmillan Company, pp. 36–47, 147–151.

[1] Hartenstein, ii. p. 131.

of psychological explanation. When, however, he had gotten well into his "sceptical" period, and later brought himself face to face with his great problem of the nature of human knowledge, we find him abandoning the old, iron-clad, bipartite division of the faculties.

The next year (1764) Kant detected a marked change in the scientific atmosphere, and also approved of it in the following words: "In the present day we have, for the first time, begun to see that the faculty of representing truth is cognition, but the faculty of experiencing the good is feeling, and also that these two faculties must not be exchanged one with the other."[1] Eight years later he writes to Marcus Herz of this psychological discovery by a deeper analysis of the "active powers," in which the feelings had been incorporated heretofore, and of the fundamental differentiation between knowledge and feeling. This change in the division of the faculties of the mind was, perhaps, most clearly and substantially expressed in the essays of Sulzer in 1751 ff. (*Miscellaneous Writings*), the *Letters on Sensation* (1755), and the *Morning Hours* (1785) of Moses Mendelssohn, the grandfather of the great musician, and in the *Philosophical Investigations of Human Nature and its Development* (1777) of Tetens. Of the latter book Kant was very fond, and it was often seen lying open on his table. All of these psychological writers persisted in pointing out the claims of "feeling" to a distinct recognition as a

Feeling first recognized as a Distinct Mental Faculty.

---

[1] Hartenstein, ii. pp. 307, 308.

basal power of mind, and gave it an application in their art theories.

Kant's acceptance of this new division grew apace with the development of his system of Critical Philoso-

The Mental Faculties and the Critical Philosophy. phy. Indeed, the main outlines of that system are to be found in this new psychological creed, which he fully set forth in 1790 in the Introduction to the third and crowning *Critique* of the system.[1] The first *Critique* explored the philosophical values of the faculty of cognition. The second *Critique* was addressed to the *a priori* nature of the faculty of will. And the third *Critique* attempted to effect a union between the first and the second by an examination of the faculty of the feeling of pleasure and pain. The following table, arranged by Kant,[2] sets forth these relations between a psychological analysis of the *higher* faculties, the philosophical or transcendental principles, and the fields of experience to which they are applied respectively.

Mental Powers.	Higher Faculties of Knowledge.	*A priori* Principles.	Products.
Knowledge.	Understanding.	Conformity to Laws.	Nature.
Pleasure and Pain.	Judgment.	Conformity to Purpose.	Art.
Action.	Reason.	Obligation.	Morals.

[1] See *A Study of Kant's Psychology*, etc., pp. 63–74.
[2] Hartenstein, v. p. 204.

The adjective "higher" in the second column of this table is most significant in this connection. Kant persistently discredited psychology, denying that it had any scientific value and that it could ever acquire any. In 1781 he abandoned the doctrinaire, rational psychology of his generation, having submitted it, as he thought, to an absolutely destructive criticism in the Transcendental Dialectic of the first *Critique*. The adjective "higher" readily points out that he introduced his own "rational" psychology in order to make the field of criticism distinct.

Empirical psychology fared somewhat differently in his hands. In 1765 it was regarded as the "peculiarly metaphysical empirical science of man," and always was a part of his lectures on metaphysics until he began, in 1773–1774, to lecture on anthropology. Four years later he gave less attention to the former science, because he was giving more to the latter; which grew up out of his lectures on physical, political, and moral geography, and thereby he became the first in Germany to raise anthropology to the rank of an academic subject. Psychology became for him more and more an affair of "mere opinion." It can never become a natural science, because mathematics cannot be applied to it: its phenomena are given in the single dimension of time. It must forever remain nothing more or less than an "historical," "natural description" of the inner sense. Kant thus threw his great interest into the empirical study of *men* (rather than of the individual man) for the sake of a working anthropology. His work on this subject was not published until 1798.

Psychology became a dubious term with him, and the critical caution already stated should not be forgotten.

If psychology became the rejected child in Kant's family of the sciences, he nevertheless continued to do the work of an excellent psychologist, for which he had unusual analytical ability. This persistent, but perhaps unconscious, reliance upon psychological insight appears in his recurrent appeal to the nature of human mental faculties. What he meant in general by these faculties can briefly be set forth as follows : " 'Cognition is the faculty of the mind for determining the existence and changes of objects.' It is a unique faculty, whose activity consists in carrying on the mechanism of representations, a mechanism into which enter both a receptivity and a spontaneity. . . . 'The capacity of having pleasure or pain with a representation is called feeling, because both contain merely the subjective relations to our ideas, but no reference whatsoever to an object of possible knowledge (not even a knowledge of our own state).' Conation is variously represented, yet all expressions may agree in these : now it is will in its highest critical meaning ; 'will can be defined as the faculty of purposes, since they are always the motives of the active powers according to principles ;' then it is the empirical activity of desire, as ' the faculty of being, through its representations, the cause of the objects of these representations.' What sort of passivities and activities is included under each is most briefly and graphically seen in diagrams." [1]

Kant's Meaning of Psychological Faculties.

---

[1] Adapted from *A Study of Kant's Psychology*, etc., pp. 206–208.

```
                      ┌ Sense (given).    ┌ External.   { " Org
                      │                   {             { " Vita
            ┌ Lower. {                     └ Internal.   " Interna
            │         │                                    from
            │         │                   ┌ Reproductive. ┌ Copyir
            │         └ Imagination       │               │ Imitati
            │           (produced).      {                │ Previsi
            │                             │                └ Symbo
            │                             └ Productive.   ┌ (Never
            │                                            {  Space
Cognition. {                                             └  Tim
            │                           ┌ A priori sensuous forms.
            │         ┌ Understanding.  { Twelve Categories.
            │         │                 { Four Principles.
            │         │                 { Three Ideals.
            │         │                 └ Apperception.
            │         │                 ┌ Determinative,—judgme
            └ Higher. │ Judgment.       {                 ┌ Æsthe
                      │                 └ Reflective.     {
                      │                                   └ Teleo
                      │                 ┌ Empirical use,—ordinary
                      └ Reason.         { Speculative use,—three i
                                        └ " Critical " use,—the fac
```

Objective. { Sight.
{ Touch.

Subjective. { Hearing.
{ Taste.
{ Smell.

...eral "bodily" feelings, heat, cold, etc.

...or consciousness of self,—to be distinguished from the feelings and
...tion.

Fantasy (invol-
  untary).

Memory (volun- { Mechanical.
  tary). { Ingenious.
{ Judicious.

e," but, for cognitions, always depending on sensations.)

...nstructing intuitions in space.   Associating intuitions in time.   Relating
  power.

...erience, or cognition.
{ Beauty.
{ { Mathematical.
{ Sublimity. { Dynamical.

...n.
  Soul.
  World.
  God.
...e moral law, Categorical Imperative.

Mind.
- Cognition.
  - Lower,—receptive, intuitive (belong to psychology).
  - Higher,—(causally) spontaneous, discursive (belong to logic).
- Feeling.
  - Lower,—mechanically empirical.
  - Higher,—rationally free : æsthetical, ethical, etc.
- Appetition and Will.
  - Lower,—the physical motivations of man.
  - Higher,—only ethical (according to the disclosures of Criticism).

The "lower" aspects of each faculty group are empirical, involuntary, and against the will ; the "higher" are rational, voluntary, and under "free" will. (See folder between pages 50 and 51.)

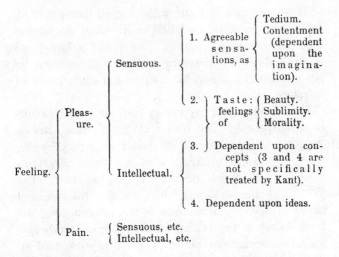

Feeling.
- Pleasure.
  - Sensuous.
    1. Agreeable sensations, as
       - Tedium.
       - Contentment (dependent upon the imagination).
  - Intellectual.
    2. Taste: feelings of
       - Beauty.
       - Sublimity.
       - Morality.
    3. Dependent upon concepts (3 and 4 are not specifically treated by Kant).
    4. Dependent upon ideas.
- Pain.
  - Sensuous, etc.
  - Intellectual, etc.

Appetition and Will.
- Empirical.
  - Desire.
  - Emotion.
    - Sthenic (strong).
    - Asthenic (weak).
  - Passion.
    - Natural : love of
      - Freedom.
      - The Sexes.
    - Acquired.
      - Ambition.
      - Imperiousness.
      - Covetousness.
- Rational.
  - This is the voluntary, ethical will, usually called "reason" in the severer "critical" sense, and is separated from all the empirical forms of motor consciousness. This is the faculty analyzed in the second *Critique*.

These schemes set forth, without great multiplicity of detail, Kant's general analytical treatment of the specific types of conscious processes. As in his pedagogy, so in his systematic philosophy and his anthropology, he has a constant fondness for division and subdivisions *ad infinitum*.

How much of this psychology crept over into his educational theory? The reader of the *Lecture-Notes on Pedagogy* will doubtless be struck by the apparent absence of any great direct influence of the former upon the latter. The human nature which supplies the recurrent theme of pedagogical idealism in the Introduction (Sections 1–30) is the human nature of broad anthropological generalizations rather than that psychological individualism which is open to introspective analysis. The

Limited Influence of his Psychology on his Educational Theory.

perfection of man, however, which sets the goal of educational efforts, he finds in the inner life, and not in any outer circumstances of life. The problems of mental culture, chiefly in the sense of intellectual training, are taken up specifically, but not until the forty-seventh section, or, more particularly, the fifty-eighth. The training of the non-mechanical faculties, so to speak, is not taken up until the sixty-third section, and then only fourteen sections present the treatment offered. Of these a little more than one-half are concerned with the rules necessary for the training, not of all psychological faculties, but only of the cognitive. The most striking feature in the attitude maintained is the persistent consideration of these faculties as standing in a hierarchy—one leads up to another, and so on. In its fundamental persuasion, no view is more conducive to the insight of the need of training and of the possibility of establishing the formula for the work of education. Here we have the genetic *spirit*, if not a full apprehension of the genetic method, in the possession of which we of to-day are educationally rich.

Within the limited circle of the range of psychological theory in his pedagogy, and also in many of the selections belonging to this theme, Kant never wearies of bringing out over and over again the essential differences between memory and understanding, whether in science or in education. This is indicative of the fact that no mechanical view of the office of instruction and the function of the school was acceptable to him. His conclusion is a psychological bulwark, which has not always been regarded in the educational theory and practice

of the century intervening between his day and ours
In 1775, near the period when he perforce began to give
his official attention to pedagogy, we have a very suggestive instance of this twofold criticism of mechanical
retention of ideas and approval of the high claims of
active thinking.   In speaking of the classification of animals, in his discussion on the various races of men, he
names two types, that of the school and that of nature.
The former "provides a school system for the memory"
and the latter "a nature system for the understanding."
"The first aims to bring creatures under titles and the
latter brings them under laws."[1]

It is superficially fair to Kant's educational theory to
say that its psychology is subordinated to his ethics,
and that the mere training of faculty is but
an episode in his great conception of education. On the other hand, it is just as
much truer, as the view is profounder, that the relative
absence of any marked influence from his psychology
upon his theory, aside from the rules laid down for the
lower and the higher faculties, has in part its explanation, and in part its justification, in the fact that
*his educational theory is pre-eminently a pedagogy of the
will.* It was this drift of his thought, perchance, which
saved him from the snare of a mere " pedagogical
psychology," that more modern invention which too
often thinks to do the work of a careful systematic
pedagogy. A count of the sections will reveal that
" will" is the one mental process most frequently

His Theory a
Pedagogy of
the Will.

---

[1] Hartenstein, ii. p. 435.

named. In his demand for a union of knowledge and power (Section 70), and in his rule of learning by doing (Section 75), this pedagogy of will receives further vindication and application. And, finally, in moral education, it is will, and not mere faculty training, which coördinates all the requirements and opportunities of securing the destiny of man in the moral behavior of the child. That this will pedagogy did not shield Kant from the dogma of formal training is apparent from Section 72, and it is often the will itself that is to be approached through the rules derivable from that dogma. The point not to be lost sight of is his genial entertainment of the view that education, to be effective, is a doing, an effort, an activity, into which our will must pour itself. The supreme expression of this aspect of human nature, both within and without the bounds of education, is *freedom* in every application to knowledge and life of which it at all admits. In this sense, then, Kant's psychology is an essential part of his educational theory.

KANT'S EVOLUTIONAL AND EDUCA-
TIONAL THEORIES

IT would be a gross injustice to our author to let it be understood that he endeavored to conceive of education Kant's Educational Theory possesses a Threefold Foundation. and to give rules for the conduct of it solely from the stand-points of a transcendental philosophy and of a psychology which represented a new advance upon the then current views of the soul. No less would it be unfair to ourselves as students of his educational ideas to rob our appreciation of them by stopping with the analyses of the two preceding sections. Kant becomes a fully accredited educational theorist by his admission of the advantages of the conception and the postulate of evolution into his discussion of the problem of the education of man. It is not a little surprising to find that he gave a threefold foundation to that all too brief discussion: (a) philosophical, (b) psychological, (c) evolutional. Thus we find him to be more and more allied to the reigning modern point of view. It is the establishment of this tripod of his educational philosophy which, perhaps, entitles him to be regarded as the author of an educational *system* rather than anything that may be worked out on the basis of the contents of the *Lecture-Notes*.

In its naturalistic, *quasi*-scientific aspects, his pedagogy previsions the much-applied current theory of development,—in gross, not in refined details, to be sure. To Kant, education essentially means a specific order of development. And, to strengthen this opinion, one finds this generic view hovering over the whole of the Introduction to the *Lecture-Notes*, forming a background for his discussion of the education of the individual. In its conception of the goal of education, as the rationalizing and freeing of man, who somehow stands in the evolutional series as a natural object, *Kant's educational theory literally becomes a synthesis of the evolutionism of anthropological science and the ethical idealism of philosophy.* He has long since been an admitted harmonizer of the speculative tendencies of his age, and we now find this intellectual temper displaying itself again in his pedagogical lectures. We should not, however, think it strange if we find Kant permitting these three bases of education to stand side by side without undertaking to render them mutually consistent. There is many a better-informed modern who displays even greater complacency than Kant in this matter.

His Theory a Synthesis of Evolution and Ethical Idealism.

Kant's relation to the theory of evolution is rather unique. To many it may seem a logical impossibility for him to have had even an interest in the theory. Here, again, the obscuration of his suggestions to the particular sciences, and their consequent neglect by his overtowering services to speculative interests, are increasingly pathetic. There is abundant evidence, however, that

Kant's Contribution to the Formation of the Theory of Evolution.

Kant entertained the theory, and that he brought education to count with it. Indeed, he was the projector of that hypothesis of physical evolution, the nebular hypothesis, which to-day underlies the science of astronomy, and which usually goes by the name of Laplace, who gave it a formulation four decades later than Kant's work of 1755, and independently thereof. He entertained the epigenetic theory of development which was propounded by C. F. Wolff in 1759, and should not be held responsible for any supposed gap between that view and those views which may now be more acceptable on the basis of the very modern science of embryology. If this were the place to enter on such a discussion, one might well question whether Kant's view of human development does not stand nearer the truth than the more refined and elaborate modern theories. The great and main point is this: Kant stood in the front rank of those who saw, and insisted upon, the need of regarding the universe as in a state of change and becoming, which follows a law of progress. This conception he articulated more or less clearly through the range of the physical and anthropological sciences as then understood, gave it an application in his educational theory, and a final interpretation in the third *Critique.*

The evidences and the scope of his concept of evolution may further be described in terms of the views expressed by him at various times. In 1764 Kant shared in the public interest in the " wild man" and his child companion of eight years of age, who appeared from the woods at Königs-

His Idea of Evolution and of its Applications.

berg.[1] His chief interest, however, was centred upon the boy, who had grown up in the woods, and whom he describes as cheerfully defying the weather, possessing a face which showed incomparable frankness and a marked absence of foolish embarrassment. He regarded this embarrassment in finer education as the effect of servitude and forced respect. Aside from the tricks at money-getting, the boy seemed to Kant to be a *complete* subject for the experimental moralist, who ought to wish for just such a subject, and who thus would have an honest opportunity to test the propositions and the beautiful chimeras of Rousseau before rejecting them. Here "child-study" was to be a touchstone of truth long before it became the waking dream of the modern scientist.

In reviewing Moscati's work on the differences between the structure of animals and man, in 1771, Kant went further in his conception of how the individual man must be connected in evolutionary thought with the race, and be compared with lower forms of animal life.[2] Man's upright position and locomotion are unnatural, being acquired. Many diseases from which four-footed animals are free may be traced to this condition of posture, which induces special deleterious strains upon various portions of man's structure. The first care of nature is to preserve man as an animal, and also his species. A "seed of reason" has been laid in man by nature, which predisposes him to take on social func-

---

[1] Hartenstein, ii. p. 209.
[2] *Ibid.*, pp. 429–431.

tions. Thus he assumes the two-footed position, and
lifts himself above his lowly neighbors, a bipedal locomotion being best adapted for social intercourse.

Four years later, as we stand at the threshold of his
pedagogical epoch, he elaborates his idea of races in
His Conception physical geography.[1] While his classifica-
of Race.   tions have long since been set aside, the
content of his idea still lingers in our modern anthropology. "Race" means the stem and its productivity;
and racial growth he traced, however imperfectly, as
dependent upon light, climate, soil, foods. Nearly a
decade later the race idea, which had grown in its integrity and served him as the background of comparison,
reappeared in his efforts to set forth the ethical conditions of the individual in his racial and historical relations to organized civic life. The two essays of interest
here are *Idea of a Universal History from a Cosmopolitan
Point of View* (1784), and *The Probable Beginnings of
Human History* (1786). Mankind is not a mere aggre-
gation; it has an organic unity. "Nature" expresses
the primitive condition of development, which is perpetuated in the instincts and other mechanisms. Man
must not remain in this raw state, but he *must* develop,
progressing in the direction of reason, law, will, freedom, morality. (See foot-notes to Sections 2, 3, 10, 26.)
Up to his own era, he regarded the race as not having
yet entered upon the last and highest stage,—namely, the
stage of ethical reason. Humanity as a whole, however, is progressing thitherward. (See Section 19.) It

---

[1] Hartenstein, ii. p. 435 ff.

should be observed that his pedagogical idea of evolution and the larger meaning he found it to give to education falls within this "race" period of his own mental development, if we may so speak.

Empirical psychology, furthermore, according to Kant's conception, approaches very closely the confines which the present age is handing over to genetic psychology. Although limited to the individual, it treats "of the origin of experience, but not of that which lies within it." [1] Anthropology, which grew into independent vigor under his hands, has the special duty laid upon it of considering man "cosmologically," and not singly. Evolution is undoubtedly a constituent in these conceptions, to the acceptance of which Kant brought himself more and more closely.

And, finally, one can cite the official passages in the *Critique of Judgment* in which the theory of evolution finds, not only definite mention, but also specific arguments offered in its favor.[2] Here it is called a "conjecture" of "a common ancestral source" for all the many species of animals. Indeed, he carries the evolutional *regressus* down "to the polyp, from this to the moss and lichen, and finally to the lowest stage of nature perceptible to us, to crude matter, from which and its forces, according to mechanical laws, the whole technique of nature appears to be derived." [3]

Evolution in the Critical Philosophy.

---

[1] Hartenstein, iv. p. 52.

[2] Section 81, Hartenstein, v. pp. 435–438.

[3] See P. Carus, "Kant on Evolution," *The Monist*, vol. ii. No. 4, Appendix, pp. 40–43.

The conception of nature determined by mechanical laws, and thus enlarged by the progressive aspect of its great changes, is what underlies the discussions of education in the *Lecture-Notes* and in some of the selections. This view bore fruit in another direction also. The moral life must be understood as standing out boldly by comparison against this great, universal background of an evolving nature. It is education, in fact, which seems to be the one type of science to which Kant gave an application of the idea of development as the law of nature which previsions the goal of human life. It was not applied in the *Critiques*, nor in his psychological analysis of man in his *Anthropology*. Here we also find some justification for the great emphasis he placed upon the individual in his educational theory. There can be no education of the race, scarcely in the æsthetical sense of Schiller, who benefited by this parallel scheme.

Evolution applied chiefly to Educational Theory.

In this way Kant's theory practically presents a third form of definition of education. Its method is comparative, which is advantageous both to the beginnings and to the endings of education. Viewed in the twofold directions, education is to surmount nature, the great mechanism ; and, in doing that, and having done that, it must proceed to transform the man-animal into a rational and moral humanity. The self-development of the race likewise offers its suggestions to pedagogy in the introductory sections. Kant always seemed to hold that evolution is better than revolution in human affairs, excepting

Education redefined in Terms of Ethics.

under some conditions of character. (See Selection X.) Human evolution, in its fullest sense, became identified with education. These thoughts, which are so germinal in the history of philosophical pedagogics, even reach an expressive suspicion of the theory of recapitulation, wherein the child is supposed to repeat the history of the race, even of the whole evolving process in organic life, now so vigorously advocated. (See Section 12.)

The connection between his philosophical account of man's action and his educational theory is further extended and illumined by the demand which both nature and ethics make upon man. By these he is called to undertake the education of humanity, not so much in himself, but rather in the next generation, his offspring. This is the demand of evolution and of progress. Kant's great forte in his evolutionary hints is upon their moral side. For him the supreme law of the universe is evolution,—not in the production of imperfect living organisms, but towards the good. And the only good for humanity is progress within man.

Having reached this point, we can see how, as a matter of fact, the tripod of educational foundation is firmly knit together in that subjectivism which is made "objective" in the work of education and moral progress. Although often sceptic both as to the ethical quality of human nature and as to the fact of human progress, Kant did hold fast to the possible solution of the moral and the pedagogical problem of the race. And no nobler conception than his of the dignity of education has since been set forth in the light of both science and human history, and, indeed, is scarce conceivable.

Having traced the history and the foundations of Kant's educational theory, we may now turn to a more detailed consideration of what that theory comprised.

KANT'S CONCEPTION OF EDUCATION

It has been a mooted question as to whether Kant can be credited with having wrought out a systematic notion of education, and especially whether the remains of his lectures can be organized into orderly discussions. Vogt, Paulsen, Lindner, Temming, and most other writers declare in the negative, while Burger probably stands alone in his suggestion that Kant did entertain an idea of education which had organizing power, but was not carried out to that length by him. One may agree with the negative view as based on a reading of his discussions, which do not touch upon all matters concerned in the practice of the schools, without thereby doing violence to a conviction which believes Kant to have had a generic conception of education, expressed with some clearness, and serving as the point of orientation in more than one way.

Is Kant's Pedagogy Systematic?

The foundation of his pedagogical views is to be found in his idea of man and of his destiny, as just sketched at some length. These represent the external goal, as it were, in terms of which one can mark the amount of advance made in any practice of education. The inner process is dynamic. No writer has more clearly set forth *a pedagogy of effort.* This spirit expressed itself in the conception of will in psychology, the factor of activity in philosophy, and the free development in evo-

lution.   Duproix is therefore right in stating that, "for
Kant, education is a constant effort, a voluntary ascension,
a progressive evolution towards an ideal which should
be more fully known and more elevated." [1]

Standing alone, this view would have little value,
being extremely schematic, and thus capable of appro-
His Chief Peda- priation by almost any detailed plan of
gogical Terms. training.   Fortunately, however, Kant gave
definite elaboration to it.   It did not stand before him
as a thin, simple conception, but as extremely rich and
complex.   The first mark of his differentiation of it can
be found in his use of the terms *Bildung*, *Kultur*, and
Erziehung, all referring to the general process which
becomes thus broken up.   (See foot-note 2, page 101.)
The chief evidence, however, is to be found in the nota-
ble fact that, when speaking in general of pedagogy and
the empirical development of man, Kant uses the following five terms : *Notwendigkeit*, *Möglichkeit*, *Wert*, *Prin-
cipien*, and *Kunst*.   He does not stop anywhere to distinguish specifically and literally between the *necessity*, the
possibility, the *value*, the *principles*, and the *art* of education.   But the rules and recommendations given upon
physical, mental, and moral training in the Treatise will
be found to be more or less in accord with these five
aspects which, with a possible sixth, exhaust the conception of education presented in the Introduction.

The Necessity of Education.—Kant first sets forth the
view that education is not optional, but compulsory.   It
is not a social luxury, but a basic national and racial

---

[1] *Kant et Fichte et le problème de l' Éducation*, p. 128.

need. Education must supply to man the lack of instincts in him, which are so fortunately present in the animal. He is "raw" and helpless (Sections 1, 2, 6). Nature alone does not educate ; but man must make his own pedagogical plans *Education a Necessity for Man.* (14). It is thus that reason appears as the ultimate source of authority in human education. Nor is it a movement in a circle to add, that it is the essence of human nature,—namely, that man is made man by education only, which finally supplies the grounds for this necessity. A good world is derived by educational development. From this point of view, Kant is able to justify pedagogy as a "natural science," and to relate the education of man to his empirical character. Do we not here find a happy approximation to that recent view of infancy, entertained on the basis of organic evolution, which regards it as the provision of nature for the introduction of formative influences to aid the individual to elevate himself above the mechanisms of an animal civilization? This necessity, according to Kant, also has its limits fixed by the age determinations of the child and by the orderly sequence which must be followed (7, 18, 26, 33). This necessity is made absolute, finally, by the great gap which exists between the human infant at birth and the human will organized into free action under law.

The Possibility of Education.—The crying need for education which human nature manifests, whether viewed *ab ante* from nature or *ad post* to the ideal of moral development, is not a delusion or a trick. The demand is met by the possibility. *Education Possible.* The ideal is, above all, "truthful." Here, again, Kant's views rest upon an analysis of human nature. Germinal reason and a *quasi*-germinal morality alone make the possibility actual. Man has innate capacities. He is equipped for perfection (7, 11). Education is a process which is exactly adapted to man rather than to animals (19). The possibility seems almost to be the divine commission to man to develop himself. So definite does the possibility become that its task is defined in the mathematical terms of "proportionate" development of the capacities. It is also so large that its achievement is not for the individual alone, or primarily, but for the entire race. So great and so certain is this possibility a provision of the natural conditions of society, that Kant, as a pedagogue, becomes prophetic, and looks forward to a future happier state of humanity as a result of true education (7). This possibility is not only "ideal," but also intellectual and practicable. Education being a possible process, it gives rise to scientific principles and to a distinct art (11, 14). The latter must be reduced to rational and directive principles for it to make any progress. The possibility of education is thus the actuality of a "science" of pedagogy,—a remarkable admission and ideal for this great determiner of all sciences.

The Value of Education.—This has already been playing upon the surface in the characterization of the two preceding items in his general view of what education is. Its value is relative. It is a means to an end. But it is also the *only* means to an *absolute* end (7, 16). This value is no less indicated by the fact that education remains up to the present (Kant's) time an undiscovered "ideal" (8). Realism

Education possesses an Ideal Value.

can scarce be the foundation of a true pedagogy, or it
would have been discovered long ago in the history of the
race. This value is not limited to the individual, for the
destiny of man is not reached in the individual alone, but
first and only in the race. To Kant, education means,
not that simple, limited interaction, shaped by the teacher,
between the individual child and the world as it is in
reality. This is the petty, parsimonious pedagogy which
becomes an inflated normalism, working blindly upon
the individual. Kant escaped this mechanical conception by incorporating it, in a subordinate way, in a vaster
regard for education. To him, education means, in the
fullest sense of the term, a progressive interaction between the individual child and humanity, as the latter is
expressed in the ultimate idea of its worth and destiny.
The chief effects of this interaction are to be traced in
the growing personality of the child, since the ideal of
humanity remains the same for both the individual and
the race, preserving a constant nature throughout the
civilizing changes of all generations (10, 15, 95a). This
does not mean a demand for pedagogical uniformity in
the race. Far from it. For it is a supreme moral idealism which is thus introduced into pedagogy. It is at this
point that his greatest service to education is to be seen.
It is morality alone which gives *meaning* to man, and at
the same time puts an *end* into educational thought and
effort. This end is not changeable with the ages in
which education may successively be carried out, and is
distinctly opposed to the temporal determinations of
utility, happiness, or any other immediate, external
result. The worth of any education, then, at once is

measurable in terms of its degree of approximation to this unalterable goal. Here, also, it is again seen how interchangeable ethics and pedagogy become for Kant (cf. Selections II., XI., XIII.).

The Principles of Education.—Kant's opportunities to lecture on education did not waste themselves on mere pedagogical idealizations. These ramblings of the rational heart, if one feels like calling them such, while appearing in the foreground, did not stand alone. He gave them the double support of offering a few positive principles, and of making the further demand that they be reduced to a scientific structure. The necessity and the possibility of training man have already presented most of the naturalistic, anthropological reasons for undertaking education. But, further, education must be reduced to a *science*, that a succeeding generation may not destroy all that its predecessor has done (14). This implies a permanent optimistic belief in the power of an accumulative science, which grows into an impersonal heritage of the race at large,—a spirit which has flourished with every discovery in the nineteenth century. The tribute paid to the value of "experts" in education is another indication of Kant's belief in the integrity of pedagogical science (17).[1]   Indeed, this belief goes so far as to make

A Science of Education demands Principles.

---

[1] The *Critique of Pure Reason*, as well as some later writings, attempted to set forth clearly just what Kant regarded "science" to be, as the complex product of constructive intellect. It would carry us too far to detail the structural aspects of science which appealed to him in these analyses, and we must be content here with these two observations. He does not introduce his technical

a demand for experimentation, which is not merely optional, but necessary in order to acquire the proper principles (20; cf. Selection III.). The *Philanthropinum* and normal schools seemed to be the hope in which this confidence rested, until their limitations became manifest.

Besides this demand for a science of pedagogy, determined on a basis of facts and reason, Kant offers a number of positive principles borrowed His Principles more or less from physiology, psychology, summarized. anthropology, and ethics, as we of to-day would say. The child must be educated according to "nature" (here following Rousseau). Civilization must underlie educational principles. The child must be educated under the dominance of the idea of humanity. The bodily powers must be cultivated to orderly independence. The mental powers must not be cultivated separately, or formally, but in mutual interdependence. Self-doing is the secret of true education, and self-education is its goal. Rules and maxims, not impulses and whims, must be the inspiration and guidance of every educational move. Age is a determinant in education. Conduct and character depend upon the establishment of good principles. Such are some of the great viewpoints from which his prescription and proscription of

conception of science in these *Lecture-Notes*, but at the same time he does declare the nature of a guiding science to be "rational" and not "mechanical" (14) or personally prejudicial (16, 17). The literalist, of course, could easily make out that the only "science" of pedagogy is that which is derived from the principles expressed in the three *Critiques*, and that the lectures are therefore non-scientific.

practices in training the infant, youth, and pupil are derived. Kant was cautious and shrewd enough to distinguish between principle and practice, between a pedagogical generalization and a pedagogical performance.

The Art of Education.—To the foregoing features in Kant's general conception of education we must add a fifth,—namely, The Art of Education (11, 14, 15). He appears among the first to recognize the practical, artistic nature of education. The large scope of education and the extreme complexity of its factors and presuppositions involve a mass of ways and means. That this is merely a haphazard and heterogeneous mass he does not seem to believe. The problem is to reduce every practice to principle, to find a rational basis for every activity. The school became to him, in all its forms, the meeting-place of pedagogical idealism and actual achievement in handling human nature. This concrete element in his theory extends far beyond his lectures on pedagogy; for it tends to reappear in his technical philosophical writings, especially those dealing with practical philosophy. (See Selection XI.) This rather constant endeavor to get his educational creed "applied" adds an unusual support to the integrity and the sincerity of the philosophical basis upon which that creed rested.

Education an Art.

The Forms of Education.—This is a sixth aspect which should be added to the above. Specific mention is not made of this by Kant, but it is integral in his educational theory, and appears in a variety of distinctions and recommendations. There is, of course, a constant danger of reading into an author

Various Forms of Education.

meanings which are not detailed in his discussions.   In such concentrated material as the *Notes* undoubtedly are one can, however, do him no real violence by gathering together the various intimations of a distinction as to the forms into which education moulds itself, and under which its work must be accomplished.   This distinction extends to a recognition of form in the external and the internal aspects of education: the types of schools, governmental *versus* philanthropic, public *versus* private (17, 22–25); the types of teachers, as parents, tutors, teachers (10, 14, 21, 24, 34); the types of education both intellectual and moral, as dependent upon age (1, 26 ff., 84, 90); and, finally, the types as to methods (especially Selection VIII.).   These types were approved, or condemned, from his stand-point of requiring education to be a full and free development of the individual man.

The Division of Educational Activities.

The difficulties involved in getting Kant's general conception of education increase as we approach the contents of the *Lecture-Notes* and attempt to systematize his views definitely expressed. The Value of Rink's Edition. We suddenly discover that the six points just inventoried do not appear in the explicit classifications which he makes of the factors, or activities, he regards as comprising education.   Again, our difficulties increase as we observe that neither the half-dozen elements in his conception nor his analyses of education into its factors serve him in the division of topics discussed in these *Notes*.   This external, or topical, division cannot be traced back beyond Rink's editing. Rink arranged the first part, here called "Introduction" (Sections 1–30), without any superscription. The second part, or the remainder (Sections 31–113), was called "The Treatise." This, in turn, was divided into two parts,—"On Physical Education" (Sections 34–90), and "On Practical Education" (Sections 91–113).[1] He also adopted the method of placing rules between certain paragraphs as a mode of still finer division of the material which came to his hand.

The question of adjusting these numerous divisions of the external and the internal educational factors has exercised the many editors and expositors of Kant's views without the end of the debate being clearly in sight. Schubert, Hartenstein, Willmann, Vogt, Fröhlich and Körner, Hollenbach, Strümpell, Richter, Kipping, Vogel, Deinhardt, Light, and others have dealt more or less—usually less—with this issue, scarcely any two arriving at the same conclusion. The question of the external division, however, is subordinate to that of the division of educational activities. It is upon the latter that all conclusions one adopts as to the former must rest.

Kant had a wonderful passion for primness, for making division upon division when treating of ideas and theo-
retical interpretations of facts. His more sys-
Kant's
Passion for   tematic treatises on philosophy are striking
Over-Analysis. on account of the almost indefinite heaping
of distinction upon distinction. This analytic refinement

---

[1] Burger, *Ueber die Gliederung der Pädagogik Kants.* Jena, 1889, p. 7.

was the mental ability which enabled him to undertake the achievement which he accomplished. This predilection reached, without doubt, its highest expression in his lectures on pedagogy, as may be gathered from the fragmentary form in which they have been preserved. In no less than a dozen sections there are given repeated divisions of those activities involved in education, and as many groupings of the particular doctrines which constitute the body of his views on this subject. We here, also, secure an insight into his method of separation and exclusion which enabled him to make so much of his work lastingly effective for the culture of his age. Indeed, as has been suggested, perhaps more of his individuality appears in this than in any other of his writings.

The following list presents the divisions of education found in the various sections :

Types of Educational Activities.

1. Care, discipline, instruction, and culture (with the age determinant broadly outlined).

4. Training = negative ; instruction = positive.

6. Care, training, instruction.

18. Discipline, cultivation, civilization, and moralization (the chief classification in the Introduction).

19. Training, teaching, thinking, acting, and a repetition of the four activities named in 18.

21. Care, discipline, culture (as instruction, direction).

22. Public and private education.

27. Obedience, freedom (the two epochs in *schooling*).

31. Physical, practical education.

32. Practical includes scholastic, pragmatic, moral ends.

47.
58. } Physical culture of the mind includes { negatively = discipline.
positively = culture.

63. { Physical culture = cultivation = nature.
Practical culture = moralization = freedom.

64. Physical culture of the mind { free = play.
scholastic = work.

72. {
1. General culture of the faculties. { Physical = p a s s i v e = practice and discipline.
Moral = active = duty and maxims.

2. Particular culture of the faculties. { Lower faculties.
Higher faculties.

Why does Kant go on making new and ever newer divisions of the content and of the aims of education? May these repeated divisions represent his annually successive approaches to the problem of education? Why does not the table of the twelve categories—the laws of science and nature—appear in these divisions? To these, and to many similar questions, it must simply be answered: we do not know. The almost inexhaustible complexity of education is strongly declared in these repeated analyses. We may choose to adopt one section or another as characteristically Kantian, and thus proceed to adapt all the others to the one selected. It is no doubt possible to bring all into agreement with Sections 18, 31, 72.

But the most important point to be observed is this: in these repeated divisions, Kant did not lose sight of the ethico-psycho-physical solidarity of the individual, and thus of the race. From beginning to conclusion, he does not forget that every phase of educational effort must proceed upon a recognition of the basis which natural and mechanical processes univer- sally present, be it in physical, psychical, cultural, or moral education, in the constant endeavor to hand the child over to a free, rational, individual independence. A second point of importance is the character of the Introduction, which, in giving some general reflections upon the nature of education, has an original cast, and approximates a logical unity. Burger is nearer the truth than most other interpreters in saying that it is truly Kantian in allowing the concepts to arise slowly before one's eyes, and in tending to give a more detailed treatment of each special type of educational activity before all are brought together into a systematic conception.[1] And, finally, the exhaustive character of his analyses is attested by the fact, that the pedagogy of the nineteenth century has not contributed a single important addition to the elements in the scheme here projected. It may have changed the rubrics in its pedagogy, from "physical" and "practical" to such as "physical," "intellectual," "moral," "social," "religious;" but these do not outstep the former's all-inclusiveness ; for within Kant's conception we find the *differentiæ* of age, sex, social condition, civic condition, and life itself co-operating directly with the more formal elements which are given an exalted position in the basal classifications. The topical and

The Solidarity of the Individual and of the Race.

---

[1] Burger, *Ueber die Gliederung der Pädagogik Kants*, Jena, 1889, p. 7.

content divisions will also readily be found to be in accordance with the philosophical, the psychological, and the evolutional bases upon which he rested his insight into the character of human education.

In view of the brevity and compactness of Kant's discussions on educational questions, it is not necessary here to pass in review the material to be found in the translation. Such observations as should be made are to be found scattered throughout the foot-notes. But the following remarks may be offered in conclusion at this point.

Kant should not be regarded as a pedagogical formalist. To him, education was not an empty process. Pedagogy

Kant not a Formalist.

meant a valuation of the ways and means at the disposal of the ruler, the parent, the teacher, which should be employed in light of the aim of education. The pedagogue should be one who, beginning with the stream of life, carefully watches its current, keeping it out of the by-pools and eddies, and guiding it onward to the greater and larger oceanic life beyond. Thus it is that the same aim is kept uppermost whether we have reference to physical development, mental activity, or the formation of character. This is the secret of the unity in Kant's theory, albeit the rules and precepts which he offers may seem to have no wider basis than a desire for a certain form of culture limited to the special activity considered under this or that topic, as the case may be.

Kant's regard for the material of education from infancy to maturity should also lead one to believe that his pedagogical ideals were not vain abstractions suspended in the air. He did not abstract physical from intellectual and moral education. Here he is both the ancient Spartan and the scientific modern. In making the first a constituent part of pedagogy, he antedated our science which shows the solidarity of the different parts of the human organism. A like vital regard for the educative material of the intellect again brings him near to the spirit of current educational progress. It is not the *a priori* intellect of the *Critique of Pure Reason*, but the empirical intelligence which comes in for directive care. There is here both matter and form. The former aspect leads to the intellectual subjects of study, about which it is remarkable he has so little to say, in view of his ripe acquaintance with the advances of science in his day. At the same time, this need not be surprising, if one may be permitted to draw a conclusion from the famous passage about the starry heavens above and the moral law within. To Kant, both physical and mental studies brought the mind to the same attitude. The latter lead to method in dealing with those subjects. In his approval of the Socratic method, and in his demand for a unification of knowing and doing, there appears a unique recognition of the need that the education of the will should penetrate all so-called intellectual education. And, finally, education for morality is described as deriving its material from the riches of human experience and of human reason in its ability to make the differentiations necessary for a recognition of duty and the organization of a firm, intelligent will. It is rather striking, however, that the educative

Margin note: But chiefly a Harmonizer of Ancient and Modern Tendencies.

material which pertains to the body and to the will is presented more fully than that which is to be coördinated with intellectual development. "The problem of the curriculum" had not arisen in his day, and the inflated hope of educational "evaluations" had not yet begun to distress the pedagogue.

THE LIMITATIONS OF KANT'S EDUCATIONAL THEORY

In expounding Kant's views on the nature of education, its presuppositions and its great purposes, and in outlining the contributions his philosophy made to the growth of educational theory in the nineteenth century, we have not been unmindful of certain limitations which characterize his conceptions, nor of the staple criticisms which have been urged against the foundations he laid. And, again, in endeavoring to make it clear that his philosophy and his pedagogy are closely related, and not widely separated, the effort has not proceeded disregardful of the schematic and partial manner in which Kant himself worked out the details of the relation, and the limited application the former was given to the latter. It has been the usual attituae towards Kant's opinions on education to regard the contents of *Ueber Pädagogik* as aphoristic, and thus as favoring the selection of those happy sayings, and the rejection of those unfortunate sayings, which may or may not agree with the critic's own views. We have sought to show the limitations of this tradition of appreciation by endeavoring to point out the larger way in which his contributions to pedagogy should be regarded.

The truest appreciation, however, is sane criticism. And Kant does not escape an application of that intellectual instrument which he taught the nineteenth century to use so successfully. The destructive critic can

Limitations due to lack of a Technical Vocabulary. perform his task with specious fruitfulness if he forgets that Kant has no fixed terminology, beyond that outlined above, in these *Notes*, and that their fragmentary character permits many gaps to appear in his arguments. The obscurity thus easily made possible does not readily justify close criticism. As to a vocabulary, however, one finds that Kant employs terms which became technical for him, at least, as may be seen in the passages in Selection IV. And, besides, a *very* partial Kantian might reply *ad hominem* that the whole field of education still remains without a fixed vocabulary. Criticism, if allowable, should also be tempered by the fact that many defects and inconsistencies may be due to the lack of his own editing of the material contained in the *Notes*. Thus making ample allowances for the character of the material available, the following criticisms are given in the sense that his theory suffers by limitation rather than by radical defect and insecurity. They can hardly be classified as belonging to the scope, material, processes, and methods of education.

1. The most persistent apparent limitation of Kant's views on education seems to be his *over-emphasis of the individual*. Duproix has pointed this out as

The Individual Over-emphasized. the distinguishing feature of Kant's ideal, which Fichte corrected by giving education an interpretation in terms of national life.ᐧ It is, indeed, true that the personal element stands out in both the *Lecture-Notes* and in the Selections, both in the generalizations and in the rules which are laid down. And this individualism goes so far that to Kant the individual will, the innermost heart of humanity, becomes the centre of educational gravitation. Free personality stands to education as effect to cause, as purpose to conditions. The " man" which Kant generically employs, especially in the Introduction, means every individual,—and also, as we shall soon see, *man*, not woman, in the literal sense. From this it is but a step to the affirmation of the doctrine of the pedagogical equality of all men. But modern education is learning more and more rapidly that such equality is truthful only so long as it is conceived ideally. Psychological diversity represents the truer account of the material upon which educational processes must effect their achievements.

It is just as true, however, that Kant's conception of the education of the individual is much wider and more complex than that conception of the individual as a static unit which is required to give force to this criticism. The individual *Kant conceived a Race Pedagogy.* was to him the individual as a representative member of the race. This racial conception marks the scope of his educational horizon (Sections 4, 11, 13), taken in its numerical or quantitative aspects. From a qualitative point of view, the individual man really becomes a true individual only as he becomes a citizen in the kingdom of moral ends. Furthermore, between the race and the moral aspects of individuality, Kant distinctly presents a conception of what might be called both state and social pedagogy, which is integrated into his ideal. Pedagogy and government are placed side by side as offering equally fundamental and difficult problems (12). The state and the school are mutually dependent institutions, and the state is roundly condemned when it advances its own ends and cares naught for the education of its citizens (16, 17, and Selection II. p. 240). This feature is carried over into the division of schools as public and private (22).

In addition to this external side of the civic organization of education, citizenship and social fitness are two significant moments in the ideal of educa- Education includes Citizenship and Social Fitness. tion which Kant demands should be constructively realized in the formation of the complete man. These appear in "civilization" (18c), in "pragmatic culture" (32b, 33), in sociability (80, note, 88), in worldly wisdom (92), in duties towards others (95b), and in the recognition of the social dangers in human development (112).

2. The second limitation, which is perhaps the chief defect in Kant's treatment of educational theory, is his complete omission of the education of Education of Woman neglected girls. The sex problem in education appeared to him, in so far as it was considered at all, in its negative aspects. The individual for whom he lays down rules positively is the boy. Sex phenomena and conditions, however, are recognized by him, and contribute several determinations to education. This is seen in various ways. The time limit of education is marked by nature herself, at the development of the sex instinct (26). Imparting a knowledge of sex relations is one of the difficult tasks of instruction (30). The development of will and the formation of character are

distinctly correlated with adolescence (84, 86), and the conclusion of the *Lecture-Notes* deals directly with the problems of the guidance and the control of adolescence (110, 111). Kant thus is one of the first moderns to think clearly in this latter regard, and to anticipate the current emphasis placed upon this phase of the individual's development and some of the problems which it hands over to education.

Kant's failure properly to conceive of, and to discuss, the education of girls is closely connected with his conception of woman. As early as 1764 we find expression of his idea of the nature of woman, and outlines of what the education of girls should be. " The fair sex has understanding, just the same as the masculine; it is only a *beautiful* understanding; ours should be a *deep* understanding, which is an expression having a meaning identical with the sublime." " The content of the great science of woman is man, and among men a particular man. Her philosophy is not subtilizing, but feeling." Education must attempt to extend her entire moral feeling, and not her memory, not by general rules, but by acts of particular judgment on her part upon her environment. He allows for her study a little history, a little geography, and feeling for expression and for music, not as art, but as mere sensation. Since she has little understanding and much inclination, she should never be given " a cold and speculative teaching, but always sensations, and, indeed, those which remain as close as possible to her sex relations. This instruction is very rare, because it demands talents, experience, and a heart full of

Kant's Idea of Woman.

feeling, and woman can very well dispense with every other, just as she can also without these educate herself very well." Hence marriage enfranchises woman, whereas it destroys man's freedom. "Laborious learning and painstaking subtilizing in a woman, even when she brings them to a high degree of perfection, destroy the prerogatives which are peculiar to her sex; they can, it is true, because of their rarity, make her an object of cold admiration, but at the same time they will weaken the charms which give her so much power over the other sex. A woman who has her head full of Greek, like Mme. Dacier, or who carries on profound discussions in mechanics, like the Marquise de Chastelet, may just as well have a beard beside; for a beard would perhaps express still more unmistakably the air of profoundness which she is trying to acquire."[1] "So far as learned women are concerned: they use their *books* in something like the way that they use their watch,—namely, carry it, in order to let it be seen that they have one; it is immaterial whether or not it runs or keeps time."[2] In fine, Kant accepted the general opinion of his age in attempting to reduce the education of girls to the formation of taste and the feelings. (See Selection I., Nos. 4, 5, 6, 7, 22, 23, 24, 47.)

Kant must, however, be credited with having insisted that the education of woman should be determined, not by the abstract possibilities of science, or of her intel-

---

[1] *Observations on the Feeling of the Beautiful and the Sublime* (1764).—Hartenstein, ii. pp. 252–254.

[2] *Anthropology*, etc. (1798).—Hartenstein, vii. p. 631.

lect, but rather in terms of the life which she is to live biologically and socially. From this conception we have not moved at the present time a single step, whatever our practices in the secondary and higher education of girls and women may be.

3. At the risk of some repetition, mention should be made of the limitation in his treatment of the so-called intellectual education. This was not ex- *Limited Treatment of Intellectual Education.* actly omitted, and yet we find but very little attention given to the subjects of study. He places the education of the intellect within the realm of "the physical," implying thereby that there are natural faculties of the mind which must be given a *quasi*-mechanical development before their true education can take place. This is also signified in the distinction between the "free" and the "scholastic" culture which the mind may have, the former being passive and the latter more active. At the same time Kant condemns turbulent curiosity in children, and fully understands the dangers of distraction and other disturbances of attention. When we come to the positive treatment of the intellect, we find it to be the logical rather than the imaginative-affective intellect which receives by far the larger share of treatment. Romances and music are interdicted as intellectual subjects. Poetry is not mentioned,—a strange omission in view of the fact that at one time Kant was offered the university chair of poetry. Mathematics and the sciences were preferred above history and language, which were also admitted into his scheme of studies.

In the *Critique of Judgment* a portion of the subject-matter of education—the literary classics of Greece and Rome—is evaluated on grounds different from those which appear in the *Lecture-Notes*. Although presenting a phase of æsthetic education, the passage may find place here.

Educative Value of Literary Classics.

" The propædeutic to all fine art, in so far as the degree of its perfection is concerned, seems to lie, not in rules, but rather in the culture of the mental powers by those kinds of knowledge which are called *humaniora;* probably because *humanity* means the universal *feeling of sympathy*, on the one hand, and the ability to *communicate* one's feelings cordially and generally, on the other; these characteristics taken together constitute mankind's appropriate happiness, whereby they are differentiated from the limitations of animals. The age as well as the nation in which the active impulse to *organized* social life, whereby a people constitutes a permanent community, struggled with the great and difficult task of combining freedom (and hence equality) with restraint (rather respect and submission from a sense of duty than fear): such an age and such a nation had to invent the art of mutual communication of ideas between the educated and the ignorant classes, combining the enlargement and refinement of the former with the natural simplicity and originality of the latter, and in this way discover that medium between the higher culture and temperate nature which constitutes the correct standard, one not to be indicated by general rules, as well for taste as for universal human understanding.

" It is not probable that a later age will dispense with this standard; for it will be less and less near to nature, and finally, without having lasting examples from her, would hardly be in a position to form a conception of the happy union, in one and the same nation, of the lawful restraint of the highest culture with the power and justice of free nature, conscious of her own value."[1]

4. The next limitation to be pointed out is twofold. It pertains to the rôle of the feelings assigned to pedagogy, and to their development under the educative material of æsthetics. The first feature of this limitation is affirmed, the other implied. *Education of Feeling neglected.* The feelings of the individual are practically banished from any share in education, and the claims of æsthetics as making positive contribution to the realization of pedagogy's ideal are neglected. These items reflect Kant's rigorous conception of human life and of the conditions under which its greatest aims are to be actualized.

In his educational theory Kant despises the feelings, both in instruction and in moralization, quite as much as in his ethical theory, in which they are forced from a contributive portion to conduct. In his psychology, as pointed out above, he came to look upon the feelings as a distinct group of mental activities,—so distinct that they gave rise to the unique philosophical problems which he discussed in the third *Critique*. In the *Lecture-Notes*, however, the explicit references to the culture of the feelings and the development of taste are only two (52, 70). At the same time it must be admitted that, according to the classifications in his psychology, much of feeling comes

---

[1] Hartenstein, v. p. 367.

under will and the mechanical development of motives through discipline and training. Beyond this, however, in so far as the feelings come in for any recognition, they are decried educationally, being looked upon as having a selfish, softening effect upon the character. In his great care for strong, virile character, he desires that the dangers of ease, indolence, and "languishing sympathy," of pride, emulation, and shame be removed as far as possible from absorption by the forming mind. At the same time, one should not forget to observe that Kant can be immeasurably tender with childhood and youth (88), whose great possibilities he idealizes into absolute worth. In his hurling defiance at the feelings, which is such a marked defect in his educational scheme, and in his profound regard for the rational heart, we find paradoxically a secret source of the great power he exercised over his own times. This negative pedagogy of the feelings is also thoroughly consistent with his ethical criticism of every form of eudæmonism as incapable of setting up adequate moral standards.

The much broader feature of this limitation is Kant's neglect of æsthetic education. This may be closely associated with the second limitation pointed
Æsthetic Values involved in his Theory. out above. To have pursued the culture of the feelings with the material of art may have meant to Kant the feminization of the should-be science of pedagogy. (See Selection I., Nos. 6, 22.) He omits the entire region of art and æsthetic appreciation as objects of training, as material for culture, and as promotive of large sections in a full moral personality. At the same time, do not æsthetic *motifs* color

his educational ideal? What else, then, are the perfection of human nature (7), the proportionate development of the capacities (10), and the ideal of the destiny
of humanity (15, 95) as found in the sublimity of moral
action (78)? But with all this implication, the nearest
approach he makes to the ideal of education as *beautify-
ing* man is his demand that man shall be " civilized"
(18c).

If we turn to the *Critique of Judgment*, we find that
the development and the formation of the æsthetical
feelings and taste, which are found by psychological
analysis to be constituent in human nature, are not
overlooked. They are also found to have their objective
counterpart in the finer arts which have developed with
civilization. This suggests what we have repeatedly seen
to be true, that the pedagogical thought and interest of
Kant the philosopher are really larger than those of Kant
the pedagogue. To the former no fundamental discipline of science and speculation is complete without its
due section on the pedagogy of itself. In this instance
we see that that which is neglected in the lectures, thus
displaying an inconsistency with the philosophical system, presents a powerful influence in his systematic
treatise on the nature of taste. It is barely possible that
his own mind had not reached, by the time of his last
course of lectures on pedagogy, the point in its development at which æsthetic analysis was undertaken with
constructive intent. And yet, there stands the essay of
1764 on the feeling of the beautiful and the sublime.

The beginnings of the modern theory of æsthetic
education can be traced to the third *Critique*. In its

preface, Kant characterizes this work as undertaking an investigation of the faculty of taste, as æsthetical judgment, merely with transcendental intent, but not for the sake of the formation and culture of that faculty. For, he opines, the latter "will continue to pursue its way, as heretofore, without any such inquiries."[1] This non-pedagogical conception of æsthetics is further expressed in the view that "there is no science of beauty, but only criticism; no beautiful science, but only beautiful art."[2] In his division of æsthetical philosophy, the usual "elements" and "method" are not retained; since "for fine art there is only a manner (*modus*), but not a method of instruction (*methodus*)."[3] As Kant worked out his views on the nature of art and its relations to the human mind these formal opinions did not prevail. His real problem assumed pedagogical meaning in addressing itself to the question of the relations between beauty and conduct. How can the good will be carried over into the world of sense? He answers by placing taste between sense and morality. The merely agreeable is wholly sensuous. The good will is wholly rational. The beautiful is the sensuous-rational.[4] In this way taste is a fit preparation for freedom. And a true lover of the beautiful is always morally good.[5]

The Founder of Modern Æsthetics.

"Now, I say: the beautiful is the symbol of the morally good; and in this respect does it give us a pleasure with which we expect others to sympathize,

---

[1] Hartenstein, v. p. 176.   [2] *Ibid.*, p. 314.
[3] *Ibid.*, p. 366.   [4] *Ibid.*, p. 214.   [5] *Ibid.*, pp. 208, 308.

whereby the mind is conscious of a certain exaltation and elevation above the mere susceptibility of desire through impressions of the senses, and at the same time estimates the worth of others according to a similar maxim of their judgment."[1] "Taste makes possible the transition from sensuous pleasure to habitual interest in morality without a too violent leap, by representing the imagination, even in its freedom, as capable of being determined in adaptation to the understanding, and teaching us to find free satisfaction with no sensuous pleasure, even in objects of sense."[2]

How completely æsthetics thus returns to the actualizing support of the ideal of education is, finally, to be seen towards the close of the *Critique*, where Kant characterizes the intentions of nature with respect to man. (See Selection IV.) The final aim of nature is not man's happi- ness, but man's *culture*, with its highest application to freedom. Discipline and the acquisition of skill are preparatory stages in this culture. In the higher education of man, the study of the humanities, art, and science must finally contribute to the actualization of this natural end. "Fine arts and sciences, which make men well-behaved, even if not morally better, by a universally communicable desire, and by politeness and social refinement, rob the sensuous inclinations of much of their tyranny, and thus prepare man for a mastery, in which reason alone shall have power; while the evils with which partly nature and partly the untamable

Art and Conduct Educationally United.

[1] Hartenstein, v. p. 364.   [2] *Ibid.*, p. 366.

selfishness of men assail us, call forth, increase, and steel the powers of the soul, that they may not succumb to these influences, and thus they make us feel a fitness, which lies hidden within us, for higher aims." [1]   It was Schiller who declared an absolute confidence in this educative power of art, and it was Herbart, borrowing from both Kant and Schiller, who labored to systematize instruction and discipline for the realization of this end.

---

[1] Hartenstein, v. p. 447.

LITERATURE

ENGLISH TRANSLATIONS OF KANT'S WRITINGS

THE following list of Kant's writings which have been translated into English is here given to aid those English-reading students of his educational theory who desire to familiarize themselves more widely with his other scientific and philosophical doctrines. It is not complete, but includes only those writings which will throw most light upon his theory and those translations which are most apt to be accessible at the present time.[1]

Kant's Cosmogony, by W. Hastie, Glasgow, 1900. (This volume contains his essay on *The Retardation of the Earth's Rotation*, and *Natural History and Theory of the Heavens*.)

Kant's Introduction to Logic and his *Essay on the Mistaken Subtilty of the Four Figures*, by T. K. Abbott, London, 1885.

Kant's Dreams of a Spirit-seer illustrated by the Dreams of Metaphysics, by E. F. Goerwitz, London, 1900.

Kant's Inaugural Dissertation of 1770, by W. J. Eckoff, New York, 1894.

Kant's Critique of Pure Reason, by Max Müller, London, 1881; reprinted with alterations, London and New York, 1896.

The Philosophy of Kant in Extracts, by J. Watson, new edition, Glasgow, 1895. (This volume contains translated selections from the *Critique of Pure Reason*, the *Fundamental Principles of the Metaphysics of Ethics*, the *Critique of Practical Reason*, and the *Critique of Judgment*.)

---

[1] It is adapted from the complete list of translations published some years ago in the *Kantstudien*, by Professor G. M. Duncan, who has kindly brought it down to date for special use in this volume.

Kant's Prolegomena, and Metaphysical Foundations of Natural Science, by E. B. Bax, London, 1883.

Kant's Prolegomena to any Future Metaphysics, by P. Carus, Chicago, 1901.

Kant's Principles of Politics, by W. Hastie, Edinburgh, 1891. (This volume contains *Idea of a Universal History from a Cosmopolitan Standpoint,* Parts II. and III. of *Upon the Common Saying: A Thing may be Good in Theory, but not in Practice,* and *Eternal Peace: a Philosophical Scheme.*)

Kant's Philosophy of Law, by W. Hastie, Edinburgh, 1887 (being Part I. of *The Metaphysics of Ethics*).

Kant's Ethical Theory, by T. K. Abbott, fifth edition, London and New York, 1898. (This volume contains *Fundamental Principles of the Metaphysics of Ethics,* the *Critique of Practical Reason,* Part I. of *On the Radical Evil in Human Nature,* Part I. of *Religion within the Limits of Mere Reason,* the General Introduction to *The Metaphysics of Ethics,* and the Preface and Introduction to Part II. of the same, and *Upon an Alleged Right to Lie from Motives of Humanity.*)

Kant's Critique of Judgment, by J. H. Bernard, London, 1892.

Kant's Anthropology Pragmatically Considered, by A. E. Kroeger, in *American Journal of Speculative Philosophy,* vols. 9 ff., St. Louis, 1875 ff.

Kant on Education, by Miss A. Churton, Introduction by Mrs. R. Davids, London, 1899.

SEPARATE EDITIONS OF "UEBER PÄDAGOGIK"

Immanuel Kant, bearbeitet von G. Fröhlich und F. Körner, Die Klassiker der Pädagogik, Bd. xi., herausgegeben von G. Fröhlich, Langensalza, 1890.

Emmanuel Kant, Traité de Pédagogie (traduction Jules Barni), avec une préface des sommaires analytiques et un lexique par Raymond Thamin.   Paris, Alcan, 1886.

Immanuel Kant, Über Pädagogik.   Mit Kant's Biographie herausgegeben von T. Vogt, 2te Auflage, Langensalza, 1883. Beyer's Bibliothek pädagogischer Klassiker, Bd. viii.

Immanuel Kant, Ueber Pädagogik. Mit Einleitung und Anmerkung versehen von O. Willmann, 2te Auflage, Leipzig. Richter's Pädagogische Bibliothek, Bd. x.

EXPOSITION AND CRITICISM

From the large mass of Kantian literature the following selections may be mentioned here.

Becker. *Immanuel Kant und die deutsche Nationalerziehung.* Worms, 1876.

Beyer, C. *Erziehung zur Vernunft. Philosophisch-pädagogische Grundlinien für Erziehung und Unterricht,* 3te Auflage. Wien, 1877.

Böhmer, O. *Die Pädagogik bei Kant und Herbart.* Marburg, 1892.

Burger, A. *Ueber die Gliederung der Pädagogik Kants.* Jena, 1890.

Duproix, P. *Kant et Fichte et le problème de l'Éducation.* Geneva, 1895.

Hollenbach, W. *Darstellung und Beurtheilung der Pädagogik Kants.* Jena, 1881.

Jahn, M. *Der Einfluss der Kantischen Psychologie auf die Pädagogik als Wissenschaft.* Neue Jahrbücher für Philologie und Pädagogik, 1884, II. Abt. Leipzig.

Kipping, F. A. *Die Grundzüge der Kantischen Pädagogik.* Pädagogische Blätter für Lehrerbildung und Lehrerbildungsanstalten, 1882, Bd. xi. pp. 370 ff.

Light, J. K. *Kant's Influence on German Pedagogy.* Lebanon, 1893.

McIntyre, J. L. *Kant's Theory of Education.* Educational Review, New York, 1898, xvi. pp. 313–327.

Phillipson, R. *Die ästhetische Erziehung, ein Beitrag zur Lehre Kants, Schillers, und Herbarts.* Magdeburg, 1890.

Prosch, F. *Die Pädagogik Kants.* Zeitschrift für das Realschulwesen, Bd. ix., 1884.

Rehorn, A. *Kant's Ansichten über den religiösen Unterricht.* Wetzlar, 1876.

Richter, A. *Kant's Ansichten über Erziehung.* Halberstadt, 1865.

Strümpell. *Die Pädagogik der Philosophen Kant, Fichte, Herbart.* Braunschweig, 1843.

Temming, E. *Beitrag zur Darstellung und Kritik der moralischen Bildungslehre Kant's.* Braunschweig, 1892.

Vogel, A. *Kant,* in *Geschichte der Pädagogik als Wissenschaft,* pp. 189–208. Gütersloh, 1877.

Vogel, A. *Die philosophischen Grundlagen der wissenschaftlichen Systeme der Pädagogik* (Locke, Kant, Hegel, Schleiermacher, Herbart, Beneke), 2te Auflage. Langensalza, 1889.

The more elaborate encyclopædias and histories of education may also be consulted, such as Buisson's, Lindner's, Rein's, Schmidt's, Ziegler's, etc.

IMMANUEL KANT'S

LECTURE-NOTES ON PEDAGOGY

FIRST EDITED BY

FRIEDRICH THEODOR RINK

1803

INTRODUCTION

1. MAN is the only creature that must be educated. By education we mean care (maintenance), discipline[1] (training), and instruction, including culture.[2] Man is thus babe, pupil, and scholar.

Types of Educational Activity.

2. Animals employ their powers, as soon as they have any, properly;[3] that is to say, in such a manner that they do not injure themselves. It is, indeed, wonderful to see young swallows, although hardly out of the eggs, and still blind, knowing how to arrange to let their excrement fall outside the nest. Animals need, therefore, no care; at the most

Care.

---

[1] Discipline is regarded by Kant as the negative part of education. Its function is to prepare the way for the later positive part, which is culture.

[2] This conception of "culture" (*Bildung*) is to be understood here in its stricter meaning of moral culture, referred to in Sections 31, 32. In Section 6 this term is used in its wider meaning, and is there translated as "education." (Cf. Section 18*c* and *d*: in *c* "cultivation" and "instruction" are fused together as the third form of educational activity.) In Section 21 culture constitutes the only positive aspect of education. (Cf. Section 58.) This term "culture" is very generally used by Kant, and is, perhaps, next to "morality," the most important item in his conception of education.

[3] Vogt rightly suggests that this kind of use of their powers is "purposive" rather than "proper."

only food, warmth, and oversight, or a certain protec-
tion. Most animals need nourishment, but no care.
By *care* is understood that foresight on the part of
parents which sees that children make no harmful use
of their powers. Should, for example, an animal cry
at its birth, as children do,[1] it would certainly become
the prey of wolves or of other wild animals, lured to
the spot by its cry.

3. Discipline, or training, changes animal nature into
human nature. An animal is already fully equipped

The Necessity
of Discipline.

through instinct; a foreign reason has made
complete provision for it. But man needs
his own reason.[2] He has no instinct, and must

---

[1] See Section 40 as to the cause of this crying.

[2] In his *Idea of a Universal History from a Cosmopolitan Point
of View* (1784) Kant gives a more formal expression of this antithesis between nature and humanity, between instinct and reason :
"Third Proposition : Nature has willed that man shall produce
everything, which is over and above the mechanical arrangement
of his animal existence, entirely from himself, and shall have part
in no happiness or perfection other than that which he, instinctively free, has procured for himself by his own reason."—Hartenstein, iv. p. 145.

"Instinct, this *voice of God*, which all animals obey, is the new-
born infant's only guide."—*Probable Beginnings of Human History* (1786), Hartenstein, iv. p. 317.

In his *Anthropology with Reference to Pragmatic Ends* the difference between man and animals is stated to consist in the fact
that "man has a character which he creates himself, since he has
the faculty of perfecting himself according to purposes derived
from himself, by means of which he can turn himself from an
animal endowed with *the capacity of reason* (*animal rationabile*)

arrange the plan of his own behavior. However, since he is not immediately capable of doing this, because he is raw when he comes into the world, others must do it for him.

4. The human race is to draw gradually from itself, through its own exertions, all the natural qualities of humanity. One generation educates another. One can, therefore, seek the beginnings [of human history] either in a barbarous or in a completely developed condition. If the latter is assumed as existing first and primarily, then man must afterwards have become wild and degenerated into barbarity.[1]

The Human Race Self-dependent.

Discipline prevents man from being turned aside by

---

into a *rational* animal (*animal rationale*) : as such he is able, *first*, to support himself and his kind, which he, *secondly*, exercises, instructs, and *educates* for domestic society ; and, *thirdly*, *governs* as a systematic totality (arranged on the basis of rational principles) belonging to society," etc.—Hartenstein, vii. p. 646. Kant then proceeds to give a much more complex differentiation of man from the animals than is implied in the simple contrast stated in Section 3. (See selections to Section 18*d* in Selection IV. p. 249.)

[1] Cf. Section 13. In his essay on the *Probable Beginnings of Human History* (1786) Kant attempted to combine what might be called the Eden theory and the Savage theory of the condition of primitive man, the stage of instinct being that of paradisaical innocency, and the stage of reason that which followed in a period of blame where human development really began. That is, human history had its beginnings with the awakening of *will*. Kant here uses his notion of the freedom of the will as the cornerstone of his philosophy of history. "Culture," with all its vices, thus follows upon a state of "nature."—Hartenstein, iv. p. 315 f.

his animal impulses from his destiny, which is humanity. It must restrain him from betaking himself wildly and thoughtlessly into danger. Training [*Zucht*], therefore, is merely negative; it is the action by which one rids man of his wildness; instruction, on the contrary, is the positive part of education.

Wildness is independence of laws. Discipline subjects man to the laws of humanity, and begins to let him feel the constraint of law. This, however, should take place early. Thus, for instance, we at first send children to school, not so much with the intention that they shall learn something there, as with the idea that they may become accustomed to sit still and to observe promptly that which is enjoined upon them, in order that in the future they may not attempt immediately to carry out their every caprice.

5. Man, however, has such a great natural instinct for freedom that he sacrifices everything for it when once he has been accustomed to it for any length of time.[1] For this very reason must discipline, as already said, be brought into use very early; for, if this is not done, it is a very difficult matter to change man later. He then follows every caprice. It is observable also in savage nations, that even though they act as servants for Europeans for a long time, they never accustom themselves to the

Discipline and the Instinct for Freedom.

---

[1] This instinct for freedom is called, in the *Anthropology*, etc., " the most violent of all the passions of savages."—Hartenstein, vii. p. 589.

latter's mode of living. With them, however, this is not a noble instinct for freedom, as Rousseau [1] and others maintain, but a certain rawness; for in this instance the animal has, so to speak, not yet developed the humanity within it. Man must, therefore, be early accustomed to subject himself to the commands of reason. If, in his youth, he is granted his own will, and opposed in nothing, he will retain a certain wildness throughout his whole life. Nor is it any advantage to him to be indulged in youth with an all too great maternal tenderness, for he will find only so much the more opposition, and will receive thrusts from all sides, when once he enters into the affairs of the world.[2]

---

[1] A French philosopher (1712–1778), author of the revolutionary doctrine of naturalism, which was violently opposed to the earlier rationalism. Kant was one of the great German thinkers who were profoundly influenced by Rousseau, whose chief educational work was the *Émile*, 1762. It is a philosophical romance, ushering in a new pedagogic era.

[2] In his conception of will training by means of meeting will resistance, which reappears throughout the *Lecture-Notes*, Kant takes a position opposite to, and critical of, that assumed by Rousseau. "So long as children find resistance only in things, and never in wills, they will become neither rebellious nor choleric, and will the better keep themselves in a state of health."—*Émile*, Payne's translation, New York, 1893, p. 29.

That Kant must have taken this process of will opposition seriously, even outside his educational theory, can be seen in the following passages found in the *Idea of a Universal History from a Cosmopolitan Point of View* :

"Fourth Proposition : The means of which nature makes use in order to effect the development of all her capacities is their *antagonism* in society, in so far as this becomes in the end the cause

It is a common defect in the education of royalty, that, since they are destined to be rulers, no one really opposes them in their youth. With man, on account of his inclination to freedom, a certain polishing of his roughness is necessary ; with the animal, however, this is not necessary, on account of its instincts.

6. Man needs care and education.[1] Training and instruction are included under education. So far as is known, no animal needs these ; none of them learn anything from their parents, except birds their singing.[2] In this they are instructed by the parent-birds, and it is affecting to ob-

A New Classification of Educational Activities.

---

of a uniform order of the same. By antagonism, I mean here the unsocial sociability of men. . . . Man has a disposition to *associate ;* since in such a state he feels himself more as a man,— that is, the development of his natural capacities. But he also has a great inclination to *detach* (isolate) himself. . . . Then occur the first true steps out of rawness towards culture, which consists really in the social value of man ; then all talents become gradually developed, the taste formed, etc. . . . Man desires peace ; but nature knows better what is good for his species : she wishes discord.

"All culture and art adorning humanity, the most beautiful social order, are fruits of unsociability, which is constrained by itself to discipline itself, and thus, through extorted art, to develop completely the germs of nature."—Hartenstein, iv. pp. 146–148.

[1] See Section 1, note 2. This division of educational activities is only partial and cursory, and is made for the purpose of fixing more closely the meaning of " education."

[2] Kant treats this question of the song of birds in his *Anthropology,* etc. In his lectures on that subject in 1790–91 this song tradition was regarded as a process corresponding to the educational

serve them sing, as in a school, before their young with all their strength ; and these, in turn, try to bring the same tones out of their little throats. In order to be convinced that birds do not sing from instinct, but actually learn it, it is worth while to make an experiment. Take away about half the eggs from a canary and replace them with sparrow eggs ; or, even exchange very young sparrows with the young of the canary. If, now, these are taken into a room where they cannot hear the sparrows outside, they learn the singing of the canary, and you have singing sparrows. It is also really very wonderful that each species of birds retains a certain song through all generations, and the tradition of song is, probably, the truest in the world.

7. Man can become man through education only. He is only what education makes him.[1] It is to be noted that man is educated only by man, and by those

---

activity of man. For an interesting study whose conclusions seem to support Kant's illustration, see "Data on Song in Birds," by Scott, in *Science*, N. S., xiv. p. 522 f.

It is probable that Kant's view of instinct *versus* learning among animals will be greatly revised when the final chapter on "learning" is written by our comparative psychologists. It has long since been known that bird-singing is not the only instance of learning, as stated in the text. This growth in more recent knowledge, however, does not do violence to the fundamental contrast Kant brings forward. (See Morgan's *Introduction to Comparative Psychology*, pp. 170, 210.)

[1] It need hardly be remarked that there is difficulty in bringing this declaration into consistency with the ethical principles contained in his writings on practical philosophy.

men who are educated themselves. Defects, therefore, in the discipline and instruction of some men make them poor educators of their pupils.[1] If a being of a superior nature were to assume the care of our education, we would then see what man could become. But, since education partly teaches man something and partly merely develops something within him, it cannot be known how far his natural qualities go. If only an experiment were to be made under royal patronage, and through the united efforts of many, there might be disclosures as to what man might accomplish. It is as important for the philosopher as it is mournful for the philanthropist to observe how royalty usually care only and always for themselves, and never take part in the important experiment of education in such a manner that nature may take a step nearer perfection. There is no one, injured by neglect in his youth, but should himself see in mature years wherein he has been neglected, either in discipline or in culture (as one might call instruction). He who is not cultivated is raw; he who is not disciplined is wild. The omission of discipline is a greater evil than the neglect of culture; for the latter can be recovered in later years, but wildness cannot be removed and a blunder in discipline cannot

Human Perfection Dependent upon Education.

---

[1] In the *Anthropology*, etc., Hartenstein, vii. p. 652, Kant regards the problem of moral education for our species as still unsolved, because our evil propensities are looked upon with disapproval and are curbed, but are not wiped out. (See Section 12, note, p. 114.)

be retrieved. It is possible for education to become better and better, and for each successive generation to take a step nearer the perfection of humanity; for behind education lurks the great secret of the perfection of human nature.[1] Henceforth this is actually possible, since now, for the first time, we are beginning to judge properly and to see clearly what essentially belongs to a good education. It is enrapturing to fancy that human nature will be better and better developed through education, and that this can be brought into a form suitable to humanity. This opens to us the prospect of a happier human race in the future.

8. An outline of a *Theory of Education* is a noble ideal, and does no harm even if we are not in a position to realize it immediately. But one should not consider the idea chimerical, and cry it down as a beautiful dream, simply because its execution meets with hindrances.

Theory of
Education
an Ideal.

An idea is nothing else than the concept of a perfection which has not yet been met with in experience; as, for example, the idea of a perfect republic governed according to the laws of righteousness. Is it for that reason impossible? Our idea must first be right, and then it is not at all impossible, even with all the hindrances which now stand in the way of its realization. If, for instance, every one should lie, would, merely for

---

[1] This affirmation, taken in connection with Sections 10, 15, is truly Kantian. The moral aspect of education appears in the foreground. (See Selection II.)

that reason, truthfulness be only a vagary? And the idea of an education which is to develop all the natural qualities in man is certainly truthful.[1]

9. Man does not fully attain the purpose of his existence with his present education. For, how differently

Present Education of Man Imperfect.

do men live! There can be a uniformity among them only if they act according to the same maxims, and these maxims would have to become second nature to them. We can labor on the plan of a more suitable education, and hand down our directions to posterity, which can realize it little by little. It is observable, for example, in the auricula, that they are all of one and the same color when grown from a root; but if, on the other hand, they are grown from seed, they are obtained with quite different and the most varied colors. Nature has so deposited the germs in them that the development of these variations depends only upon the proper sowing and transplanting. So with man.

10. There are germs in human nature, and it becomes our concern to develop the natural capacities proportion-

---

[1] The conceptions of "idea" and "ideal" form the basis of considerably more than a third portion of the *Critique of Pure Reason*,—namely, the Transcendental Dialectic, which endeavors to present the illusory nature of the transcendental ideas of the soul, the world, and God. The illustration of the perfect republic appears there also, with particular reference to the Republic of Plato. In the *Critique* all "ideas" are not regarded as "truthful," since they lead human reason persistently into error.

ately, to unfold humanity from its seeds, and to see to it that man attains his destiny. Animals attain their destiny of themselves, and without being aware of it. Man is obliged to make an effort to attain his; but this cannot be done if he never has a concept of it. In the case of the individual the attainment of this goal is also utterly impossible. If we assume a really cultivated primitive pair, let us see how they would teach those intrusted to their care. The first parents give their children an example; the latter imitate it, and so some natural qualities are developed. All cannot be trained after this manner, since, at the very best, the times are only occasional in which children see examples. In ancient days men had no conception of the perfection to which human nature can attain. We ourselves are not yet perfectly clear about this conception. But this much is certain, that individuals, no matter how highly they may culture their pupils, cannot make them fulfil their destinies. The race, and not the individuals, can succeed in doing this.[1]

The Purpose of Education: Attainment of Destiny.

---

[1] Strong and valid exception can be taken to this racial conception of education, in that it tends to misrepresent the true limits of any and all education, which must primarily be that of the individual; on the other hand, there is no other way than that of education (unless we make exception of the way of genius) for the individual to reach his own destiny. Kant expressed the same thought in his *Idea of a Universal History from a Cosmopolitan Point of View* (1784), Hartenstein, iv. p. 144: "Second Proposition: In man (as the only rational creature on earth), those natural capacities, which have in view the use of his reason, can be

11. Education is an *Art* the practice of which must be brought to perfection in the course of many genera-

---

completely developed only in the race, and not in the individual."
". . . Reason in a creature is a capacity to extend the rules and purposes of the uses of all its powers far beyond natural instinct, and there are no limits to its possibilities. It, however, does not act instinctively, but needs trials, practice, and instruction, in order to make progress gradually from one stage of insight to another. Therefore every man would have to live an excessively long time in order to learn how to make a complete use of all his natural capacities ; or, if nature has assigned him a short term of life (as it actually has), she needs, perhaps, an interminable series of generations, of which one will transmit its enlightenment to another, in order finally to urge her germs in our species to that degree of development which is appropriate to her intention."—*Ibid.*, p. 145. In his review the next year of the second part of Herder's *Ideen zur Philosophie der Geschichte der Menschheit* (*Ibid.*, p. 191), Kant presents a more acceptable modification of this thought, which should not be omitted here : ". . . It is no contradiction to say, that it [the human race] is in all its parts asymptotic to this [its destiny], and yet on the whole it does come together with it ; in other words, that no individual member of all the offspring of the human race, but only the species fully reaches its destiny. The mathematician can explain this ; the philosopher would say : the destiny of the human race as a whole is *unceasing progress*," etc.

In its balder form this view forces the whole problem of education to disappear, leaving no trace behind it (as Temming observes). Kant's pedagogy does not fare as badly, however, as a simpler evolutional pedagogy, which primarily attemps to be a race pedagogy. This is subject to the same limitations ; but the superiority of Kantian pedagogy lies in its concept of the moral destiny of the race, which, of course, breaks with all development. Kant conceived of education as a conscious struggle, in which the end is known from the beginning. Evolutional pedagogy puts the

tions. Each generation, provided with the knowledge of its predecessors, can always produce an education which shall develop, proportionately and purposively, all the capacities of man, and thus lead the entire race towards its goal.

Education a Concern for the Race.

Providence has decreed that man shall bring the good out of himself, and, as it were, says to him, " Go out into the world; I have equipped you with every disposition for the good.[1] It is your affair to develop them, and thus your own happiness and unhappiness depend upon yourself." Somewhat in this fashion could the Creator have spoken to man.

12. Man is to develop first his native capabilities for the good. Providence has not placed them in him already perfect and complete; they are only bare potentialities, and without the distinction of morality.[2] Man is to seek to make himself better, to cultivate himself, and, if he is evil, to develop morality within himself. If one gives this ma-

Education: Man's Greatest and Hardest Problem.

---

struggle down as going on unconsciously and without reference to the end.

[1] To speak of a plurality of dispositions for the good might be proper empirical pedagogy, but it is not in harmony with Kant's ethical theory, which held "the good will"—only one factor—to be the sole basis of morality.

[2] This statement is not in harmony with Kant's ethically established doctrine of transcendental freedom. The apparent fact of man's psychological (i.e., as rational) development, and the ethical necessities of Criticism come into conflict more than once in these *Lecture-Notes*. (See note above and Section 102.)

ture reflection, he finds it to be very difficult. Education, therefore, is the greatest and hardest problem that can be proposed to man; for insight depends upon education, and education, again, depends upon insight. Thus education can advance only step by step, and a proper idea of the peculiar nature of education can arise only as each generation hands down its experience and wisdom to the one following, and this, in turn, adding something, gives it over to *its* successor. But how great a culture and experience does this idea presuppose! It could, accordingly, arise only late, and we ourselves have not yet brought it into perfect clearness. I wonder, indeed, whether the education of the individual should imitate the development of the race in general through its various generations.

Two human inventions can be regarded as the most difficult,—namely, the art of government and that of education; and yet we are still contending among ourselves as to their fundamental nature.[1]

13. But where shall we begin to develop the human capacities? Shall it be with a barbarous or with an already cultured state? It is hard to conceive of an unfolding out of barbarity (that is why the concept of the primitive man is so difficult), and we see that in the case of a development from such

Education and Civilization.

---

[1] While Kant indulges in representations of the extreme difficulty of the problem of education, it must not be thought that he regarded it as wholly unsolvable. To the end of his life he did not cease to look upon the race as making some definite progress towards the ideals of ethics.

a condition man has always relapsed into barbarity, from which he has again elevated himself. We also find a very close adjacency to barbarity among very well civilized people in the earliest information they have left to us on record. But how much culture is already presupposed by writing! In regard to civilized people, the beginning of the art of writing can be called the beginning of the world.

14. Since the development of human capacities does not take place of its own accord, all education is an *art*. Nature has bestowed no instinct for that.[1]   Education a The origin, as well as the progress, of this   Necessary Art. art is either *mechanical*,[2] without plan, being arranged according to given circumstances, or *rational*. The art of education has a mechanical origin solely at those occasional times when we learn whether something is injurious or beneficial to man. Every art of education which arises merely mechanically must carry with it many faults and deficiencies, since it has no plan for its foundation. The art of education, or pedagogy, must therefore become

---

[1] Modern pedagogy is coming more and more to ally the fundamental qualities of the real teacher to the characteristics of the maternal instincts, an extension of which should pass upward into the work of education. Kant's view, then, is here rather to one side.

[2] This conception of "mechanism" is a characteristic Kantian term in accounting for events. For the most part, aside from its being a synonym for "nature," it is employed for the purposes of destructive criticism, when directed towards human efforts. (Cf. Section 20.)

rational if it is to develop human nature so that it attain its goal. Parents already educated are examples which the children imitate. In order to improve children, it is necessary that pedagogy become a study, otherwise there is nothing to hope from it, and he who has been educated corruptly trains others in a like manner. The mechanism in educational art must be transformed into science, otherwise there will never be a united effort, and one generation will pull down what its predecessor has built up.

15. One *principle in the art of education*, which those men who devise educational plans should especially
The Idea of Humanity: a Principle in Pedagogy. have in mind, is this: children should be educated, *not* with reference to their present condition, but rather with regard to a possibly improved future state of the human race,—that is, according to *the idea of humanity* and its entire destiny. This principle is of great moment. Parents usually educate their children for the present world, corrupt though it be.[1] They should, however, educate them

---

[1] To illustrate, by way of contrast, the simplicity of ends in ethics, Kant makes the following remark in the *Fundamental Principles of the Metaphysics of Morals* (1785), Hartenstein, iv. p. 263 : "Since it is not known in early youth what aims may be adopted later in life, parents try above all to have their children learn a great many different things, and provide for *skill* in the use of the means for all kinds of purposes, of none of which can they determine whether it could not perhaps be in the future the object of their pupil, but which it is still *possible* that he may have at some time ; and this is so great that they usually neglect to form and to correct their judgment about the value of the things

better, that an improved future condition be thereby realized.

16. But here we come upon two hindrances to this end: (*a*) Parents are usually anxious only that their children should prosper in the world, and (*b*) Princes regard their subjects as mere instruments for the accomplishment of their own purposes.

Defective Aims of Parents and Princes.

Parents exercise forethought for the home, princes for the state. Neither have for their ultimate aim the good of the world and the perfection for which man is intended, and for which he also has the capacity. But the plan of an educational scheme should be made cosmopolitan. And is, then, the good of the world an idea

---

which they might like to adopt as their purposes in life." (Cf. Section 95*a*.)

The method by which Kant arrives at the pedagogical principle summarized in this section should be compared with the method by which he establishes one of his important ethical postulates,— namely, that of immortality. The highest good is held to be in a process of infinite or gradual realization ; therefore the necessity of the postulate to provide a time and place for that infinite realization. This line of reasoning was developed in his mind nearly a decade later than the method which appears in these *Notes*. Education being subject to the same conditions of slow progression, children should be brought under a scheme which looks to the future and not to the present. This "future" is not the mere sequent in biographical time, but the future of moral expansion and security. Kant's regenerative principle for education can scarce be regarded as formalistic, but is rather literally filled with an empirical, psychological content,—if one might speak of "principles" in such a paradoxical manner.

which can be injurious to us in our private welfare? Never! For, even if it seems necessary that something be sacrificed for it, nevertheless, one promotes through it the advantage of his present condition. And then, what splendid consequences attend it! *Good education is exactly that whence springs all the good in the world.* It is necessary only to develop further the germs which man possesses; for the elements of evil are not found in man's natural capacities. The only cause of evil is this, that nature is not brought under rules. In man there are only germs of good.[1]

---

[1] If Rink properly edited this *Note*, it stands in contradiction with Kant's views expressed later in these *Notes* (see Section 102) and with his more mature ethical views. For example, in his *Religion within the Limits of Mere Reason*, Part I. (first published 1792, Hartenstein, vi. p. 113 f.), Kant held that human inclinations are enemies of the morally good, but also that these evil forces can be won over by the ideas of that good, germs of which are found in human nature. He almost travesties this conception here expressed as a foundation for educational theory—in which the influence of Rousseau may be seen most strongly at work—in the following passage which stands almost at the opening of the above-named writing : "Newer, but much less wide-spread, is the opposite heroic opinion which has taken root probably among philosophers alone, and in our times especially among educators : that the world is continually moving forward in just the opposite direction,—namely, from bad to good (though almost unnoticeably) : at least the capacity for this is to be met with in human nature. But they certainly have not derived this opinion from experience, if they mean *morally* good or bad (not civilization) ; for the history of all times speaks too loudly against it ; but it is probably merely a good-hearted presupposition of the moralists from Seneca to Rousseau, in order to incite to the patient cultivation of the seed of

17. But whence shall come the improved condition of the world,—from princes or from subjects?[1] Should the latter improve themselves and meet a good government half-way? If it is to be brought about by sovereigns, there must be an improvement in the training of the princes,—a training which for a long time has had this defect, that in their youth they met with no opposition. A tree standing alone in a field grows crooked and spreads its branches in every direction; on the other hand, a tree which stands in the midst of a forest grows straight upward, because the trees near it offer it resistance, and it seeks the air and sun from above. So it is with princes. It is always better that they should be educated by some one from among their subjects rather than by one of their own rank. Only as their education is superior can we expect good from the nobility. Hence the world's improvement depends chiefly upon private endeavors, and not so much upon the co-operation of princes, as Basedow,[2] and others think, since

Education of Princes Imperfect.

good which we perhaps possess, if one could only count upon a natural groundwork for this in man.'' (Cf. also Selection X.)

[1] Kant gives to this question an answer that is in direct opposition to the reigning view of his time, which expected much progress in education from the efforts of royalty. In spite of this contrary answer, Kant gives preference for public education. (See Section 25.)

[2] (1723–1790.) Basedow, for a time a professor of ethics and literature in Denmark, developed an educational system inspired by Rousseau, and, under the patronage of the Prince of Anhalt-Dessau, established his model school at Dessau in 1774, giving it the name of *The Philanthropinum.* Kant took an unusual interest in this experiment for a pedagogical laboratory, as may be seen in

experience teaches us that the ultimate aim of princes is not the promotion of the world's good, but rather the well-being of their own state, so that they may attain their own individual ends.   When they provide money for educational enterprises, they reserve the right to control the plans.   So it is in everything which concerns the development of the human mind and the extension of human knowledge.   Money and power do not create, but at most only facilitate.   Yet they might bring it about, if only national economy did not credit in advance the state's income in favor of its own treasury.   Up to the present time even universities have not brought about the world's improvement, and never was the probability of their doing it less than it is now.[1]

Therefore the management of the schools should be left entirely to the judgment of the most intelligent Experts in experts.   All culture begins with the indi-
Education. vidual and thence extends itself.   The gradual approach of human nature to its true end is possible only through the efforts of liberally inclined propagandists who take an interest in the world's welfare and who are capable of conceiving the idea of a future improved state.   But many a ruler still looks upon his

---

his appeal to the public in its behalf, translated in Selection III. As another biographical instance of the close interest between philosophy and pedagogy, which did not originate in, but has displayed a peculiar triumph in the modern era, one can cite the enthusiasm at a later date which Fichte showed at Pestalozzi's Institute at Yverdun.

[1] See Selection IX., p. 264, for another criticism of the universities of his day.

people as only a part of the kingdom of nature, and has an eye to nothing but their propagation. At the most he wishes them to have ability, but solely in order to make of them better instruments for the accomplishment of his own purposes. It is true that individuals also should have in mind the great purpose of nature; but they should reflect especially upon the development of humanity, and see to it that it become not only skilful but moral, and try to advance posterity further than they themselves have gone, which is the most difficult of all.

18. In his education man must therefore be:[1]

(a) *Disciplined.*—"To discipline" means to attempt to prevent the animal nature from becoming injurious to human nature in the individual as well as in the member of society. Discipline is, hence, only the taming of wildness.

The Four Types of Educational Activity.

(b) *Cultured.*—Culture includes instruction and teaching. It furnishes skilfulness, which means the posses-

---

[1] This is the earliest complete division of educational activities given in these *Notes*, and is perhaps the most exhaustive of all the many divisions in which Kant indulges. At the same time, the terms of this division render it the only one that is in agreement with his usual mode of empirical and psychological analysis and of his adoption of technical terms. (See the passages gathered in Selection IV.)

This division returns to that given in Section 1, which is rather "popular" in form. The distinctions of "cultivation," "civilization," and "moralization" correspond to those of "technical," "pragmatic," and "moral" in Section 32. (On the relation of this division to that in Section 72, see note to the latter.)

sion of a faculty sufficient for the execution of any
desired purpose. It determines no goal whatever, but
leaves that to circumstances.

Some kinds of skilfulness are good in all cases,—for
example, reading and writing; others for a single purpose
only, as music, which makes us agreeable in company.[1]
Because of the multitude of aims, skilfulness becomes,
in a certain sense, indefinitely varied.

(c) *Civilized.*—It must also be seen to that man acquire
prudence,[2] be a suitable member of the social community,
be well liked, and have influence. To this end there is
necessary a certain form of culture which we call " civilization."[3] Essential thereto are manners, politeness,

---

[1] Kant did not regard music as a means of education in any
sense of the term. He looked upon it as a negligible art, and
seldom attended concerts. (See Selection V.)

[2] The conception of "prudence" playing rather an extended and
important part in Kant's division of educational activities (see
Sections 32, 33, 91, 92) and having a *quasi*-ethical aspect, his own
definition of it in 1785 may here be in place : "The word *prudence*
is used in two senses : in one it can bear the name of worldly
prudence, in the other that of private prudence. The first means
a man's ability to have influence upon others, in order to use
them for his purposes. The second is the insight to unite all these
purposes for his own lasting benefit. The latter is especially that
to which the value of the first is reduced, and of him who is prudent in the first sense of the term, but not in the second, it could
better be said : he is clever and cunning, but on the whole impru-
dent."—*Fundamental Principles of the Metaphysics of Ethics*,
Hartenstein, iv. p. 264.

[3] This factor in education is here an addition to those factors
mentioned in Sections 1, 6. It is the pragmatism of Sections
32, 33, and the "worldly wisdom" of Sections 91, 92. In

and a certain judiciousness by virtue of which all men may be used to one's own ultimate aims. This form of culture adjusts itself to the changeable taste of each age. Thus, a few decades ago people were still very fond of ceremonial in social intercourse.

(*d*) *Moralized.*—Moralization must not be neglected. Man should not only be qualified for all sorts of purposes, but he should acquire that type of mind which chooses good aims only. These are such as are necessarily approved by every one, and which at the same time can be the purpose of every one.

19. Man can be either merely trained, taught, mechanically instructed, or really enlightened.[1] Dogs and horses are trained and human beings can be trained   Learning to Think. also. (This word, *dressiren*, "to train," is derived from the English, "to dress," *kleiden*. Thus the place where the preacher changes his robes should be called *Dresskammer*, and not *Trostkammer*.[2])

It is not enough that children be trained; the most important thing is that they learn *to think*. This leads

---

Section 63 this "certain form" disappears entirely, being absorbed by the elaboration there of 18*d*. The word is taken rather in an active sense.

[1] This is only a cursory division of education, which seems to find its purpose in a desire to emphasize the moral factor by bringing it into strong contrast with mechanical instruction.

[2] To play upon words was a source of great delight to Kant. The reader is free to believe him or not, as he was often by punning led to false etymologies. His point is that this kind of education is altogether *external* in character.

to those principles from which all actions arise.[1] Thus
it becomes apparent that there is very much to be done
in a really worthy education. In private education,
however, it usually happens that the *fourth* and *most
important* point is but seldom observed, for children are,
for the most part, reared in such a manner that their
moralization is confided to the pastor. And yet how
infinitely important is it that children learn to abhor
vice while they are young, not merely on the ground
that God has forbidden it, but because it is in itself
abominable![2] Otherwise they will very easily fall into
the way of thinking that it could always be practised, and
would be permitted if only God had not forbidden it,
and that, therefore, God can easily make an exception for
once. God is the holiest Being; He wills only that which
is good, and commands that we practise virtue for its own
inherent worth, and not merely because He demands it.

We live in the epoch of disciplining, culturing, and
civilizing, but we are still a long way off from the epoch

**Moral
Education
lacking.**

of moralizing.[3] Under the existing conditions of society, it can be said that the for-
tunes of the state grow with the distress of
men. And it is yet a question whether we would not

---

[1] Particularly those moral principles the search for which constituted Kant's great quest in his technical labors. To Kant,
"thinking" was something directly opposite to mechanical action.
(See Sections 72, 103, and Selection XII.)

[2] Cf. Sections 77, 105.

[3] In the *Reflections on Anthropology*, p. 216, Kant says, "the
pedagogical concepts of morals and religion are yet in their infancy."
(Quoted from Vogt, p. 68.)

be happier in the savage state, where all our culture would find no place, than we are in our present condition.[1] For how can we make man happy unless we make him wise and moral? Otherwise the quantity of evil is not diminished.

20. We must have *experimental schools* before we can establish *normal schools*. Education and instruction must not be merely mechanical, but must rest upon principles. Yet they are not to be affairs of mere reasoning, but they must also in a certain manner be a mechanism. In Austria there have been, for the most part, only normal schools which were established according to a plan against which much was said, with good reason; and especially were they reproached with being blind mechanisms.[2] All

Experiments Necessary in Education.

---

[1] In discussing, in 1754, the question of the aging of the earth from a physical point of view, Kant contrasts the cold-blooded character of his century with the enthusiasm of ancient peoples for "large things," expressing the following doubt : "Then when I think how great an influence the art of government, instruction, and example have upon mental and moral life, I doubt whether such ambiguous characteristics are proofs of a real change in nature."—Hartenstein, i. p. 206.

In 1786, in the essay on *Probable Beginnings of Human History* (Hartenstein, iv. p. 321), Kant reaches the opinion that the step out of the raw condition of the life of instinct was a loss for the individual but a gain for the race.

[2] The first of the normal schools was established in Vienna in 1771. The plan referred to is that projected by Abbot Felbiger in 1774. It is also interesting to note that Kant's call for "experimental schools" was first actually answered by his successor Herbart, who founded a "pedagogical seminary" at Königsberg.

other schools had to be modelled after these normal schools, and those who had not been in these schools were refused any advancement. Such ordinances indicate to what extent the government occupies itself in this matter, and under such constraint it is impossible for any good thing to thrive.

It is often imagined that educational experiments are unnecessary, and that a judgment as to whether a thing will be good or not can be reached on rational grounds alone. This is a great error, and experience teaches that with our experiments there very often appear effects entirely different from those which were expected. Since it all depends upon experiments, it is clear that no one generation can present a complete educational plan. The one experimental school which, in a measure, began to break the way was the Institute at Dessau.[1] In spite of the many defects with which one can reproach the Institute (defects which are found in all conclusions drawn from experiments), we must give it the honor of having made experiments continually. It was, in a certain way, the only school in which teachers had the freedom to work out their own methods and plans, and where they were united among themselves as well as with all the scholars in Germany.

---

[1] Kant here speaks of the Institute as having done its work,—in the past tense. The Institute closed in 1793, but we need not necessarily conclude that this *Note* dates from that year, since the Institute dragged along an existence after its real work had been accomplished. Philanthropinism, however, extended widely beyond the Institute in the labors of Salzman (1744–1811) and Campe (1746–1818).

21. Education includes the care which infancy demands, and schooling.[1] The latter is,—

(a) *Negatively*, the discipline which merely prevents faults. Division of Education.

(b) *Positively*, instruction and direction,[2] and so far forth, belongs to culture. Direction is guidance in the execution of that which has been taught. Hence arises the difference between a teacher [*Informator*], who merely instructs, and a private tutor [*Hofmeister*], who is also a director. The former educates for the school merely, the latter for life.

22. Education is either public or private. The former has to do only with instruction, which can always remain public. The practice of the precepts given to the pupils is left to the latter. A complete public educa-

---

[1] This new division does not repeat the suggestion towards a similar division stated in Section 4, but seems to be made in order to make emphatic the distinction between "instruction" and "direction." Here is also to be found the basis for his distinction between private and public education presented in the sections following. (Cf. Section 58.)

[2] With "direction" compare "cultivation," Section 18c, and "pragmatic culture," Section 32b. The present-day distinction is made in terms of "theory" and "practice." The distinction between "teacher" and "tutor," here introduced to illustrate a principle in a division of educational aims and activities, reappears in Sections 32, 34. The limits of Kant's pedagogical horizon might seem to be the activity of the private or family tutor; but the public school teacher—who is a social and professional creature of the nineteenth century—comes in for a fair share of consideration. (See Sections 20, 81, 88.)

tion is that which unites both instruction and moral culture. Its aim is the promotion of a good private education. A school in which this is found is called an Educational Institute. There cannot be many such institutes, nor can the number of their pupils be large, for they are very costly, and their mere establishment requires a great deal of money. It is with them as with almshouses and hospitals : the necessary buildings, the salaries of the directors, managers, and attendants, take half of the money appropriated ; and it is certain that if this money were sent to the poor in their homes they would be much better provided for. Thus it is very difficult for other than the children of the rich to attend such institutes.

Public and Private Education.

23. The purpose of such public institutes is the completion of domestic education. If parents or their assistants were well educated, the expense of public institutes would not be necessary. In these establishments we should make experiments and train subjects, and it is thus that a good domestic education will result.

Private Education.

24. Private education is conducted either by the parents themselves or, if they do not, as frequently happens, have the time, capability, or perhaps even the desire to do it, by paid assistants. When there are assistants to conduct the education, there arises the very difficult situation that the authority is divided between the parents and the tutors. Now the child is governed by the commands of the tutor, and

Parents versus Tutors.

then it must follow parental caprice. In such education it is necessary that the parents yield their authority entirely to the family tutor.

25. But how far is private education to be preferred to public, or *vice versa?* In general, it appears that public education is more advantageous than Public Education Preferable. domestic, not only from the view-point of skilfulness, but also as regards the character of a citizen. Domestic education not only brings out family faults, but also fosters them.

26. How long should education continue? Until that time when nature herself has arranged that the human being shall guide himself,—until the develop- Time Limit of Education. ment of the sexual instinct,—until the youth himself can become a father and can educate,—until about the sixteenth year.[1] After this period auxiliary

---

[1] Cf. Section 111. In commenting on Rousseau's conception of the strife between culture and human nature, Kant observes as an illustration of this strife, in his *Probable Beginnings of Human History* (1786), Hartenstein, iv. pp. 322, 323, foot-note :

"The sixteenth or seventeenth year has been determined by nature as the epoch of maturity,—*i.e.*, of the impulse as well as of the ability to beget his kind ; an age in which the youth, in a crude state of nature, literally becomes a man, for he is then able to support himself, to beget his kind, and to support it together with his wife. The simplicity of his needs renders this easy for him. But under civilized conditions many means of earning are necessary, skill as well as favorable circumstances, so that this epoch is postponed, on the average, at least ten years. Nature has not, however, changed her period of maturity to make it agree with the progress of social refinement, but she rather follows ob-

means of culture can be used and a secret discipline may be practised, but there can be no further education, properly speaking.

27. The *first* epoch in the pupil's life is that in which he must show submissiveness and positive obedience; the *second* is that in which he is permitted to make use of his powers of reflection and of his freedom, but under laws. In the former there obtains a mechanical, in the latter a moral constraint.[1]

Two Epochs in Schooling.

---

stinately her law which she has laid upon the preservation of the human species as animal species. From this results an unavoidable rupture from the aims of nature by morals, and from morals by the aims of nature; for the natural man is at a certain age already a man, while the citizen (who has not, however, ceased to be a natural man) is still only a youth, yes, only a child; for it is quite proper so to designate him who, on account of his age (in the civil condition), cannot support himself, much less his kind, although he has the impulse and the ability, consequently the call of nature, to beget it. Nature has certainly not implanted instincts and powers in living creatures in order that they should be fought and suppressed. Hence the disposition was not at all placed upon the civilized condition, but merely upon the preservation of the human species as animal species, and the civilized condition is hence in inevitable conflict with the latter,—a conflict which could be avoided only through a perfect civil constitution (the highest aim of culture), since now the interim is usually filled with vices and the manifold human misery which results from them."

Kant reverts to this great gap between the demands of nature and of the state, and points out the same difficulties in moralization, using almost the same language, in the *Anthropology*, etc., vii. p. 650.

[1] As to the earlier epoch, Kant remarks, in *Reflections on Anthropology*, "Man must be weakened in order to be tame and later

28. The submissiveness of the pupil is either *positive* or *negative*. It is *positive* when he must do that which he is commanded, because he himself cannot judge, and the mere capacity for imitation still exists in him. It is *negative* when he must do that which others desire, if he wishes others to do things to please him. In the first instance he risks being punished; in the second, not obtaining what he wishes. In the latter instance, although he is able to think, he is still dependent upon others for his pleasures.

Kinds of Constraint.

29. One of the greatest problems in education is, How can subjection to lawful constraint be combined with the ability to make use of one's freedom ? For constraint is necessary. How shall I cultivate freedom under conditions of compulsion? I ought to accustom my pupil to tolerate a restraint upon his freedom, and at the same time lead him to make good use of his freedom. Without this all is mere mechanism, and he who is released from education does not know how to make use of his freedom. At an early age he must feel the inevitable opposition of

The Antinomy between Constraint and Freedom.

---

virtuous. The constraint of education and government makes him soft, pliable, and submissive to laws. Later the reason stirs itself.'' (Quoted from Vogt, p. 71.)

With the chronological divisions of Sections 27–30 compare in detail the more ethical and logical divisions of character organization of Sections 80–88. Here the school life of the child is considered, while there the life of the child as a citizen of the moral world is emphasized.

society, in order to learn the difficulty of self-support, economy, and acquisition, so as to be independent.

30. Here the following must be observed:

(*a*) The child should be left perfectly free, from earliest childhood, in everything (except in such instances where he might injure himself; as, for, example, when he reaches for an open knife), unless the manner of his freedom interferes with that of others; as, for example, when he screams, or is merry in too noisy a way, he discommodes others.

Education towards Freedom.

(*b*) The child must be shown that he can attain his aims only as he permits others to reach theirs; as, for example, he will be granted no pleasure if he does not do what others desire, that he must learn, etc.

(*c*) It must also be shown to the child that he is under such constraint as will lead him to the use of his own freedom; that he is cultivated, so that one day he may be free,—that is, not dependent upon the foresight of others. This is the child's latest acquisition. For the consideration that each must rely upon himself for his own sustenance comes to the child very late. They fancy it will always be as it is in the parental home; that food and drink will come without any thought on their part. Without such treatment, children, and especially those of rich parents and princes, become like the inhabitants of Tahiti, who remain children their whole life long.

Here public education has the most evident advantage, since in it one learns to measure his powers and the limitations which the rights of others impose upon him. In this form of education no one has prerogatives, since opposition is felt everywhere, and merit becomes the only standard of preferment.   This education produces the best prototype of the future citizen.

Here must be considered another difficulty, which consists in anticipating the knowledge of sexual relations, in order to avert vice before the age of manhood. More will be said on this later.[1]

---

[1] See Sections 110, 111.

THE TREATISE[1]

31. PEDAGOGY, or the Science of Education, is either physical or practical.[2] Physical education includes that

---

[1] Rink placed the superscription *Abhandlung* before Section **31**, which some editors of Kant's *Lecture-Notes on Pedagogy* have stricken out. The question involved in the retention or omission of the superscription is : whether Kant had succeeded in making all his preliminary distinctions hitherto and now turns to begin the systematic exposition of his views on education, or whether any division of education Kant makes is really fundamental. I have preferred to retain the superscription, without attempting to decide the point at issue otherwise than as indicated in the notes to those sections in which the divisions of educational activities are made. (See Sections 1, 18, 72, *et al.*)

[2] We have here presented an analysis of the theory of education which has its sole basis in the Kantian doctrine of freedom. Everything that is related to nature and is constituted by natural processes is called "physical," whereas everything connected with freedom is called "practical" or "moral." Kant labored hard with this cleavage, which is fundamental, and thus, for him, eternal in human thought, in the Third Antinomy of the Dialectic of the *Critique of Pure Reason*. It is the battle between freedom and causation, both of which are "transcendental ideas."

This radical distinction could hardly have appeared fully fledged in Kant's thinking when he began lecturing on pedagogy in 1776, being a product of his critical system which was in the making in that decade. It is fairly possible that we have here the antithesis between nature and freedom, in terms of which Kant sought, apparently, to work over the whole of educational theory. It is needless to add that the execution of this effort is far from complete in these *Notes*.

maintenance which man has in common with animals.[1]
Practical, or moral, education is that by which man is to
be so formed that he can live as a freely   The Science of
acting being.   (All that which has reference   Education.
to freedom is called "practical.")   It is the education
towards personality, the education of a free being who
can maintain himself and become a member of society,
but who can also have an inner worth peculiar to himself.

32. Hence practical education consists of:

(*a*) *Scholastic-mechanical* culture, which relates to skilfulness, and thus is *didactic* (the work of the teacher);

(*b*) *Pragmatic* culture, which relates to   Scope of
prudence (the work of the private tutor);   Practical
and   Education.

(*c*) *Moral* culture, which relates to good conduct.[2]

---

[1] Cf. Section 2.   "Physical" education is also employed in radically different senses in Sections 47, 63, and following.   In the
former section the conception is given a wider range, so as to include the culture of the soul ; in the latter sections it particularly
comprehends the effects of a teacher upon a pupil, and to which
the pupil passively adjusts himself.   The rendering given in the
text follows the reading adopted by Vogt rather than that given by
Rink, which would read : "Physical education is that which man
has in common with animals, or maintenance," and is difficult to
harmonize with the trend of Kant's views as to the meaning of
"physical education."

[2] It is difficult to harmonize the inclusion of *a* and *b* under
"practical" education here with the later treatment of them under
the "physical" education of the mind in Sections 58, 63, 68,
72 ; the intelligence, as well as the body, is regarded as having a

Man needs scholastic culture, or instruction, in order to become qualified for the attainment of all his ends. It gives him a value considered as an individual. But through the culture of prudence he is formed for citizenship; then he attains a public worth. Then he learns not only to use civil society for his purposes, but also to conform himself to civil society. Through moral culture he finally attains a value with reference to the whole human race.

33. Scholastic education is the very earliest, for all prudence presupposes skilfulness. Prudence is the ability to turn one's skilfulness to account. Moral education, in so far as it rests upon principles which should be apprehended by each one, is the latest; but, in so far as its rests on common sense, it must be observed from the beginning, even along with physical education; for otherwise faults are easily engrafted with which afterwards all educational power labors in vain. Skilfulness and prudence, however, must correspond to the age of the pupil. For a child to be skilled, prudent, good-natured, and cunning in a mature way is worth as little as for an adult to be childish in his mode of thinking.

Relations between its Factors.

"mechanical," hence a "physical" nature. At the same time Kant does not deny that there is a physical preparation for education to freedom, and it may be this which is specifically understood in Section 32, as the second paragraph endeavors to present. (Cf. Sections 77, 91.) The division in Section 32 is identical with *b, c,* and *d* of Section 18, though under slightly different terms. (See Selection IV.)

PHYSICAL EDUCATION

34. Although the person who assumes the position of a tutor in a family does not have the oversight of the children early enough to enable him to super- *Utility of* intend their physical education, yet it is very *Physical* useful for him to know all that is necessary *Education.* to observe in education from beginning to end. Even though he has, as a tutor, to do with older children only, yet it may happen that more children be born into the family, and if he conducts himself well he has always a right to be the confidant of the parents, and to be consulted by them in regard to the physical education of their children ; and, besides, he is often the only learned person in the house. Hence a knowledge of this subject is very necessary to a family tutor.

35. Properly speaking, physical education consists only in the care given children either by parents, nurses, or attendants.[1] The mother's milk is the *Physical Care:* food which nature has intended for the *Nursing.* child. That the child imbibes dispositions with it—as the adage runs : " You drank that in with your mother's

---

[1] " Physical" is here used in its narrower sense, and is not comprised under the activities outlined in Section 18. Sections 35–47 show the influence of Rousseau.

In his *History of the Kantian Philosophy* (p. 271) Rosenkranz derisively speaks of Kant's " stepmotherly solicitousness" for suckling and rocking. This derision is rather unwarranted, first, in view of the general interest in those topics created by Rousseau ; second, in view of Kant's personal interest in the care of the body

milk"—is a mere prejudice. It is most salutary to both if the mother suckles her child. There may, however, be exceptional instances owing to sickly conditions. It was formerly believed that the first milk which the mother has after the child is born, and which is whey-ish, is injurious to the infant and must be gotten rid of before the child could be given suck. It was Rousseau who first called [1] the attention of physicians to the question as to whether this first milk might not be good for the child, since nature has arranged nothing aimlessly. And, in truth, it has been found that this milk is highly beneficial to infants, and is the best remover of the ordure in newly-born babes which doctors call *meconium*.

36. It has also been inquired whether the child cannot be nourished equally as well on animal's milk. Human milk is very different from that of animals.

Milk the Proper Food for Infants.

The milk of all grass- and vegetable-eating animals readily curdles upon the addition of an acid, as, for example, vinous acid, lemon acid, or particularly the acid which is called *rennet* and is found in a calf's stomach ; ordinarily human milk does not curdle. If, however, mothers or wet-nurses partake of only vegetable food for several days at a time, their milk curdles

---

because of his own physical weakness ; and, finally, in view of the paramount importance of those subjects at the proper time of infancy. Kant, furthermore, implies here as elsewhere in these *Lecture-Notes* that education is a subject as wide as all human interests and needs : nothing "human" can be indifferent to it.

[1] In his *Émile*. (See Miss Worthington's translation of Steeg's Extracts, Boston, 1894, p. 18.)

like cow's milk, etc.; but if they then eat meat for a certain time, the milk attains its former quality. From this it has been concluded that it is best, and especially so for the child, for mothers or nurses to eat meat during the nursing period. Any milk vomited by infants is found to be curdled. The acidity of the child's stomach is the chief agent which causes the curdling of milk; human milk can be curdled in no other manner. Then how much worse it would be if the child were given milk which curdles of its own accord! That everything does not depend upon this we see in other nations. The Tunguses,[1] for example, subsist on meat almost entirely, and are strong, healthy people. Such people, however, are short-lived; and a large, grown youth, who does not appear to be light in weight, can be lifted from the ground with little effort. The Swedes, on the other hand, and especially the nations in India, eat almost no meat, and yet they are on the whole very well developed. Thus it appears that it depends entirely on the good condition of the nurse, and that that food is the best which keeps her healthy.

37. After the child is weaned there is the question as to what shall be his food. For some time trials have been made with all sorts of gruels. But it Proper Foods is not good to nourish the child from the for Children. beginning with such foods. Especial care must be taken not to give children anything pungent, such as wine, spice, salt, etc. But it is very singular that they have

---

[2] A tribe in Northeastern Siberia.

such a great desire for all these things. The cause is this, that poignant foods give an agreeable stimulus and animation to their as yet blunt sensations. Russian children partake freely of the brandy of which their mothers are very fond; and the Russians are strong, healthy people. To be sure, those who can endure this must possess good physical constitutions; yet many perish thus who might otherwise have lived. Such a premature stimulus of the nerves produces many disorders. There must even be a careful watch against too warm foods and drinks for children; for these, too, cause weakness.

38. Moreover, children should not be kept too warm, as their blood is in itself much warmer than that of adults. The temperature of children's blood is 110° Fahrenheit, that of adults only 96°.[1] The child is stifled in the warmth to which parents are accustomed. A cool dwelling makes men strong, anyhow. It is not good for adults, even, to dress and to cover themselves too warmly and to become accustomed to too hot drinks. Thus a cool and hard couch is best adapted to the child. Cold baths are also good. Children's hunger must not be stimulated, but be rather only the natural consequence of activity and occupation. In the mean time, the child must not be allowed to become accustomed to anything to such an extent that he

Care of the Body.

---

[1] This error may be due to Kant or to Rink; for the average temperature of the infant, as now determined, is only 99° Fahrenheit, and of the adult 98.6° Fahrenheit.

come to regard it as a necessity. Even the morally good must not be presented to him under the form of habit.

39. Swaddling is not found among barbarians. The savage nations in America, for example, place their young children in holes dug in the earth, in which is strewn the dust of decayed trees in *Swaddling condemned.* order that the urine and uncleanness may be absorbed and the children may have a dry place, and cover them with leaves; further than this, they allow them the free use of their limbs. It is only for our own convenience that we swaddle children like mummies, in order that we may be freed from giving them constant attention lest they become misshapen; and yet that is just what often happens as a result of swaddling. It is very distressing to children, and they fall into a sort of despair, since they cannot use their limbs at all. Then we think that merely speaking to them will quiet their cries. Let an adult be swaddled, and then see whether he, too, will not cry out and fall into distress and despair!

It must in general be observed that the earliest education should be purely negative,—that is, that one should not add anything to the precautions which nature has taken; that nature itself be not interfered with. If any tampering with nature is to be permitted in education, it is only in the process of physical hardening. This is another reason why swaddling should be abandoned. If, indeed, one wishes to exercise a little precaution, the most appropriate thing is a kind of box, covered with straps, which is used by Italians, and by them called *arcuccio*. The child is left in this box all the time, and is even given suck while lying in it. Thus there is prevented any possibility of the mother smothering the child, should she fall asleep while nursing at night. Many of our children lose their lives in this manner. This precaution is preferable to swaddling-clothes, since the children have more freedom and all deformation is prevented; the effect of swaddling is often to deform children.

40. Another custom in early education is the use of the cradle. The simplest kind is that used by some peasants: the cradle is suspended by cords from a beam, and requires only a push to keep it swinging back and forth of its own accord. The cradle, however, is of no value whatsoever, for the swinging is injurious to the child. It is noticeable even in grown persons that swinging produces nausea and vertigo. The aim is to lull the child in this way so that he will not cry. Crying, however, is beneficial to children. As soon as they are delivered from the womb, where they had no air, they take their first breath. The course of the blood thus changed produces painful sensations.[1] But crying is a great aid in developing the inter-

The Cradle condemned.

---

[1] In his *Anthropology*, etc. (Hartenstein, vii. p. 589), Kant finds a cause other than physiological for this phenomenon, in which he seems to have been greatly interested. The infant "regards his inability to make use of his limbs as restraint, and so immediately announces his claim to freedom (of which no other animal has any idea)." See the longer note, p. 652, where the first cry is further described as being one of "indignation and irritated anger," not

nal constitutional parts and canals of the child's body. The custom of nurses and mothers to hurry to a crying child and to sing to him, etc., is very injurious. This is usually the first spoiling of the child; for, if he sees that he obtains everything by crying for it, he cries all the more.

41. Leading-strings and go-carts are usually employed to teach the child to walk. It is very remarkable that children are taught how to walk, just as though man would never have learned it without being taught. Leading-strings are very injurious. A certain author once complained of being narrow-chested, which he attributed entirely to leading-strings. When the child reaches for everything, and picks up everything from the floor, the leading-strings about the chest support the weight of its body. As the bones are very soft at this period, the chest is pressed flat, and later in life retains this shape. Children do not learn to walk with the same steadiness by the use of such means as when they learn it by their own efforts. It is best to allow them to creep about on the floor until they begin to walk of their own accord.

Leading-strings and Go-carts condemned.

---

of "pain, but vexation, probably because he wishes to move his limbs and immediately feels his inability to do so as a bondage whereby he is robbed of his freedom." Kant proceeds to deal further with this physiological phenomenon of "the first cry" as a datum from which to speculate as to its meaning and utility in preserving the species in an evolutional scale, whose goal seems to be "social cultivation" on the basis of reason, of which there must have been an earlier germ.

As a precaution, the floor can be provided with a thick covering; thus the children cannot injure themselves with splinters nor by falling.

It is usually said that children fall very heavily. Aside from the fact that children cannot fall heavily, it does them no harm if they do fall now and then. They thus learn all the better how to maintain an equipoise, and how to turn themselves so that the fall will not injure them. The child is often made to wear the so-called *Butzmütze*,—a kind of cap which projects so far forward as to prevent him from falling on his face. But that is a negative education where artificial instruments are employed, replacing the natural means which the child possesses. In this case the hands are the natural instruments which the child extends when falling. The more artificial instruments are employed the more does man become dependent upon them.

42. It is much better, anyway, if fewer instruments be used in the beginning, and the children permitted to learn more by themselves; then they learn many things much more thoroughly. It is quite possible, for example, that the child would learn to write by himself. For some one discovered it at first; nor is the discovery such a very great one. It would suffice, for example, to say to a child who asks for bread, "Can you draw a picture of it?" Then the child would draw an oval figure. Now, one would need only to ask whether that were to represent a loaf of bread or a stone, and he would attempt thereupon to make the letter B, etc.; and in this manner the

Self-education as early as Possible.

child would gradually discover his own A-B-C's, which he would afterwards exchange for other signs.[1]

43. There are some children who come into the world with certain defects. Are there not means for improving these faulty, misshapen forms? It is proved by the researches of a great many well-informed authors that corsets are not helpful here, but serve only to aggravate the evil by hindering the circulation of the blood and the humors, as well as the necessary development of the external and internal parts of the body. When the child is left free he at least exercises his body; but the individual who wears a corset is much weaker when he lays it aside than one who has never put it on. It can possibly be helpful to those who are born distorted if a greater weight be placed on the side where the muscles are stronger. But this also is very dangerous, for who is able to establish an equilibrium? The best thing is for the child to exercise himself, and to assume a position, though it does become painful to him; for no machine is of any value here.

Corrective Instruments condemned.

---

[1] Great men are only too easily and often intentionally misunderstood. This is especially true of Kant. And that is why I remark here only that he by no means intends that each child shall invent his own alphabet; but he merely means thus to indicate how children actually and, indeed, analytically proceed in reading and writing without being or becoming conscious of it themselves, even as they grow older, and how, under certain circumstances, they would proceed. . . . [A note by Rink.]

44. All similar artificial contrivances are of all the greater detriment in that they run directly counter to the

Nature to be
followed.
end that nature purposes in organized and rational beings, according to which they must retain their freedom so as to learn to use their powers. It is the duty of education to prevent children from becoming weak. Hardening is the opposite of softening. Too much is ventured if one tries to accustom children to everything. The education of the Russians goes very far on this point. An incredible number of children die because of this.

Habit is a pleasure or action which has become a necessity through frequent repetition of that pleasure or that action. There is nothing to which children accustom themselves more easily, and therefore there is nothing of which less must be given them than piquant things; for example, tobacco, brandy, and warm drinks. Afterwards it is very difficult to disaccustom one's self from them; and at first the attempt to do so occasions distress, since a change in the functions of our body has been introduced by the repeated indulgence.

The more habits a man has the less is he free and independent. It is the same with man as with all other animals. He always retains a certain inclination for that to which he was early accustomed. The child must be prevented from habituating himself to anything, and he must not be allowed to form any habits.

45. Many parents wish to accustom their children to everything. This is of no value. For human nature in general, and in a measure that of individuals, does not

accustom itself to everything, and many children always
remain in apprenticeship. Parents wish, for example,
that children shall be able to go to sleep and   The Doctrine
to arise at all times, or that they eat at will.   of No Habits.
But, in order to endure this, a particular regimen is
necessary,—a regimen which strengthens the body and
repairs the injuries done by this system. We find in
nature many examples of periodicity. The animals have
their definite time for sleep. The human being should
also accustom himself to sleep certain hours, in order
that his body be not deranged in its functions. As for
the other item, which is, that children shall be able to
eat at all times, it is not possible to cite the animals as
examples; for, as the food taken by herbivorous animals, for example, is but slightly nourishing, eating becomes their ordinary occupation. But it is very salutary
to man if he always eats at a certain hour. And many
parents wish that their children shall be able to endure
great cold, bad odors, all sorts of noises, etc. This is
not necessary in the least; the one thing is this, that they
acquire no habits. To this end it is very expedient to
place children in various circumstances.[1]

46. A hard bed is much better for the health than a soft
one. A severe education has great value in strengthening
the body. But by severe education we un-   Physical
derstand simply the prevention of all indo-   Hardening.
lent ease. There is no lack of remarkable examples for

---

[1] This inconsistent return to the practice condemned at the beginning of the section must simply be left standing, unless one
wishes to question the accuracy of Rink's editing.

the confirmation of this assertion, but unfortunately they are not heeded, or, to be more exact, people will not heed them.

47.[1] In regard to that which concerns the culture of the mind (which can also in a certain sense be called The Negative physical),[2] it is of chief importance to Aspect of Physical observe that discipline be not lavish, but Education. that the child always feel his freedom, in such a manner, however, that he does not hinder the freedom of others; thus he must be accustomed to meet with resistance. Many parents deny their children everything, in order to exercise their patience, and accordingly demand more patience of their children than they themselves possess. This is cruel. Give the child

---

[1] The question of arranging Kant's *Lecture-Notes* has been troublesome to the editors of them, most of whom complain of the unsatisfactory editing of the loose and fragmentary material by Rink. Vogt has, perhaps, been the most successful in effecting a rearrangement of the sections, which clings to the topical divisions of the *Notes*. Thus, at this point, Rink scattered the discussions on "discipline." But Kant's conception of discipline (Sections 3, 5) is definite enough to accept Vogt's order, followed in the translation, as the more acceptable one. Rink placed Sections 48 and 51 between 40 and 41 ; Sections 52–56 between 76 and 77 ; and Sections 47, 49, 50 were grouped in this place.

[2] "Physical" is here used in the broader sense. (Cf. Sections 31, note 2, 63, 72.) It includes the psychical nature as opposed to the practical, or the psychical in so far as it is a part of nature. It is specifically "discipline," which Kant here projects as the first step in education. Herbart's division of "government" follows this conception of Kant, and has almost the identical aim of subduing instinctive wildness.

sufficient for his needs, and then say to him, "You have enough." But it is absolutely necessary that this be irrevocable. Pay no attention to the cries of children, and do not yield to them when they wish to obtain anything by this means; but that which they request in a friendly manner give them, if it is for their good. Thus the child will form the habit of being frank; and, since he is not troublesome to any one by crying, every one in turn will be friendly to him. Providence truly appears to have given children cheerful manners so as to beguile people. Nothing is more injurious than a vexing and slavish discipline which is administered in the hope of breaking stubbornness.

48. Children do not have perfect vision during the first three [1] months. They have the sensations of light, but cannot distinguish one object from another. *Early Crying and Discipline.* This can easily be demonstrated: hold before them some glittering object, and they do not follow it with their eyes. With the power of vision there develops the ability to laugh and to cry. When the child is in this condition, he *cries with reflection*, be it as obscure as it may. He thinks that he is suffering some positive injury. Rousseau says, that if a six-months'-old child be struck on the hand, it cries just as if a firebrand had fallen on its hand. Here the conception of offence is actually present. Parents speak ordinarily a great deal about breaking the will of children. Their will may be broken if it has not already been spoiled. The first

---

[1] Vogt's edition reads "eight,"—evidently a misprint.

step towards spoiling children is to yield to their des-
potic will, and to allow them to extort everything by
crying. It is an extremely difficult matter to correct
this later, and the attempt seldom proves successful.[1]
The child can be compelled to keep quiet, but he feeds
on his spleen and fosters his internal fury. By this
means the child is habituated to pretence and to concealed emotions. It is very strange, for example, that
parents should desire children to kiss their hands after
having been punished with the rod. Children thus
become trained to dissimulation and falsehood; for the
rod is not exactly a beautiful present, for which one
may expect thanks, and one can easily imagine with
what sort of a heart the child will kiss the hand that
punishes him.

49. One often says to children, " Fie ! Aren't you
ashamed of yourself? What a naughty thing to do !"
etc. Such things, however, should not appear in early education. The child as yet
has no notion of shame and propriety. He
has no need to be ashamed, and he is only intimidated
by being spoken to in such a manner. He becomes em-
barrassed when others look at him, and likes to hide
from them. As a result there develop reserve and detrimental dissimulation. He does not venture to ask for
anything, and yet he ought to feel free to ask for everything; he conceals his feelings and always appears to be

Misuse of Shame in Discipline.

---

[1] Cf. Horstig, *Soll man die Kinder schreien lassen ?* (Shall we let
children cry ?) Gotha, 1789. [A note by Kant.]

otherwise than he is, instead of saying everything frankly. Instead of always being with his parents, he shuns them, and throws himself into the arms of the more complacent domestics.

50. Trifling and continual caressing are no better than such a vexing education. This strengthens the child in his own will and makes him false ; and, since it reveals to him a weakness in his parents, it robs them of the reverence he should necessarily have for them. But, if he is educated in such a manner that he is unable to obtain anything by crying, he will be free without being bold, and unassuming without being timid. *Dreist* ("bold") should be *dräust*, since it is derived from *dräuen*, from *drohen*, which means "to menace." [1] An overbearing (*dräust*) person is unendurable. Many men have such bold faces that one constantly fears an incivility from them ; on the other hand, there are those in whom it can be seen at once that they are incapable of saying a coarse thing to any one. A frank appearance is always possible, but a certain goodness should go along with it. People often say of a distinguished man that he looks like a king. But this look is nothing more than a peculiar bold expression which he has always worn from his youth because no one then opposed him.

Evils of Pampering.

51. It can certainly be said with truth that the children of common people are much more spoiled than

----

[1] See Section 19, note 2, p. 123.

the children of the aristocratic class; for the common people play with their children like monkeys. They sing to them, hug and kiss them, and dance with them. They imagine that they benefit a child if, as soon as he cries, they hurry and play with him, etc. But this makes him cry only so much the more. If, on the contrary, his cries are not heeded, they finally cease; for no creature readily continues in a fruitless labor. If children are accustomed to see all their caprices satisfied, the subsequent breaking of the will comes too late. If they are simply permitted to cry, they will become tired of it themselves. Concession to all their fancies in early youth ruins their heart and manners.

The Danger of Fostering Whims.

The infant, to be sure, has no conception of morality; but his natural disposition is spoiled in such a way that afterwards very hard punishment is necessary in order to repair the evil.[1] When later it is desired to break children of the habit of expecting all their whims to be satisfied, they express in their screams as great a rage as that of which adults only are capable, and which is without effect merely because they lack the power to put it into activity. For so long a time they have needed only to cry in order to obtain what they wished, that now they rule despotically. When this domination ceases, they are quite naturally fretful. When men have been in possession of power for a long time, they find it very difficult to relinquish it all at once.

---

[1] See Section 102.

52. The culture of *the feeling of pleasure* or *of pain* properly belongs here.[1] This should be negative; but the feeling must not be spoiled by too much tenderness. An inclination for indolent ease is worse for man than all the evils of life. It is therefore extremely important that children should learn to work. If they are not already effeminated by fondling, children really love amusements which are combined with fatiguing exertions and occupations which demand strength on their part. One should not make children fastidious in their enjoyments, nor allow them to choose their pleasures by themselves. Mothers usually spoil their children in this particular, and pamper them generally. Still, it is noticeable that children, especially the sons, love their father more than their mother. This may be due to the fact that mothers do not permit them to spring about, run around, etc., for fear that they might be injured. The father, on the contrary, who scolds and even whips them when they have been unruly, takes them now and then into the fields and there lets them run around, play, and be boyishly frolicsome.

Education of Feeling.

---

[1] This "feeling" represents one of the three divisions of the mental faculties—the others being understanding and desire—which Kant's authority sanctioned for almost a century as the starting-point of psychological science. This feeling forms the basis of his *Critique of Judgment*, which treats of the æsthetic factors of experience, and also forms the key-stone to the whole system of Criticism. It is surprisingly strange that in these *Lecture-Notes* there appear only two references to the cultivation of the æsthetic "powers,"—viz., Sections 52, 70. (See Selection V.)

53. We think we discipline the patience of children by compelling them to wait a long time for anything. Training in This is, however, hardly necessary. But Patience. they have need of patience in sickness, etc. Patience is twofold: it consists either in abandoning all hope or in taking new courage. The first kind of patience is not necessary when one desires only that which is possible; the second kind may always be had if one desires only what is right. In sickness, hopelessness aggravates just as much as courage tends to ameliorate. He who is capable of understanding this in its relation to his physical or moral condition does not abandon hope.

54. The will of children should not be broken, as stated above, but merely directed in such a manner that it will afterwards yield to natural hin-Will-breaking. drances. Of course, at first the child must blindly obey. It is unnatural that the child should command by his cries, and the strong obey the weak. One should, therefore, never yield to the cries of children in their first years, and never allow them to obtain what they wish by this means. Parents usually deceive themselves in this, and later think to make amends by denying children everything for which they ask. But this is absurd,—to deny them without reason that which they expect from the kindness of their parents, merely to oppose them and to let them, the weaker ones, feel the superior force of their parents.

55. Children are *badly* educated if their wills are gratified, and quite *falsely* educated if one acts directly

contrary to their wills and their desires. The former
ordinarily happens so long as they are the playthings of
parents, especially at the time when they   Negative Will-
begin to talk. This indulgence works great   training.
harm for the entire life. It is true that by opposing
the wills of children we prevent them from exhibiting
their ill-humor,—that we must do,—but they rage all
the more inwardly. They have not yet learned how
to conduct themselves. The rule which should be observed with children from their earliest years is this:
go to their assistance if you believe they are crying
because something is really hurting them, but let them
cry if they are doing it merely out of ill-humor. And
a similar course must later constantly be followed.
The opposition which the child meets with in this
case is quite natural and peculiarly negative, since he
is simply not yielded to. Many children, on the contrary, receive everything they desire from their parents
merely by recourse to entreaties. If they are permitted to obtain everything by crying, they become ill-
natured; but if by entreaties, they become gentle. If,
therefore, there is no important reason for a contrary
course, the child's wishes should be granted. But if
one has reasons for not granting them, he must not allow himself to be moved by repeated entreaties. Every
refusal must be irrevocable. The result will be that
the necessity for frequent refusals will be done away
with.

56. Let us suppose—what can be conceded only
very seldom—that the child naturally tends to be stub-

born; then it is best not to do anything to please him
if he does nothing to please us. Will-break-

Stubbornness.

ing results in creating a servile disposition;
natural resistance, on the contrary, produces docility.

57. All this is still a part of *negative* culture; for
many of the weaknesses of man result, not from his
having been taught nothing, but from the

**Dangers of.
False
Impressions.**

false impressions which he has received.
Thus, for example, nurses inculcate upon
children a fear of spiders, toads, etc. Children would
be just as apt to reach out for spiders as they do for
other things. But since nurses, as soon as they see a
spider, show their terror by their looks, this fright is communicated to the child through a sort of sympathy.
Many retain this fear throughout their whole life and are
always childish in this respect. For, while spiders are
without doubt dangerous to flies, their sting being poi-
sonous to them, they do not harm human beings. And
a toad, likewise, is as harmless as a green frog or any
other animal.[1]

---

[1] Since at this point in the *Notes* the attention seems to be turned
from infancy and to be directed more to the features of childhood
and youth, the following selection on the development of the child
may be in place here. In the opening section of the *Anthropology*, etc., which treats of "the consciousness of one's self," Kant
observes,—

"It is remarkable that the child who can talk very well begins
rather late to speak in the first person (perhaps a year later), but
has always spoken of himself in the third person (Charles wants to
eat, to go, etc.), and that something seems to dawn upon him
when he begins to speak with 'I'; he never returns to the

58. The *positive* aspect of physical education is *culture*.[1] In this respect man is different from the animal. It consists principally in the exercise of his mental faculties. That is why parents should give their children

---

earlier form of speech. Formerly he merely *felt* himself, now he *thinks* himself. The explanation of this phenomenon may be difficult for the anthropologists.

"That a child neither weeps nor smiles before he is three months old, as has been observed, seems to rest upon the development of certain ideas of offence and injustice which hint at reason. [See Section 48.] That in this period he begins to follow with his eyes any brilliant objects that may be held up before him is the crude beginning of the progress of perceptions (apprehension of the idea of sensation) which is later extended to knowledge of the objects of the senses,—*i.e.*, of experience.

"That, further, when he tries to talk, his mutilation of words seems so adorable to mothers and nurses, and makes them inclined to hug and kiss him all the time, and to make him a little autocrat by fulfilling his every wish : this lovableness of the child during his development into manhood must be credited partly to his innocence and the frankness of all his as yet faulty expressions, in which there is no concealment and nothing malicious, but also in part to the nurse's natural inclination to be kind to a creature who engagingly resigns himself to her authority, for he is given a play-time, the happiest of all, in which the educator again enjoys himself by making himself a child once more.

"The child's memory of his early years does not, however, reach so far back, for this was not the time of experiences, but merely of scattered perceptions which had not as yet been united under the concept of an object."—Hartenstein, vii. pp. 437, 438.

[1] Kant places "culture" in strong contrast with "moralization ;" that has *many* ends, this has only *one* end,—viz., the selection of the good. (Cf. Sections 1, note, and 21.)

Sections 58–76 deal with "intellectual education," which ought to be inserted here as a superscription.

every opportunity for such exercise. The first and principal rule here is : all instruments shall be dispensed with as far as possible.[1] Therefore, leading-strings and go-carts should never be used, and the child should be permitted to creep until he learns to walk by himself, for then he will walk much more steadily. Instruments, in fact, only ruin natural ability. Thus, we use a string to measure a given distance, but it can be done just as well by the eye ; we use a clock in order to tell the time, but it is necessary only to note the position of the sun ; we use a compass in order to know the directions when we are in a forest, but it is possible to know this by the position of the sun during the day and of the stars by night. It might even be said : instead of using a boat to go on the water, one can swim. The illustrious Franklin[2] marvelled that every one did not learn to swim, since it is so agreeable and useful. He even indicates an easy way by which one can learn it by himself. Let an egg drop into a brook where the learner's head is just out of the water when he is standing on the ground ; now attempt to reach the egg. In bending over, the feet are raised and the head is laid back in the nape of the neck, so that the water does not enter the mouth, and thus the learner has exactly the position which is necessary for swimming. The essential thing is the cultivation of

The Positive Aspect of Physical Education.

---

[1] This rule may be regarded as an excellent summary of the *Émile.*

[2] Benjamin Franklin (1706–1790), the printer, the statesman, the scientist, and the great American exemplar of wisdom and common sense, as found in his *Poor Richard's Almanac.*

natural ability. Mere instruction is often sufficient, or the child himself is often inventive enough and makes his own instruments.

59. That which must be observed in physical education, consequently in that which concerns the body,[1] has reference either to the use of voluntary movement or to the use of the organs of sense. The important thing in the case of voluntary movement is that the child always help himself. For this he needs strength, skilfulness, agility, confidence. For example, one should be able to go over narrow bridges, walk along precipitous heights where one looks down into a deep abyss, or walk on an unstable support. When a man is not able to do such things, he is not completely what he might be. Since the *Philanthropinum* of Dessau has set the example, many experiments of this sort have been made with the children in other institutes. One is astonished when he reads how the Swiss accustom themselves from their infancy to climb the mountains, and of the agility they possess in walking on the narrowest foot-paths with complete safety, and in leaping chasms over which their visual

Movement and the Senses.

---

[1] This phrase is the exact rendering of the text, which brings confusion into Kant's conception of "physical education," as expressed in Section 31 and elsewhere. That which is *implied* by the phrase—namely, that physical education is identical with bodily care—is excluded from the prevailing conception of education in the suggestions presented in Section 34 and following. The phrase, then, should have specified this portion of physical education as that which is connected naturally with mental activity.

judgment tells them they will pass in safety. Most men, however, fear even an imaginary fall, and this fear paralyzes their limbs in such a manner that it would be really dangerous for them to make any such attempt. This fear ordinarily grows with age, and is usually found among those who are engaged in much brain work.

Such experiments with children are really not very dangerous ; for they have, in proportion to their strength, far less weight and do not fall as heavily. Moreover, their bones are not as brittle and fragile as they grow to be later. Children try their own strength themselves. Thus, for example, they are often seen climbing without any apparent purpose. Running is a healthy movement and strengthens the body. Leaping, lifting, carrying, hurling, throwing at a mark, wrestling, racing, and all such exercises are excellent. Dancing, in so far as it is technical, seems to be less suitable for young children.

60. Practice in long-distance throwing and in hitting targets also results in training the senses, especially that
Training the of visual perception of distance. Playing
Senses. ball is one of the best sports for children, since it involves running, which is very healthful. In general, those plays are the best which, along with the skilfulness they develop, also train the senses ; for example, those which exercise the eye to judge distance, size, and proportion accurately, or to find the cardinal points of any place when one must rely upon the sun, etc.[1]

---

[1] See *Émile*, Payne's translation, pp. 96 ff., 115.

All such are good exercises. The local imagination, by which is meant the skill to represent anything in the place where it was actually seen, is something very advantageous; for example, the ability to find one's way out of a forest by noticing those trees which were passed previously. It is the same with the *memoria localis*,[1] by which one knows not only in what book something has been read, but also the exact location of the passage. Thus, the musician has the keys in his mind, and does not need to concern himself about them. It is just as requisite to cultivate the hearing of children, that by this means they may discern whether a thing is near or far and on which side it is.

61. The play of blindman's-buff among children was known even among the Greeks, by whom it was called μυίνδα. Children's plays are very universal, anyway. Those which are used in Germany are found in England, France, etc. They are based upon a natural impulse of children. In the play of blindman's-buff, for example, this impulse manifests itself in the desire to know how they can help themselves when deprived of one of their senses. Top-spinning is a particular play; but children's plays of this kind give men material for wider reflection, and sometimes are the occasions of important inventions. Thus, Segner[2] has written a dissertation on the top, and the top has given to the captain

The Plays of Children.

---

[1] The memory of place.

[2] Johann Andreas von Segner (1704–1777), a German naturalist and mathematician, a professor at Jena, and later at Göttingen.

of an English ship the occasion to invent a mirror by means of which the height of stars can be measured aboard ship.

Children love noisy instruments, such as little trumpets, drums, etc. But these instruments are worth nothing, since children make themselves very troublesome to others. It would be much better if they should learn to make whistles out of reeds.

Swinging, also, is a good movement; adults themselves use it for their health; but in this sport children must be watched, since the movement can become very rapid. Kite-flying is a faultless play. It cultivates dexterity; for the height to which the kite rises depends upon its position relative to the wind.

62. His interest being absorbed in these plays, the boy denies himself other needs, and thus learns gradually to

The Moral Value of Plays.

impose other and greater privations upon himself. At the same time he becomes accustomed to continuous occupation; but, for this very reason, his plays must not be merely plays; they must be plays having a purpose and an end; for the more his body is strengthened and hardened in this manner the safer is he from the disastrous consequences of pampering. Gymnastics should simply be confined to guiding nature, and ought not, therefore, to try to bring about affected elegance. It is discipline, and not instruction, which should appear first. In cultivating the body it must not be forgotten that children are also being formed for society. Rousseau says, "You will never make an excellent man, unless you have a little scamp to begin with." A vivacious child can become a good man much sooner than can a pert, artful boy. The child must be neither troublesome nor insinuating in his social relations. When he has an invitation from others, the child must be confident without being forward, candid without being saucy. The way to accomplish this is not to undo anything, not to give him those ideas of decorum by which he is intimidated and rendered unsociable, or, on the other hand, which suggest the desire of making himself of some account. Nothing is more ridiculous than precocious modesty or impertinent conceit in a child. In the latter instance, the child must be allowed to feel his weakness, but not too much of our superiority, that he may by his own efforts perfect himself as a man who is to live in society ; for if the world is large enough for him, it must be large enough for others too.

Toby, in *Tristram Shandy*,[1] says to a fly which had annoyed him for a long time, as he lets it out of the window, "Go, you bad thing, the world is large enough for you and for me." Every one could take these words for his motto. We must not annoy one another; the world is large enough for us all.

63. We now come to the *culture of the soul*, which can, in a certain sense, also be called physical. It is necessary, however, to distinguish between nature and freedom. Giving laws to freedom is something entirely

---

[1] *The Life and Opinions of Tristram Shandy*, by Laurence Sterne (1713–1768).

different from cultivating nature. The nature of the body and that of the soul agree in this, that in our cultivation[1] the effort must be made to prevent impairment to either, and that art add something to the body as well as to the soul.[2] Thus, in a certain sense, it is possible to call the culture of the soul, as well as that of the body, "physical."

Physical Culture of the Soul.

This physical culture of the soul is to be distinguished from the moral culture in that the former aims solely at nature, the latter solely at freedom. A man can be highly cultivated physically; he may have a highly perfected mind, but at the same time be wanting in moral culture, and hence be an evil being.

But it is necessary to distinguish *physical* culture from *practical* culture, which is *pragmatic* or *moral*. In the latter case it is *moralization* and not *cultivation*.[3]

64. We divide the *physical culture of the mind* into the *free* and the *scholastic*. The free culture is, so to speak, only a play; and the scholastic, on the other hand, is a serious affair. The former is that which must always be observed in the pupil; in the latter he must be considered as subjected to constraint. One may be busy in play; this is called "busy in leisure;" one can also be employed under compulsion, and this is called "work." The scholastic culture should be work, and the free should be play, for the child.[4]

Free and Scholastic Culture.

---

[1] That is, by discipline.   [2] By culture.   [3] Cf. Section 32.

[4] In the division of the "scholastic-mechanical" culture of Section 32, Kant is aiming a sharp criticism against a method, pre-

65. Various educational plans have been devised in order to try to find—something very laudable—which is the best method in education. It has been suggested, among other things, to let children learn everything as in play. Lichtenberg,[1] in a number of the *Göttingen Magazine*, ridicules the opinion of those who would teach boys everything in the form of play, while really they should be

Play in Educational Method.

---

vailing in his time, which, wherever possible, sought to teach children in the form of play. This criticism has not lost its force against the same tendency in method which has a thriving survival in current education.

Elsewhere in his writings Kant utters protests against the effort among his contemporaries to do away with any and all constraint in learning. In the *Critique of Judgment* (1790), Hartenstein, v. p. 314, he observes, in treating of the mechanical factor in free art, that "many modern educators think they promote a free art best by removing from it all constraint and changing it from work into mere play." In the *Anthropology*, etc. (1793), Hartenstein, vii. p. 543, definite mechanical rules are regarded as absolutely essential, even in the case of genius: "Mechanism of instruction, since it forces the pupil to imitation, is, to be sure, disadvantageous to the germination of genius,—*i.e.*, as far as his originality is concerned. But yet every art requires certain mechanical fundamental rules ; that is to say, it needs conformity of the product to the underlying idea,—*i.e.*, *truth* in the representation of the object which is thought of. This must be learned with scholastic strictness, and is of course an effect of imitation. But to free the imagination from this constraint, and to allow the peculiar talent, even contrary to nature, to proceed irregularly and to *run riot*, would perhaps yield original madness, but of a sort which would not be exemplary, and which would certainly not be reckoned as genius."

[1] Georg Christoph Lichtenberg (1742–1799), a well-known German natural scientist and satirist, a professor at Göttingen.

early accustomed to serious occupations, because they will one day enter upon a serious life. This has a perverse effect. The child should play, he should have hours of recreation ; but he must also learn to work. The culture of his skill is certainly good, like the culture of his mind ; but each kind of culture should be practised at different times. It is, moreover, especially unfortunate for man that he is so greatly inclined to indolence. The more a person has idled away his time the more difficult it is for him to make up his mind to work.

66. In labor the employment is not agreeable in itself, but it is undertaken with another end in view. Employ-

Play *versus* Work.

ment in play, on the contrary, is agreeable in itself without having a further purpose. When we go out for a walk, the walk itself is the purpose, and the longer the walk the more agreeable it is to us. If, however, we wish to go somewhere, the society which is to be found in that place, or something else, is the purpose of our going, and we choose the shortest way. The same applies equally to card-playing. It is strange indeed to see how rational men are capable of sitting and shuffling cards by the hour. This shows that men do not cease so easily to be children ; for in what particular is this play any better than the children's game of ball? It is true that adults do not ride a stick, but they none the less ride other hobby-horses.[1]

---

[1] Kant remarks on the meaning of play as follows in the *Anthropology*, etc. (Hartenstein, vii. p. 596): "The plays of the boy (ball, wrestling, running races, playing soldier) ; further, those of the man (chess, cards, where in the case of the former the mere

67. It is of the greatest importance that children learn to work. Man is the only animal that must work.[1] He is obliged to make a great deal of prepa- Work and ration before coming to the enjoyment of Education. that which is necessary for his sustenance. The question whether heaven would not have provided for us much better by offering us everything already prepared, so that work would not be required of us, must certainly be answered negatively; for man craves employment, even such as entails a certain constraint. Just as erroneous is the idea that if Adam and Eve had only remained in Paradise, they would have had nothing to do but sit together, sing Arcadian songs, and contemplate the beauty of nature. *Ennui* would as certainly have tormented them as it does other people under similar circumstances.

Man must be occupied in such a manner that, so en-

---

superiority of the understanding, in the latter the net gain is the one object in mind); finally, those of the citizen, who tries his luck in public, with faro or dice,—are all spurred on unconsciously by wiser nature to daring feats, to try their strength in conflict with others, really in order that the vital force may be preserved from exhaustion and kept active. Two such opponents think that they are playing with each other; whereas, as a matter of fact, nature is playing with them both, of which their reason can easily convince them when they consider how badly the means they choose suit their purpose."

[1] The exaggeration in this statement can readily be permitted to stand in spite of the facts in the lives of bees, ants, the nest-building of birds, the dam-building of beavers, etc. Work as instinct expression and work as a rational necessity are doubtless the radical distinctions Kant here conveys. (See Section 3.)

grossed by the purpose which he has in mind, he becomes oblivious of himself, and the best rest for him is that which follows labor; hence the child must be accustomed to labor. And where else than in the school is it possible to give the inclination to work a better cultivation?[1] The school is a forced culture. To lead the child to look upon everything as play is very injurious. There must be a time for recreation, but there must also be a time for work. Even if the child does not see the utility of this constraint immediately, he will become aware of its great benefits later. It would only indulge children's indiscreet curiosity always to answer their questions, Why is this? and Why is that? Education

---

[1] "So far as *excessive study* is concerned, it is not necessary to warn young people against it. In this matter youth needs the spurs rather than a bridle. Even the most violent and the most persistent exertion in this regard can well *tire* the mind, so that as a result man may take a dislike to science, but will not put it out of tune where it has not already been disconcerted, and therefore found pleasure in mystical books and in manifestations which go beyond healthy human understanding. To this also belongs the inclination to devote one's self to the reading of books which have received a certain holy anointing, merely on account of this liberalism, without aiming at the moral, for which a certain author has coined the phrase, 'He is writing mad.'" [Foot-note by Kant.] "It is a common experience that merchants engage in too much business and lose themselves in too extensive plans. But anxious parents need not fear excess of industry in their young people (if their heads are level to begin with). Nature herself guards against such overloading of knowledge in this way: the things over which he has racked his brains, but all to no purpose, disgust the student."—*Anthropology*, etc. (1798), Hartenstein, vii. pp. 535, 536.

must be full of constraint, but this does not mean that it shall be slavish.[1]

68. As for the free culture of the faculties of the mind,[2] it must be observed that it is continuous. It has

---

[1] Kant herein departs from Rousseau in thus denying the great value of the principle of utility as a motive for learning. The following passage in the *Anthropology*, etc. (Hartenstein, vii. p. 459), could well be taken as directed against the great effort of the Philanthropinists to rob work of its true characteristics : "*To make something difficult easy is a service ; to represent it as easy, though one is not able to do it one's self, is deceit.*" (Cf. Section 64, note.)

[2] Kant here means the "intellectual" powers, excluding the "affective" and "active" powers. He followed the old doctrine of the mental faculties,—indeed, he established the doctrine by giving it his authoritative adoption,—which he rather regarded as real powers. The basal differentiation between Kantian and Herbartian pedagogy is first to be sought in Herbart's critical overthrow of this psychological doctrine of the faculties.

Kant here, as elsewhere, accepts the theory of the equilibrium of the mental faculties, which has been, and remains *an undemonstrable ideal* of psychology. The corresponding theory in physics was established in the past generation as the working principle of the conservation and correlation of energy. This ideal has played an enormous rôle in pedagogy, usually in terms of the old pedagogical maxim, which Kant here probably most nearly approximates, of the "harmonious development of the mental powers as an end and a duty in education." (See Section 10.) In one of his earliest observations upon the structure of the human mind he found psychological features which, if true, rob this maxim of all its empirical worth : "In the perfection of the human understanding there is no such proportion and similarity as, for example, in the structure of the human body. In the case of the latter it is, indeed, possible to estimate the size of the whole from the size of one and the other members, but in mental ability it is entirely

the higher powers particularly in view. The lower powers are cultivated at the same time, but only with reference to the higher; wit, for example, with reference to the understanding. The principal rule to be followed here is that no power of the mind shall be cultivated in isolation, but each with reference to the others; for example, the imagination only for the benefit of the understanding.

Education of the Mental Faculties.

The lower faculties have no worth in themselves; for example, a man may have a great memory, but no judgment. Such a one is a living lexicon. But such pack-mules of Parnassus are necessary; for, although they themselves are unable to produce anything rational, they can drag along the material out of which others can bring something good.[1] Wit becomes outright silliness

---

different. Science is an irregular body, without evenness and uniformity. A learned man of a dwarf's stature often excels in this or that division of knowledge another who towers far above him with the whole range of his science. The vanity of men does not extend so far, according to all appearances, as not to be aware of this difference."—*Thoughts on the True Valuation of Living Forces* (1747), Hartenstein, i. p. 7.

[1] There occur many allusions in Kant's writings to empty and lifeless learning, of which these are a few instances :

"There is also *gigantic* learning, but which is often *cyclopean*, —that is to say, lacking an eye,—namely, that of true philosophy, in order to use purposively through reason this mass of historical knowledge, the burden of a hundred camels."—*Anthropology*, etc., Hartenstein, vii. p. 545.

" He who cannot *think* himself, although he can learn a great deal, is called a dull (stupid) man. A person can be a *vast* scholar (a machine for the instruction of others, as he himself was instructed), and yet be very *stupid* so far as the rational use of his historical

if it is unaccompanied by judgment. Understanding is the knowledge of the universal. Judgment is the application of the universal to the particular. Reason is the faculty of perceiving the union of the universal with the particular.[1] The free culture continues its course from childhood until the time when the youth is liberated from all education.[2] If, for example, a youth adduces a

---

knowledge is concerned.—He whose procedure with that which he has learned betrays publicly the restraint of the school (hence the lack of freedom in his own thinking) is a *pedant*, be he scholar, soldier, or even courtier."—*Anthropology*, etc., Hartenstein, vii. p. 449.

"The obtuse person lacks wit, the stupid person lacks understanding. Quickness in grasping and in remembering a thing, also ease in expressing it properly, have a great deal to do with wit; hence he who is not stupid can be very obtuse in so far as it is difficult to get something into his head, although the next moment he may be able to see it with greater ripeness of judgment; and difficulty in expressing one's self is no proof of lack of understanding, but only that the wit did not furnish sufficient aid in clothing the thoughts in the most suitable symbols."—*Essay on the Diseases of the Head* (1764), Hartenstein, ii. p. 214.

[1] In the *Anthropology*, etc. (Hartenstein, vii. pp. 545, 546), Kant distinguishes these three faculties in terms of the peculiar question each is supposed to ask : "The understanding asks : What do I will? (*i.e.*, in the theoretical sense : What will I affirm as *true?*) ; the judgment asks : What's it about? the reason asks : What is its result?"

[2] On the time limit. (See Section 26.)

"The age when man attains the complete use of his reason can, with reference to his *skill* (ability in any direction), be fixed at about the twentieth year, with reference to *prudence* (ability to use other men for his own purposes) in the fortieth year, and finally, with reference to *wisdom*, at about the sixtieth year; but in the

universal rule, he should be permitted to cite instanc
in history or in fables in which it is concealed, a
passages in poetry where it is already expressed, and
thus induced to exercise his wit, memory, etc.

69. The maxim, *tantum scimus, quantum memoria tene-*
mus,[1] is without doubt quite correct, and that is why the
Importance of culture of the memory is very necessary.
Memory and All things are so made that the understand-
Rôle of
Mechanical ing first follows the sensuous impressions
Methods. and the memory must retain them. Thus
it is, for example, with languages. They can be learnec
either by formal[2] memorizing or by conversation, and
in the case of modern languages the latter is the best
method. The acquisition of a vocabulary is really in-

---

last epoch it is more *negative*, seeing all the foolishness of the
first two," etc.—*Anthropology*, etc. (1798), Hartenstein, vii. p.
517.

It should be observed how Kant here works his doctrine of freedom into the intellectual processes,—a tendency hardly in accord
with the *Critique of Pure Reason.* This view is definitely affirmed
in the *Anthropology*, etc. : "The inner perfection of man consists
in this, that he has the use of all his faculties in his power, so as
to subject them to his free will."—*Ibid.*, p. 455.

[1] We know only so much as we hold in the memory. As for
the correctness of this maxim, that it might serve as a basis for
pedagogical practices, there has been much debate. We of to-day
would probably invert the order of dependence, and say that we
really remember only that which we know, and therefore easily
forget what we do not understand.

[2] "Formal" and "material" are important concepts in Kant's
philosophical thinking, which appear in his pedagogy. (Cf. the
type of division in Section 100.)

dispensable; but it is best to have the pupils learn those words which occur in reading an author. It is necessary that the pupils have a fixed and definite task. Geography also is best learned by a mechanical method. The memory especially loves this form of mechanism, and in a multitude of cases it is very useful. Up to the present time there has been contrived no mechanism to facilitate the study of history; the attempt has been made with tables, but these do not appear to have very good effects.[1] History, however, is an excellent means of exercising the understanding in judging. Memorizing is very necessary, but as a mere exercise it has no value, —for example, memorizing a speech word for word. In any case, it only helps towards the encouragement of confidence; and, besides, declaiming is something for adults only.[2] Here belong also all those things which are learned merely for a future examination, or *in faturam oblivionem*.[3] The memory should be employed only with

---

[1] Rink cites in a note the historical tables of Schölzer, and suggests that Pestalozzi's idea and practice appear to have been expressive of the mechanical aims here discussed by Kant.

[2] To be sure, there are men of intelligence and insight who seem to be incapable of declaiming. But it is certain that that is more easily remembered which is read with the necessary expression, or which, at least, could be so read, and the latest method of reading has proved that the foundation for this can be laid easily and successfully. See Olivier, *Ueber Character und Wert guter Unterrichtsmethoden*, Leipzig, 1802, and his *Kunst, lesen und recht schreiben zu lehren*, Dessau, 1801. (On the Character and Worth of Good Methods of Instruction, and Art of Teaching Reading and Correct Writing.) [A note by Kant.]

[3] To be soon forgotten.

such things as are important for us to remember and which have relation to real life. Novel-reading is most injurious to children, since it only serves to amuse them for the time being. Such reading weakens the memory. It would be absurd to wish to remember romances and to repeat them to others. Thus all novels should be taken out of the hands of children. While reading them they fashion for themselves in the story a new romance; for they rearrange the circumstances, and fall into reveries and become empty-minded.[1]

Distractions must never be tolerated, least of all in the school, for they end in producing certain inclinations and certain habits. Even the most beautiful

Distraction.

talents perish in him who is subject to distraction. If children become heedless in their pleasures, they soon compose themselves; but they appear most distracted when they have some naughtiness in mind, for then they are thinking how they can conceal or

---

[1] Kant remarks repeatedly on the evils of novel-reading. (Cf., for example, *Anthropology*, etc., Hartenstein, vii. p. 525.) "Novel-reading, besides causing many other depressions of the spirits, makes distraction habitual. For although, by descriptions of characters which are really to be found among men (although the descriptions are exaggerated), it gives the thoughts a coherence (connection, continuity), as in a true history whose exposition must always be in a certain way *systematic*, yet at the same time it allows the mind, while the reading is going on, to insert digressions (for example, still other events as imaginings) and the current of thought becomes *fragmentary*, so that the ideas of one and the same object are allowed to play about in the mind in a scattered way (*sparsim*), not connected according to intellectual unity (*conjunctim*)." (See also Selection VI. p. 255.)

repair it. Then they only half hear, do not know what they are reading, etc.[1]

70. The memory must be cultivated early, but care must be taken to cultivate the understanding at the same time.[2]

Methods of Memory Training.

The memory is cultivated:

(*a*) By retaining the names which appear in narratives.

(*b*) By reading and writing; the child must practise the former by mental effort without having recourse to spelling.

(*c*) By languages, which the child must learn first by hearing before he reads anything.

Then a suitably arranged *orbis pictus*, so called, would be of great use, and a beginning can be made with botany, mineralogy, and a description of nature in general. To make sketches of these objects gives occasion for drawing and modelling, for which a knowledge of mathematics is necessary. The earliest scientific instruction is connected most advantageously with geography, mathematical as well as physical.[3] The narration of travels, illustrated by maps

Science Instruction.

---

[1] In the *Reflections on Anthropology*, p. 121 (cited by Vogt, p. 92), Kant recognizes two kinds of distraction, both of which are real enemies of attention in the best pedagogical sense of the term: one is thoughtlessness, which is negative, and to which the remarks on novel-reading are directed; the other is distraction proper, which is positive.

[2] See Selection VI. for passage on Memory.

[3] This preference for geography as a subject and means for intellectual education runs back in Kant's life to a period as early as

and engravings, leads to political geography. From a study of the present surface of the earth the student goes back to its former condition, and comes upon ancient geography, ancient history, etc.

In the instruction of children we must try to effect a gradual union of knowledge and power. Among all the sciences, mathematics appears to be the one which best accomplishes this purpose.[1] Moreover, knowledge and language should be united (eloquence, rhetoric, and oratory). But the

Union of Knowledge and Power.

1765–66, as is indicated in his announcement of his university lectures for that winter semester, a part of which is translated in Selection VII. Wallace remarks in his *Kant* (p. 31) that Kant and Hamann, the "Magus of the North," "seem in 1759 to have entertained the idea of a joint-work—a natural philosophy for children (*Kinder-physik*)."

[1] On this separation of knowledge and ability, which Kant simply postulates here as existing and as constituting a problem for all instruction, he makes a special remark in the *Critique of Judgment* in trying to determine the intimate nature of art:

"Art as the skill of man is also to be distinguished from science (power from knowledge), as practical from theoretical faculty, as technique from theory (as surveying from geometry). And even that which one *can* do, as soon as he *knows* what should be done, and therefore is sufficiently familiar with the desired effect, cannot be called art. Only that which one, even though he knows it most thoroughly, has not yet the skill to make, belongs in so far to art." —Hartenstein, v. p. 313.

This unusual pedagogical selection of mathematics as capable of overcoming the contradiction usually affirmed to exist between theory and practice had more light thrown upon it, according to Willmann (p. 122), in Bernhardi's *Mathematik und Sprachen, Gegensatz und Ergänzung*, 1818, whose foundation was derived from Kant's theory of knowledge. (Cf. Section 75, below.)

child must also learn to distinguish clearly between knowledge and mere opinion and belief.[1] In this way there is formed a correct understanding, and a taste that is *correct* rather than *fine* or *delicate*. The taste which is to be cultivated first is that of the senses, especially that of the eye, and lastly that of ideas.[2]

71. Rules must appear in everything that is to cultivate the understanding.[3] It is also very useful to ab-

---

[1] See the third section of the second part of the Methodology of the *Critique of Pure Reason*, where Kant treats at length of the relations between "opining, knowing, and believing."

[2] Cf. Section 52 and note. In these two paragraphs of Section 70, which tend to summarize the content of a course of study, it is rather amazing not to find anything selected from poetry, music, and the other fine arts, as containing educative material. (See Selection V.) One is tempted to ask, Was the last paragraph of Section 70 written after the *Critique of Judgment* (1790), especially its Introduction, which treats critically of the union of man's psychological powers in æsthetical experiences and its expression in judgments of taste?

[3] "The natural understanding can, through instruction, be enriched with many concepts and furnished with rules ; but the second intellectual faculty—namely, that of knowing whether something falls under a rule or not, judgment (*judicium*)—cannot be taught, but only practised ; therefore its growth is called maturity, and that understanding which, we say, does not come before the years. It is also easy to see that this could not be otherwise ; for instruction takes place by communication of rules. In case one should attempt to instruct judgment, universal rules would be necessary according to which one could decide whether a given case falls under a rule or not," etc.—*Anthropology*, etc. (1798), Hartenstein, vii. p. 515.

stract them, so that the understanding may not proceed in a merely mechanical fashion, but rather with a consciousness of the rule which it is following.

It is also very good to arrange the rules into certain formulas and to intrust them in this form to the memory. Then, if we remember a rule and have forgotten its application, we will not be long in recovering it. Here occurs the question : whether rules should first be given *in abstracto* and learned only when their application has been completed, or should rule and use go together. The latter course alone is advisable. In the other instance the use remains very uncertain until one reaches the rules. The rules should also occasionally be arranged into classes ; for they are not retained if they have no relation to one another. Thus grammar must always be a little in advance in the study of languages.

Training the Understanding.

72. We must now give a systematic concept of the whole aim of education and of the manner in which it is to be attained.[1]

1. *The general culture of the faculties of the mind*, distinguished from their particular culture. It aims at dexterity and perfection : the pupil is

Final Division of Educational Activities.

---

[1] This section, taken with Section 31, constitutes the chief division of educational theory which Kant makes, his whole treatment being subordinated to or regulated by this division. This section presents his conception of the parts of education,more scientifically, so to speak, than do any of the other sections treating this point. Sections 31, 72 should be closely compared with Section 18, between which one does not find any lack of harmony, the latter

not merely informed in some particular thing, but his mental powers are strengthened.[1] It is either

(*a*) Physical or

(*b*) Moral.[2]

(*a*) *Physical.*—Here everything depends on practice and discipline, without it being necessary for the child to know any maxims. It is *passive* for the pupil, who must be obedient to the direction of another. Others think for him.

(*b*) *Moral.*—This does not depend on discipline, but on maxims.[3] Everything is lost if one attempts to base

---

being more empirically exhaustive, the former more philosophically schematic. Thus we catch a glimpse of the severely systematic character of Kant's mode of thinking. We also here discern the *real pedagogical system* which Kant gives evidence of having actually thought out,—a credit which has too often been withheld from him.

[1] This conception of mental faculties, which regards them like separate muscles in the body, lies at the basis of the doctrine of formal training, here apparently adopted by Kant without modification. This is also rather a logical sequence to the aim of education presented in Section 10.

[2] One should not fail to note that that portion of physical education which is presented in Section 31—viz., "maintenance"—does not appear in this systematic exhibition of educational ends. It seems to have been intentionally excluded as early as Section 34. "Pragmatic instruction," likewise, disappears here. (Cf. Section 33.) It is well to observe how this division of educational theory really contains everything which Kant has already affirmed to be a factor in education. (Cf. Section 18.)

[3] "Maxim" is a most important technical term in Kant's theory and practice of ethics. It stands in contrast with, yet in close relation to "law." Thus: "*Maxim* is the subjective principle

it upon examples, threats, punishments, etc. Then it would be nothing but mere discipline. We should see to it that the pupil behaves well from his own maxims and not from habit, and that he not only do the good, but do it for the reason that it is good; for the moral worth of actions consists in the maxims of good. The difference between physical education and moral education is this: the former is passive for the pupil, the latter active. He must always perceive the principles of action and the bond which attaches it to the idea of duty.[1]

73. 2. *The particular culture of the faculties of the mind.*[2] This includes the culture of the intellect, the senses, the imagination, the memory, the strengthening of the attention, and the wit, and thus whatever concerns the lower powers of the understanding. We have already mentioned the culture of the senses; for example, the visual perception of space. As for the culture of the

Culture of the Lower Mental Faculties.

---

of willing; the objective principle (*i.e.*, that which would also serve all rational beings subjectively as a practical principle if reason had full power over the active faculties) is the practical *law*."— *Fundamental Principles of the Metaphysics of Ethics*, Hartenstein, iv. p. 248. (Cf. the first section of the *Critique of Practical Reason*.) A maxim, being the formula which dictates an action for a reasonable being, is opposed to the principle of mechanical action. It is likewise an important element in his theory of moral education. (See Sections 77, 78.)

[1] See Section 19.

[2] Cf. Sections 52–66 and 68–71 for the earlier discussions of the culture of the lower faculties of the mind.

imagination, the following is to be remarked: children have an extremely powerful imagination, which has no need of being further stretched and strained by fairy-tales. It has much more need of being governed and brought under rules; but, at the same time, it should not be left entirely inactive.

Geographical maps have something in them which charms all children, even the smallest. When they are tired of everything else, they still learn something when maps are used. And this is an *Value of Maps.* excellent diversion for children, where their imagination is not allowed to wander, but must be fixed on a definite figure. It is really possible to begin with geography. Pictures of animals, plants, etc., can be added at the same time; these will enliven geography. But history should not appear until later.

As for strengthening the attention, it should be observed that this must not be neglected. To attach our thoughts fixedly to an object is not so much *Attention.* a talent as a weakness of our inner sense, because it is inflexible in this case and cannot be applied at will. Distraction is the enemy of all education; but memory is based upon attention.[1]

---

[1] Following the passage from the *Anthropology*, etc., translated in note 1 to Section 69, p. 174, Kant gives this illustration:

"The teacher from the pulpit, or in the academic class-room, or the legal prosecutor, or advocate, if he wishes to show presence of mind in free delivery (impromptu), eventually in relating something, must give proof of three kinds of attention: first, regard for that which he is *now saying*, in order to represent it clearly; second, reference to that which he *has said;* and third, provision for that

74. As for *the higher faculties of the understanding*, we have to do here with the culture of the understanding, the judgment, and the reason. In a certain sense, the training of the understanding can begin passively with the citation of examples which apply to a rule or, *vice versa*, with the discovery of the rule which applies to particular cases. The judgment indicates what use is to be made of the understanding. The understanding is necessary in order to comprehend what has been learned or spoken, and in order to repeat nothing without comprehending it. How many read and hear things without understanding them, even though they believe them! Pictures and things are necessary to understanding.

Culture of the Higher Mental Faculties.

The reason discerns principles. But it must be remembered that we are here speaking of a reason that is still under guidance; hence it must not always wish to reason, but it must be on its guard against reasoning too much about that which transcends its concepts. We are not here speaking of the speculative reason, but of reflection upon that which occurs according to its causes and effects. It is a reason which, in its economy and arrangement, is practical.[1]

---

which he *wishes to say* later. If he neglects attention to these three things,—*i.e.*, if he neglects to arrange them in this order,—he distracts himself and his hearer or reader, and even a usually intelligent man cannot help getting confused."

[1] This every-day "practical" reason must not be confused with the speculative reason in its ethical aspects, which Kant also calls "practical."

75. The best method of cultivating the faculties of the mind is that each one himself do all that which he wishes to accomplish;[1] for example, to put immediately into practice the grammatical rules which he has learned. A geographical map is best understood if one can draw it himself. The best way to understand is to do. That is most thoroughly learned and best remembered which one learns himself. There are, however, but few men who are capable of this. They are called self-taught men (αὐτοδίδακτοι).

Learning and Practice.

76. In the culture of the reason, one must proceed according to the Socratic method.[2] Socrates,[3] who called himself the intellectual midwife of his hearers, gives in his dialogues, which Plato[4] has in a certain sense preserved for us, examples of how one can lead even old people to pro-

Socratic Method in training the Reason.

---

[1] In this rule Kant probably reached the highest point in his pedagogy of intellect, which was to prepare the way for the autonomy of the will in its organization of character.

[2] See Selection VIII., Section 119. An early modification of this method appears in Kant's own pedagogical activity. In announcing his lectures for the summer semester of 1758, he states his intention to pursue the following method in metaphysics : "In the Wednesday and Saturday hours I shall consider polemically those propositions treated on the preceding days. In my opinion, the polemical method is the best method for obtaining fundamental insights."—Hartenstein, ii. p. 25.

[3] A Greek philosopher (470–399 B.C.). His teaching and death revolutionized philosophy. His maxim was : Know thyself. His method was that of interrogation.

[4] The most distinguished disciple of Socrates (429–347 B.C.) and the author of the immortal *Dialogues*.

duce considerable from their own reason. There are many points on which it is not necessary that children should exercise their reason. They must not reason about everything. They do not need to know the reasons of everything which is to contribute to their education; but as soon as duty comes into question, the principles must be made known to them. We must see to it, anyway, that rational knowledge be drawn out of them rather than introduced into them. The Socratic should furnish the rule for the catechetical method.[1] It is, to be sure, rather slow; and it is difficult so to arrange it that at the same time that knowledge is being drawn out of one mind the others shall learn something. The mechanically catechetical method is also good in many of the sciences; for example, in the instruction in revealed religion. In universal religion, on the contrary, it is necessary to employ the Socratic method. In respect to that which must be learned his-

---

[1] This proceeds solely by means of questions and answers which have been prepared in advance of the pupil's study. In its pure form the teacher does not speak otherwise than to ask the questions. Its "mechanical" character appears when the questions and answers alternate as an aid to memory. (See Kant's model of a "Moral Catechism," Selection XI., and Selection VIII., Section 119, where Kant does not seem to hold the catechism in very high esteem.)

Willmann (p. 124) supposes Kant in these observations in Section 76 to have had in mind Bahrdt's *Philanthropinischer Erziehungsplan*, Frankfurt-am-Main, 1776, which introduced the consideration of the Socratic method.

J. F. C. Grässe published a work in 1795 bearing the title *Lehrbuch der allgemeinen Katechetik nach Kant'schen Grundsätzten*.

torically, the mechanically catechetical method is found to be preferable.[1]

MORAL EDUCATION.[2]

77. Moral culture must be based upon maxims, not upon discipline. Discipline prevents defects ; moral culture shapes the manner of thinking. One Moral Culture must see to it that the child accustom him- and Maxims. self to act according to maxims and not according to cer-

---

[1] In these *Notes* Kant has little or nothing to say about "learning" (see Sections 70, 73, 75), a topic of importance in the general theme. A note on this point, with somewhat wider and different bearings, is found in the Dialectic of the *Critique of Practical Reason*, has pedagogical interest, and is here transcribed :

"*Learning* is really only the totality of *historical* sciences. Consequently only the teacher of revealed theology can be called a *God-learned* man. But if one wishes also to call him who is in possession of rational sciences (mathematics and philosophy) learned, although this would at once contradict the meaning of the word (as at all times only that can be reckoned as learning which one must be *taught*, and which, therefore, one cannot discover by himself through reason) ; even so the philosopher with his knowledge of God, as a positive science, would make too poor a figure to let himself be called *learned* on this account."—Hartenstein, v. pp. 143, 144.

See foot-note 1, p. 170 ; Selection I., Nos. 8, 18, 20 ; also Selections VIII. and IX.

[2] In several editions of the *Lecture-Notes*, as in Rink's, Hartenstein's, Vogt's, etc., which retain any headings to the divisions of Kant's discussions, the superscription "Practical Education" is placed before Section 91. The intervening sections are so patently concerned with this topic that I have placed the heading "Moral

tain impulses. Discipline leaves habits only, which fade away with years. The child should learn to act according to maxims whose justice he himself perceives. It is easily seen that it is very difficult to accomplish this in the case of young children, and that therefore moral education demands the utmost sagacity on the part of parents and teachers.

When the child is untruthful, for example, he should not be punished, but treated with contempt, and should be told that he will not be believed in the future, etc. But if he is punished when he does wrong and is rewarded when he does right, he does right in order to be treated well. And when later he enters the world where things do not happen in that way, but where he can do right or wrong without receiving any reward or chastisement, he becomes a man who thinks only of how he can best make his way in the world, and will be good or bad just as he finds it most profitable.

78. The maxims must spring from man himself. In moral education, the attempt to introduce into the child's
Morality *versus* mind the idea of what is good or evil must
Discipline. be made very early. If one wishes to establish morality, there must be no punishment. Morality is something so holy and sublime that it must not

---

Education'' before Section 77, following Kant's analysis in Section 72, and accepting Burger's very proper suggestion. Sections 77–90 present the intellectual basis, and hence the passive aspect of character ; Sections 91 ff. consider the active acquisition of character by the child.

be degraded thus and placed in the same rank with discipline.[1] The first endeavor in moral education is to establish a character. Character consists in the readiness to act according to maxims. At first these are the maxims of the school and later they are those of humanity. In the beginning the child obeys laws. Maxims also are laws, but subjective; they spring out of the human reason itself. No transgression of the law of the school should go unpunished; but, at the same time, the punishment must always be commensurate to the fault.

---

[1] Kant does not regard the moral law as "beautiful," but as "sublime." In the *Critique of Judgment* beauty is the type of judgment that can be applied to *nature*, and sublimity is the type which pertains specifically to *man*. This peculiarly high regard for morality appears in its best expression in the famous apostrophe to duty in the *Critique of Practical Reason*:

"Duty! Thou sublime great name, thou that dost embrace nothing popular which bears insinuation with it, but dost demand submission, yet without threats which excite natural aversion in the mind, or arouse fear in order to move the will, but that dost merely set up a law which of itself finds entrance into the mind, and yet wins for itself reluctant esteem (if not always adherence), before which all inclinations are silent, even though they secretly work against it—what is the origin worthy of thee, and where shall one find the roots of thy noble descent, which proudly rejects all relationship with natural inclinations; a root to spring from which is the indispensable condition of that worth which men alone can give themselves?"

"Two things fill the mind with ever new and increasing admiration and awe the oftener and more steadily I think about them: *the starry heaven above me and the moral law within me.*"— Hartenstein, v. pp. 91, 167.

79. If one wishes to form a character in children, it very important that in all things they be shown a certai

Character-forming by Rules.

plan, certain laws which they must follow exactly. They should, for example, have a fixed time for sleep, for work, and for recreation; the time, being once fixed, must be neither lengthened nor shortened. In the case of indifferent things, children may be permitted to exercise their own choice, but they must always continue to observe what they have once made a law for themselves. One should not attempt to give children the character of a citizen, but rather that of a child.

Those persons who have not laid down certain rules for themselves are untrustworthy; it frequently happens that it is impossible to explain their conduct, and one never knows exactly where to find them. It is true that those people are often blamed who always act according to rules; for example, the man who regulates his every action by the clock; but this blame is often unjust, and this preciseness, although it looks like painful punctiliousness, is a disposition favorable to character.[1]

80. Obedience, above all things, is an essential trait in the character of a child, particularly that of a pupil.[2] It

---

[1] It is said that Kant was so regular in taking his daily afternoon walks that passers-by would take out their timepieces to regulate them by his appearance! This note might be taken as his justification of his regularity.

[2] This conception is almost a direct transcription of his ethics into his pedagogy; for morality, according to Kant, means self-

is twofold: first, it is an obedience to the *absolute* will of him who directs; but it is, secondly, an obedience to a *will regarded as rational and good.* Obedience can be derived from constraint, and then it is *absolute*, or from confidence, and then it is of the other kind. This *voluntary* obedience is very important; but the former is also externally necessary, since it prepares the child for the accomplishment of such laws as he will have to fulfil later as a citizen, even if they do not please him.

Obedience: First Step in Character-formation.

81. Children must, therefore, be under a certain law of necessity; but this law must be a universal one which is to be especially observed in schools. The teacher must show no predilection, no preference for one child; for otherwise the law ceases to be universal. As soon as the child sees that all others are not subjected to the same law as he, he becomes presumptuous.

Universal Laws in School.

82. It is always said that everything should be presented to children in such a manner that they will do it from *inclination.* Without doubt this is good in many

---

determination in the light of an absolutely unchanging principle, —that is, morality is obedience to the reason behind conduct.

Kant's double treatment of the pedagogical unit as both "child" and "citizen" indicates that his conceptions of morality were elaborated in the light of their usefulness for all social as well as individual ends,—a phase of educational thought in which present-day efforts are engaged. (See Sections 12, 17, 18c, 25, 29, 88, 112, etc.)

cases; but there is also much that must be prescribed for them as *duty*.[1] This will be of very great value Duty *versus* Inclination. during their whole life; for, in public duties, in the labors of an office, and in many other instances, duty alone, not inclination, can guide

---

[1] Kant's view of the psychological affinity of the concept of duty and its pedagogical usage appears in the following passages:

"For the pure conception of duty, mixed with no foreign addition of empirical incitements, and especially the conception of the moral law, has upon the human heart, by means of the reason alone, . . . an influence so much more powerful than all other motives which one may offer from the field of experience, that it, in the consciousness of its own dignity, despises the latter and can gradually become their master," etc.

In a foot-note to this passage Kant gives an interesting observation on the inadequacy of the current instruction in morals:

"I have a letter from the late excellent Sulzer [1720–1779], in which he asks me why lessons in morals accomplish so little, however convincing they may seem to the reason. My answer was delayed by my preparation to give it complete. But it is no other than that the teachers themselves are not clear in their own ideas, and they destroy them, while trying to make up for this, by hunting up motives for being morally good, in order to make the medicine powerful. For the most ordinary observation shows that when one represents an action of uprightness, free from any idea of an advantage of any sort, in this or another world, performed faithfully amid the greatest temptations of need or enticement, it leaves every similar action which was in the least degree affected by a foreign motive far behind, and overshadows it; it elevates the soul and arouses the wish to be able also to behave thus. Even children of moderate age feel this impression, and duties should never be represented to them in any other way."—*Fundamental Principles of the Metaphysics of Morals* (1785), Hartenstein, iv. pp. 258, 259.

us. Even if we suppose that the child does not perceive the duty, it is none the less better if he be given the idea of it; and, while he can easily see his duty as a child, it is much more difficult to perceive that something is his duty as a man. If he could see this also, which is not possible before maturer years, his obedience would be more perfect.

83. All transgression of a command by a child is a lack of obedience, and this entails punishment. Even if the transgression is due simply to negligence, correction is not useless. This punishment is either *physical* or *moral*.[1]

Punishment: Physical and Moral.

Moral punishment is that which effects our desire to be honored and loved, this being auxiliary to morality; for example, when the child is shamed and treated coldly and reservedly. These inclinations should be preserved as far as possible. This kind of punishment, therefore, is the best, since it comes to the aid of morality; for example, if a child lies, a look of scorn is sufficient and most suitable.

Physical punishment consists either in the refusal of

---

[1] In his treatment of this topic, much of Rousseau's influence can be traced. (See *Émile*, Payne's translation, p. 65.) At the same time, Kant adds to Rousseau's scheme of punishment by natural consequences a more positive means of education, regarding the former as inadequate. This is an interesting feature in Kant's moral theory, which stoutly protested against the *utility* feature of Rousseau's scheme : those acts are good which are useful. To Kant, the outcome of an action is incidental and indifferent ; the morality resides in the motive or intention generating the action.

that which the child desires or in the infliction of chastisement. The former is closely related to moral punishment, and is negative. The other forms should be practised with caution, in order that they may not result in *indoles servilis*.[1] It is not good to distribute rewards among children; it makes them selfish, and results in *indoles mercenaria*.[2]

84. Obedience, moreover, is either that of *the child* or of *the adolescent*. Disobedience entails punishment. This is either really *natural*, brought by man upon himself by his own conduct; for example, the child falls ill if he eats too much; and these forms of punishment are the best, for man experiences them, not only in his childhood, but throughout his whole life; or it is *artificial*. The desire to be esteemed and loved is a sure means of making chastisements durable. Physical means should serve merely to supplement the insufficiency of moral punishments. When the latter are of no avail, and recourse is had to the former, the formation of a good character ceases. But in the beginning physical constraint supplies the deficiency of reflection in the child.

Punishment: Natural and Artificial.

85. Punishments which are angrily inflicted have perverted effects. Children then regard them as merely the consequences, but themselves as objects, of another's emotion. Children should always be corrected cautiously, that they may see that the only aim in view is their improvement. It 'is absurd to de-

Mode of Punishment.

---

[1] A servile disposition.　　　[2] A mercenary disposition.

mand of children, when they have been chastised, that
they shall thank you, that they shall kiss your hand, etc.;
this only makes them servile. If physical punishments
are often repeated, they make a child stubborn; and if
parents chasten their children for wilfulness, they only
make them more wilful. Stubborn people are not always
the worst, but often yield easily to kindly remonstrances.

86. The obedience of *the adolescent* is different from
that of the child. It consists in submission to the rules
of duty. To do anything for the sake of Conduct of the
duty means to obey reason. It is useless to Adolescent.
speak of duty to children. They come to look upon it
as something the transgression of which is followed by
the rod. The child could be guided by his instincts
alone; but as soon as he begins to develop, the idea of
duty must be added. One should not have recourse to
the sentiment of shame with children, but should reserve it until the period of adolescence; for shame can
be present only when the idea of honor has taken root.

87. A second chief trait in the formation of the child's
character is *veracity*.[1] Indeed, this is the principal

---

[1] Lying is an anthropological and a moral phenomenon which
had great interest for Kant, as is indicated in numerous passages
and fragments. (See Selection I., No. 33.)

"The transgression of the duty of truthfulness is called a lie;
wherefore there may be external, but also internal lies, so that
both can occur together, or even as contradicting each other.

"But a lie, be it internal or external, is twofold: (1) when one
asserts as *true* something which he knows to be untrue; (2) when

feature and the essence of a character. A man who lies has no character at all, and if there be anything

---

one asserts as *certain* something of which he knows himself to be subjectively uncertain.

"*Lying* ('from the Father of lies, through whom all evil is come into the world') is the really corrupt spot in human nature," etc.—*Announcement of the Early Conclusion of a Tractate on Everlasting Peace in Philosophy* (1796), Hartenstein, vi. p. 498.

"The greatest violation of man's duty towards himself, regarded merely as a moral creature (towards humanity in his own person), is the reverse of truthfulness, or *lying. . . .* A lie may be an external or an internal one. By the former, man makes himself an object of contempt in the eyes of others ; by the latter, which is still more, in his own eyes, and injures the dignity of humanity in his own person. . . . Lying is rejection and, as it were, destruction of his human dignity. . . . Man as a moral being (*homo noumenon*) cannot use himself as a physical being (*homo phœnomenon*), as a mere means (speaking machine), not bound to the internal purpose of the communication of thoughts, but he is bound to the condition of the agreement with the declaration of the former, and is pledged to truthfulness towards himself," etc.—*The Metaphysics of Morals*, Pt. II. (1797), Hartenstein, vii. pp. 234–236.

In the same year appeared his essay *On a Supposed Right to Lie from Humanitarian Motives*, in which he reached the conclusion that there can be found no excuse for any sort of lying.

"One can class with the unintentional play of the productive imagination, which may then be called *fantasy*, the inclination to guileless *lying* which is *always* met with in children, *now and then* in adults, otherwise good, sometimes almost like an hereditary disease, where, in relating something, events and alleged adventures, growing like an avalanche, emerge from the imagination, with no other intention whatsoever than merely to be interesting," etc.—*Anthropology*, etc., Hartenstein, vii. pp. 494, 495.

good in him, he owes it entirely to his temperament. Many children have a disposition to lie, which has no other cause than a vivacious imagination. It is the father's affair to see to it that they break off this habit, for mothers usually consider it a thing of no, or at least very small, importance; they even look upon it as a flattering proof of the superior talents and capacities of their children. Here is the place to make use of shame, for here the child comprehends it perfectly. The blush of shame betrays us when we lie, but it is not always a proof of lying. We often blush at the shamelessness with which another accuses us of wrong. Under no condition should the attempt be made to exact the truth from children by punishment; their lying will necessarily entail its own damaging consequences, for which they may then be punished. The withholding of respect is the only suitable punishment for lying.

Veracity: Second Step in Character-formation.

Punishments may also be divided into *negative* and *positive*. The first should be inflicted in cases of idleness or immorality; as, for example, lying, being disobliging and quarrelsome. But the positive punishments are for ill-natured naughtiness. Above all things one should avoid treasuring up spite against the child.

Punishment: Negative and Positive.

88. A third feature in the character of the child must be *sociability*. He must have friendships with others, and not always live for himself alone. Many teachers, it is true, are opposed to this in school; but that is unjust. Children should prepare themselves for the

sweetest of all the pleasures of life. But teachers should not prefer one pupil above another because of his talents, but only because of his character; for otherwise there arises jealousy, which is incompatible with friendship.

Sociability: Third Step in Character-formation.

Children should also be candid, and their faces should be as serene as the sun.[1] A happy heart alone is capable of finding pleasure in the good. A religion which makes men gloomy is false; for they should serve God with a joyous heart and not from compulsion. The happy heart must not always be held strictly under the restraint of the school; for then it will soon be destroyed. When it has freedom, it recovers itself again. Those plays wherein the heart brightens and the child endeavors always to surpass his comrades are serviceable for this end. Then the soul becomes serene once more.

89. Many people think that their youth was the happiest and the most agreeable time of their whole life; but this is certainly not so. It is the hardest period, because one is under discipline, and can seldom have a true friend and less rarely freedom. Horace has already said, *Multa tulit, fecitque puer, sudavit et alsit*.[2]

Limitations of Childhood.

---

[1] " Children, especially girls, must be early accustomed to frank, unforced smiling; for the cheerfulness of the features is gradually imprinted internally, and begets a *disposition* to joyousness, friendliness, and sociability which this approach to the virtue of good-will early prepares."—*Anthropology*, etc., Hartenstein, vii. pp. 585, 586.

[2] The boy has endured much and done much,
He has sweated and he has frozen.

90. Children should be instructed only in such things as are suitable for their age. Many parents are glad when their children can talk precociously; but nothing usually comes of such children. A child should have only the wisdom of a child. He must not be a blind imitator. But one who is supplied with precocious maxims is entirely beyond the limitations of his years, and he simply imitates, mimics.[1] He should have only a child's understanding, and not be in evidence too soon. Such a one will never become a man of intelligence and serene understanding. It is just as intolerable to see a boy wishing to follow all the fashions; for example, to curl his hair, to wear handfrills, and even to carry a snuffbox. He thus acquires an affected air, which does not beseem a child. Polite society is a burden to him, and manliness is finally completely lacking in him. For this very reason should his vanity be counteracted very early; or, more properly speaking, he must not be given occasion to become vain. But this happens when very young children are told how beautiful they are, how charmingly this or that finery becomes them, or when this is promised and given to them as a reward. Finery is not suitable for children. They should regard their neat and simple clothing merely as indispensable needs. But parents themselves should attach no value to these things, and should avoid all self-admiration; for here, as elsewhere, example is all-powerful, and strengthens or destroys good teaching.

Education according to Age.

---

[1] Cf. Section 74.

91. Practical education includes:

Elements of Practical Education.

(*a*) Skill,

(*b*) Worldly wisdom, and

(*c*) Morality.

It is essential that skill be thorough and not transitory. An appearance of the possession of a knowledge of things which cannot afterwards be realized must not be assumed. Thoroughness should be a quality of skilfulness, and gradually become a habit of the mind.   It is the essential point in the character of a man.   Skill is essential to talent.

92. Worldly wisdom consists in the art of applying our skill to man,—that is, to use men for our own ends.   To acquire this, many conditions are necessary.

Worldly Wisdom.

It is really the last thing to be acquired ; but, according to its worth, it occupies the second place.

If the child is to be given over to worldly wisdom, he must dissemble, make himself impenetrable, and yet be able to penetrate others.   Especially must he conceal his character.   The art of external appearance is propriety, and this art must be possessed.   It is difficult to penetrate others, but it is necessary to understand this art and at the same time to make one's self impenetrable.   This includes dissimulation,—that is, concealing one's faults, and the above-mentioned external appearance.   Dissimulation is not always hypocrisy, and can sometimes be permitted, but it borders very closely upon immorality.   Simulation is a desperate means.[1]   Worldly

---

[1] The extreme and almost unethical position taken here in the *Lecture-Notes* is fairly saved by the following passage in the *Critique of Pure Reason* (1781) :

wisdom requires that a man shall not fly into a sudden passion; but neither must he be altogether too indolent. Thus one must not be vehement, but yet strenuous, which is not the same thing. A strenuous (*strenuus*) man is he who has pleasure in willing. It is a question of the moderation of the emotions. Worldly wisdom is a matter of temperament.[1]

93. Morality refers to character. *Sustine et abstine*[2] is the best preparation for a wise moderation. If one

---

"There is a certain form of dishonesty in human nature which, after all, like everything that comes from nature, must contain elements of good,—namely, a disposition to conceal one's true feelings and to make a show of certain assumed feelings which are regarded as good and honorable. Most certainly men have, by means of this inclination to dissemble, as well as to assume an advantageous appearance, not merely civilized themselves, but to a certain extent gradually moralized themselves; since one could not penetrate the varnish of propriety, respectability, and modesty, he therefore found, in the supposedly true examples of goodness seen round about him, a school for his self-improvement. However, this disposition to represent himself as being better than he is, and to express sentiments which he does not possess, merely serves provisionally, as it were, to bring man out of rawness, and to permit him at least to take on the manner of goodness, as he knows it; later, when real principles are once developed and established in his mode of thought, every form of falsehood must be powerfully combated, because otherwise it destroys the heart and does not permit good sentiments to come up amid the rank weeds of fair appearance."—Hartenstein, iii. p. 498.

[1] That type of feeling which is, and in so far as it is, dependent upon our physical constitution was held by Kant to be "temperament."

[2] Bear and forbear.

desire to form a good character, he must begin by banishing the passions. Man must so train himself that his inclinations do not grow into passions, and he must learn to do without that which is denied him. *Sustine* means: suffer and accustom yourself to endure.

Morality.

Courage and inclination are necessary in order to learn to do without something. One must become accustomed to refusals, opposition, etc.

Sympathy is a matter of temperament. Children must be kept from a yearning, languishing sympathy. Sympathy is really sensibility; it is in keeping only with a character which is sensitive. It is also different from compassion; it is an evil which consists in merely bewailing a thing. Children should be given some pocket-money with which they could do good to the needy; then it would be seen whether or not they are compassionate. When they are generous only with the money of their parents, this quality perishes.[1]

Sympathy condemned.

---

[1] Kant has hardly given a proper place to sympathy as a means of great pedagogic importance, even empirically regarded. In Herbart's scheme, for example, sympathy is made one of the cardinal features in educational growth. Kant here apparently excludes sympathy as a constituent of character and morality, because psychologically he regarded it as merely a derivative form of the feeling of pleasure-pain, and therefore as having no connection with will. In his later writings he gave a higher place to this form of feeling, as may be seen in the following selections from the *Metaphysics of Morals*, Pt. II., Hartenstein, vii. pp. 264–266 :

"*Sympathy* (*sympathia moralis*) is indeed a sensuous feeling of pleasure or displeasure (hence æsthetic) with respect to the enjoy-

The maxim *festina lente*[1] indicates a continuous activity; one must greatly hasten in order to learn much, —that is, *festina;* but things must also be learned thoroughly, which requires time,— **Thoroughness.** that is, *lente.* It is a question which is preferable: to have a great range of information or only a small range, but one which is thorough. It is better to know little, but to know this little well, than to know much and to know it superficially; for, in the latter case, the shallowness of one's knowledge will finally become patent. But the child cannot tell under what circumstances he may need this or that knowledge, and, therefore, it is best that he know thoroughly a little of everything, otherwise he will impose upon and dazzle others with his show of learning.

94. The final thing in practical education is the foundation of character.[2] This consists in the firm resolu-

---

ment, or the pain, of others (fellow-feeling, sympathetic sensation), sensibility to which has been implanted in man by nature. But to employ sympathy as a means for the advancement of active and rational kindness is a special, although only a conditional duty, under the name of *humanity* (*humanitas*); because here man is regarded not merely as a rational being, but also as an animal endowed with reason. . . .

"But although to have sympathy with others is not in itself a duty, yet active interest in their fate is duty, and hence to cultivate to this end the sympathetic, natural (æsthetic) feelings in ourselves, and to employ them as so many means for interest, from moral principles and feeling appropriate to those principles, is at least indirect duty."

[1] Make haste slowly.   [2] See Selection X.

tion of the will to do something, and then in the actual
execution of it. *Vir propositi tenax,*[1] says Horace, and
Firmness of that is a good character. If, for example,
Will. I have promised anything, I must keep my
promise, even if it does me harm. The man who forms
a certain resolution, but does not carry it out, can no
longer trust himself. If, for example, having taken the
resolution always to arise early to study,[2] or to do this
or that, or to take a walk, one then excuse himself in
the spring-time because the mornings are still too cold
and it might be injurious to him ; in summer because it
is so favorable for sleeping, and sleep is particularly
agreeable to him, and thus from day to day defer the
execution of his resolution, he finally ends by destroying
all confidence in himself.

That which is contrary to morals should be excluded
from resolutions of this kind. The character of a wicked
man is very bad, its chief quality being its perversity ;
yet we admire seeing him executing his resolutions and
being firm, although one would prefer to see him display
an equal persistency in good conduct.

There is not much to esteem in him who is constantly
deferring the performance of his purposes. The so-
called future conversion is of this sort. The man who
has always been vicious, and who wishes to be converted
in an instant, cannot possibly succeed ; for only a miracle
could make him instantly like one who has conducted

---

[1] A man firm in his resolutions.

[2] This is another little personal allusion. For years his servant
uniformly called him a few minutes before five o'clock every morning, and without exception, the story runs, Kant obeyed the call.

himself well during his whole life and has never had other than upright thoughts. For the same reason, there is nothing to be expected from pilgrimages, castigations, and fastings, since it is impossible to conceive how pilgrimages and other practices can contribute anything towards making, at a moment's notice, a virtuous man out of a vicious one.

What shall it profit for uprightness and improvement of character to fast during the day only to eat so much more during the night, or to inflict a penance on the body which can contribute nothing to a change of soul?

95. In order to establish a moral character in children, we must note the following:

The duties which they have to fulfil must be shown them as much as possible by examples and regulations. The duties which the child has to perform are none other than the ordinary ones towards himself and towards others; they must therefore be drawn from the nature of things. Hence we have to consider more closely at this point,— *Doctrine of Duties in Pedagogy.*

(*a*) Duties towards one's self;

(*b*) Duties towards others.[1]

(*a*) Duties towards one's self. These do not consist in procuring fine clothing, giving splendid dinners, etc., although neatness must be aimed at in everything. Nor do they consist in the attempt to satisfy one's desires

---

[1] This is the division of duties which Kant makes in the second part of the *Metaphysics of Morals* (1797), Hartenstein, vii. pp. 202, 217.

and inclinations; for, on the contrary, one should be very temperate and abstemious, and maintain a certain dignity within himself which ennobles him above all creatures, and it is his duty not to deny in his own person this dignity of humanity.[1]

Human Dignity.

But we do deny the dignity of humanity when, for example, we become addicted to drink, commit unnatural sins, practise all manner of immoderation, etc., all of which degrade man far below the animal. No less is it contrary to the dignity of humanity for a man to cringe before others, or to overload them with compliments, in the hope of ingratiating himself by such undignified conduct.

The child should be made sensible of this human dignity in his own person; for example, in the case of uncleanness, which, to say the least, is not befitting humanity. But the child can also really degrade himself below the dignity of humanity by lying, since he is already able to think and to communicate his thoughts to others. Lying makes man an object of universal scorn, and is a means of robbing himself of the esteem for, and confidence in, himself which every one ought to possess.

(b) Duties towards others. Reverence and respect for the rights of men should be instilled into the child at a very early age, and he should be made to put them into practice. If, for example, a child meets another child poorer than himself, and haughtily pushes him out

---

[1] As may be traced in the introductory *Lecture-Notes* (see Section 15), and as clearly elaborated in his ethical theory, "the dignity of humanity" is a highly specialized and important phrase. It is the great objective content of conduct under the subjective law of "duty." It is thus not a trite and meaningless expression.

of his way, or gives him a blow, one should not say to him, "Do not do that, it hurts him; but be compassionate, he is a poor child," etc.; but he in turn should be treated just as haughtily and forcefully, because his conduct is contrary to the rights of humanity. But children do not have any generosity. This can easily be seen, for example, when parents command their child to give half of his lunch to another, without being promised so much the more; either they do not obey, or very seldom and unwillingly. It is also useless to speak much about generosity to the child, since he has as yet no possessions of his own.

96. Many writers have entirely omitted, or have falsely expounded, like Crugott,[1] that section of ethics which contains the doctrine of duties towards one's self. Duty towards one's self consists, as has been said above, in preserving the dignity of humanity in one's own person. A man censures himself when he keeps the idea of humanity in mind. In this idea he finds an original with which he compares himself. As he grows older, and the sexual instincts begin to develop, then is the critical moment in which the idea of human dignity is alone capable of holding the young man within bounds. The youth should early be warned as to how he must guard himself against this or that.

97. There is something that is almost entirely lacking in our schools, which, however, would greatly promote the formation of uprightness in children,—

---

[1] A German theologian (1725–1790).

namely, *a catechism of right.*[1] It should contain, in popular form, cases of conduct which are met with in ordi-

A Moral Catechism. nary life, and which always naturally call up the question whether something is or is not right. If, for instance, some one, who ought to pay his creditors to-day, is touched at the sight of a needy person and gives him the sum which he is owing and should now pay,—is that right? No! It is wrong; for I must be free before I can be generous. In giving money to the poor I perform a meritorious deed, but in paying my debt I do only that which I ought to do. Further, can necessity ever justify a lie? No! There is not a single conceivable case in which it is excusable, and least of all before children, who would look upon every trifling thing as a necessity and would often allow themselves to lie. If there were such a book, an hour each day could be devoted very usefully in teaching children to know and to take to heart the right of men,—this apple of God's eye on earth.[2]

---

[1] By "right," Kant means the good considered from the view-point of human relations. Kant was quite attached to this idea of a catechism, as may be seen in the translation of the model for the same which he prepared in Selection XI.

It is interesting to note that he here makes, perhaps, the only definite recommendation with respect to the content of the school curriculum,—another instance of the complete ethical saturation of his educational theory. What he has to say in Section 70 may be regarded as a passing comment upon the school studies of his day. One need not marvel, therefore, at the proneness of our present-day subject-evaluaters and curriculum-makers to miss the point of Kant's contribution to education.

[2] We no longer lack catechisms of rights and duties, and many of them are very useful. In many schools attention is already

98. As for the obligation of being benevolent, it is only an imperfect one.[1] One should make children stout-hearted rather than effeminate, so that they shall not be too greatly affected by the misfortunes of others. Let them be filled, not with sentiment, but with the idea of duty. Many persons, indeed, have become hard-hearted because, having formerly been compassionate, they often found themselves deceived. It is useless to attempt to make the meritorious side of an action intelligible to a child. Clergymen often commit the fault of representing benevolent deeds as something meritorious. Putting aside the fact that we can do no more than our duty with respect to God, it is nothing more than our duty to do good to the poor; for the unequal prosperity of men comes only from accidental circumstances. If I possess a fortune, I owe it to the fact that advantage was taken of them, which proved favorable either to me or to my predecessor, but my relation to the whole remains the same.[2]

The Pedagogy of Benevolence.

99. A child's envy is aroused when he is constantly reminded to value himself according to the standard of

---

given to this necessary part of instruction, but much remains to be done in order to realize Kant's fine idea. [A note by Rink.]

[1] "Obligation" is a technical term in Kantian ethics, and means the great and prevailing characteristic of "duty," which is absolute and conditionless. Interest and prudence, for example, always "depend" upon something else ; but duty commands conduct without any hypothetical conditions ; hence the "categorical imperative," the supreme formula of duty.

[2] That is, ethical obligations are universal, and cannot find any limitation in external circumstances.

others. He should, on the contrary, consider himself
according to the ideas of his own reason.[1] Humility,

Envy and
Humility in
Education.

therefore, is nothing else than a comparison
of one's worth with moral perfection. The
Christian religion, for example, makes man
humble by leading him to compare himself with the
highest model of perfection rather than by teaching
humility directly. It is absurd to make humility consist in valuing one's self less than others : " See how such
and such a child behaves," etc. To speak to children in
such a manner produces only an ignoble turn of mind.
When a man estimates his value according to others, he
attempts either to lift himself above them or to diminish
their worth. The latter is envy. When a person is en-
vious, he tries to impute faults to another ; for, were the
latter not there, there could be no comparison between
him and one's self. A badly applied spirit of emulation
produces only jealousy. The only case in which emulation could be of any use would be that of persuading
another that a thing is practicable ; as, for example, if I
require a certain task of a child and show him that
others are able to do it.

---

[1] "Nothing could be more unfortunate for morality than to wish
to derive it from examples. For every example of it which is presented to me must itself be previously judged by principles of morality, whether it is worthy to serve as an original example,—*i.e.*, as
a pattern ; but in nowise can it furnish supremely the concept of
morality."—*Fundamental Principles of the Metaphysics of Morals*,
Hartenstein, iv. p. 256.

See Section 95 and Selection XI., "Ethical Didactics," Section
52, for Kant's conception of the weakness of example as a pedagogical means.

In nowise must a child be permitted to put another
to shame. One should endeavor to avoid all arrogance,
which is based on mere advantages of fortune. At the
same time the effort must be made to develop frankness
in children. Frankness is a modest confidence in one's
self. It places man in a position in which he can display
all his talents in a proper manner. It is entirely different from impudence, which consists in indifference, towards the judgment of others.

100. All the desires of man are either formal (freedom
and power) or material (related to an object); Desires and
they are desires of opinion or of pleasure; Vices.
or, finally, they relate to the bare continuance of these
two things as elements of happiness.

The desires of the first kind are ambition, imperious-
ness, and covetousness. The desires of the second kind
are those of the pleasures of sex (voluptuousness), of
things (luxurious living), or of society (taste for amuse-
ment). The desires of the third kind, finally, are the love
of life, of health, of ease (freedom from care in the future).

The vices are those of malice, of baseness, or of nar-
row-mindedness. To the first kind belong envy, in-
gratitude, and malicious joy at the misfortune of others;
to the second kind belong injustice, perfidy (falseness),
dissoluteness, as well in the dissipation of one's goods
as of health (intemperance) and of honor. The vices of
the third kind are uncharitableness, stinginess, indolence (effeminacy).[1]

---

[1] See *Anthropology*, etc., Sections 78–84, Hartenstein, vii. pp.
586–597, where Kant presents rather an exhaustive account of

101. The virtues are those of merit, of mere obligation, or of innocence. To the first kind belong magnanimity (in conquering one's self as well in revenge as in the love of ease and of covetousness), beneficence, and self-control; to the second, honesty, propriety, and peaceableness; to the third, finally, faithfulness, modesty, and temperance.[1]

Virtues.

102. We now come to the question whether man is by nature morally good or bad. He is neither; for he is by nature not a moral being at all; he becomes a moral being only when his reason raises itself to the concepts of duty and of law.[2] It can be said, however, that he has originally impulses for all vices, for he has inclinations and instincts which incite him, although his reason impels him in the opposite direction at the same time. He can, therefore, become morally good only by means of virtues,—that is, by self-restraint,—although he can be innocent as long as his passions slumber.

Man by Nature non-Moral.

---

human passions. Because of this thoroughness, Herder called him "the great observer in the pathology of our souls." With some slight deviations, the divisions in the *Anthropology* are the same as those presented here.

[1] It is something to cause remark, that Kant seems to be satisfied in his *Notes* with a mere enumeration of the vices and the virtues, without going into the pedagogical question of how the former can be eliminated and the latter perpetuated in the growth of the individual.

[2] There is great difficulty, if not impossibility, in removing the contradiction between this statement and the theoretical doctrine of transcendental freedom. It also does violence to some early views in these *Notes*. (Cf. Selection X.)

Vices result, for the most part, from the fact that civilization does violence to nature; and yet our destination as men is to emerge from the raw state of nature in which we are nothing more than animals. Perfect art returns to nature.

103. Everything in education depends upon one thing: that good principles be established and be made intelligible and acceptable to children. They must learn to substitute abhorrence of that which is revolting and absurd for the abhorrence of hatred; fear of their own conscience for the external contempt of men and divine punishment; self-estimation and internal dignity for the opinions of others; inner worth of action and conduct for words and emotions; understanding for feeling; finally, joyousness and serene piety for sullen, timorous, and gloomy devotion.

Necessity of Good Principles.

But, above all things, children should be guarded from estimating too highly *merita fortunæ.*[1]

RELIGIOUS EDUCATION [2]

104. When we come to consider the *religious education* of children, the first question is, whether it is possible to inculcate religious ideas upon young children. This is a point in pedagogy over which there has been much dispute. The concepts of religion always presuppose a theology. Now,

Religion versus Theology in Education.

---

[1] The merits of fortune.

[2] Religious education, it is hardly necessary to note, is not made an organic factor in education (see Section 72), but appears as a

would it be possible to teach a theology to young people who, far from having a knowledge of the world, do not know even themselves? Would youth, which does not yet know what duty is, be capable of comprehending an immediate duty to God? This much is certain, that if it were possible so to arrange that children should witness no act of adoration towards the Supreme Being, and that they should not even hear the name of God, the proper order of proceeding would be to lead their attention first to final causes and to that which is fitting for man, to exercise their judgment, to instruct them in the *order and beauty of the works of nature*, then to add an extended knowledge of the structure of the universe, and, finally, to reveal to them the idea of a Supreme Being, a Lawgiver. But, since this is not possible in the present state of society, the result would be, if one desired not to teach them anything about God until later, and yet they heard His name mentioned and saw demonstrations of devotion to Him, that this would produce in them either indifference or perverted ideas, as, for example, fear of divine power. Now, since it is necessary to prevent this idea from nestling in the fantasy of children, the inculcation of religious concepts must be

---

subtopic in moral education. In the rules laid down under this topic, Kant seems to reflect more or less influence from Rousseau on the same theme. At the same time it must be observed that Kant does not advocate that a one-sided moral education should replace all religious instruction, as the experiments in French schools have attempted during the last two decades. Kant simply argues against *dogma* in favor of *duty* as having prime pedagogical importance.

attempted very early. But this should not be an affair of memory, imitation, and pure mimicry; but the way which one selects must always be in harmony with nature. Children will comprehend, even without having the abstract concepts of duty, of obligations, of good or evil conduct, that there is a law of duty; that it is not the agreeable, the useful, and the like which determine it, but something universal which does not adjust itself according to the fancies of men. But the teacher himself must develop this concept.

At first everything should be attributed to nature, and then nature itself attributed to God; how, for example, in the first place, everything was arranged for the conservation of the species and their equilibrium, but also remotely for man that he be able to make himself happy.

The best means for first making clear the idea of God is to employ the analogy of a father under whose care we are placed; from this the transition to the idea of the unity of man, as in a family, can happily be made.[1]

---

[1] Kant does not confuse the pedagogy of religion with the pedagogy of morals, although the former may be subordinated to the latter. In the "Ethical Didactics" (Selection XI. pp. 280, 285) he explicitly states that the moral catechism and the religious catechism must not be mixed.

It should also be noted that his suggestions here as to the foundation of religious education, aside from their theology, have received full justification, if they have not even borne fruit directly, in the later history of pedagogy. Fichte was the first to carry out Kant's idea of the dependence of religion upon morality. Schleier-

105. But, then, what is *religion ?* Religion is the law in us, in so far as it is imprinted upon us by a legislator and a judge; [1] it is morality applied to the knowledge of God. If religion is not united with morality, it becomes nothing more than an endeavor to gain divine favor. The singing of praises, prayers, and church-going should only serve to give man new strength and new courage for improvement, or be the expression of a heart inspired by the idea of duty. These things are only preparations for good works, but not good works themselves, and one cannot please the Supreme Being otherwise than by becoming a better person.

Religion and Morality.

With the child it is necessary to commence with the law which he has in himself. Man is contemptible in his own eyes when he is vicious. This contempt springs from his own nature, and not from the fact that God has forbidden evil; for the legislator is not necessarily the author of the law. Thus a prince can forbid thievery without being regarded on this account as the author of the prohibition of theft. From this man learns to understand that his good conduct alone makes him worthy of

---

macher's pedagogy of religion, as well as his theology, was based on the feeling of dependence, here so well described by Kant. And on downward through the Herbartian movement in its successive stages this point of departure for religious instruction has been steadily maintained, until it is now fully accredited even by the "higher criticism" or the science of religion.

[1] See Selection XIII. "Religion (subjectively considered) is the knowledge of all our duties as divine commands."—*Religion within the Limits of Mere Reason* (1793), Hartenstein, vi. p. 252.

blessedness. The divine law must appear at the same time as a natural law, for it is not arbitrary. Religion, therefore, is a part of all morality.

But one must not begin with theology. That religion which is founded merely upon theology can never contain anything moral. There will arise from it only fear, on the one hand, and selfish purposes and sentiments, on the other, which will produce nothing more than a superstitious cult. Morality must precede, theology follow, and then we have religion.

106. The law in us is called *conscience*.[1] Conscience is, properly speaking, the application of our actions to this law. The reproaches of conscience will be without effect if it be not considered as the representative of God, who has His lofty seat above us, but who has also established a tribunal in us. On the other hand, if religion is not joined with a moral conscientiousness, it is without effect. Religion without moral conscientiousness is a superstitious worship. People imagine that they serve God when, for example, they praise Him and extol His power and His wisdom, without thinking how they can fulfil the divine laws ; yes, without even knowing and searching out His power and His wisdom, etc. These praises are an opiate for the conscience of such people and a pillow on which they hope to sleep tranquilly.[2]

Conscience and Religious Education.

---

[1] See Selection XIII., on Conscience.

[2] Many of these strictures upon the content of religious instruction doubtless reflect Kant's critical memory of the excessive pietistic practices in the school which he attended in his youth.

107. Children cannot comprehend all *religious concepts*, but a few, notwithstanding, must be imparted to them; only these should be more negative than positive. To make children repeat formulas is of no use, and produces only a false concept of piety. True reverence consists in acting according to God's will, and it is this that children must be taught. Care must be taken with children, as with one's self, that the name of God be not so often misused. Merely to use it in congratulation, even with pious intentions, is a profanation. The thought of God should fill man with reverence every time he speaks His name, and he should therefore seldom use it, and never frivolously. The child must learn to feel respect for God as the master of his life and of the whole world; further, as the protector of man; and, finally, as his judge. It is said that Newton[1] always stopped and meditated a moment whenever he spoke the name of God.

Method in Religious Pedagogy.

108. By a unified elucidation of the concepts of God and of duty the child learns all the better to respect the care which God takes for His creatures, and is thus restrained from the inclination for destruction and cruelty which expresses itself so much in the torture of small animals. At the same time, youth should be taught to discover the good in evil; for example, animals of prey and insects are models of

Duty and God.

---

[1] Sir Isaac Newton (1642–1727), the English mathematician and physicist.

cleanliness and industry; wicked men make us think of the law; birds which seek worms are protectors of the garden, etc.

109. One should also give children some concepts of the Supreme Being, so that whenever they see others pray, etc., they may know to whom they are praying and why they do it. But these con- *Social Uses of Religious Instruction.* cepts should be very few in number, and, as already said, only negative. One should, however, begin to inculcate these in the earliest years, but at the same time guard against children estimating men according to their religious practices; for, in spite of its varieties, there is, after all, everywhere unity of religion.

CONCLUSION

110. In closing, we will add a few remarks as to the course to be pursued with *youth just entering adolescence.*

The Pedagogy of Adolescence. About this time the boy begins to make certain distinctions which he has not made before. First, *the distinction of sex.* Nature has thrown a veil of secrecy over this matter, as though it were something indecent and merely an animal need. But nature has tried to combine it with every possible kind of morality. Even savages conduct themselves in this matter with a sort of modesty and reserve. Children sometimes ask their elders inquisitive questions about it; for example, as to where babies come from. But they are easily satisfied, either when given answers which mean nothing or when told that they are asking foolish questions.

The development of these inclinations in the boy is mechanical, and, as is the case with all instincts, they are developed with no knowledge of an object.[1] Thus it is impossible to keep the adolescent in ignorance and in the innocence which is inseparable from it. Silence on the subject only makes matters worse. We can see

---

[1] "Next to the instinct for nourishment, by means of which nature preserves each individual, the instinct of sex, by which it provides for the preservation of each species, is the most important."—*The Probable Beginnings of Human History* (1786), Hartenstein, iv. p. 318.

that in the education of our ancestors. In our times it
is rightly assumed that the boy must be talked to openly,
plainly, and positively. This is, indeed, a delicate point,
because one does not like to look upon it as a matter of
publicity. But all will be well if one is sympathetic
with the boy's inclinations.

The thirteenth or fourteenth year is usually the time
when the sexual instinct is developed in a boy. (When
it occurs earlier, children have probably been debauched,
or corrupted by bad examples.) By that time their
judgment is formed, and nature has prepared them for
the time when they can be spoken to about these things.

111. Nothing so weakens the mind, as well as the
body, of man as that kind of voluptuousness which is
directed to himself, and it is entirely opposed to man's nature. This also must
not be concealed from the adolescent. It
should be represented to him in all its abominableness,
and he should be told how it renders one useless for
the propagation of the race, how it destroys the physical
powers, how it results in premature old age, how it
harms the mind, etc.

Guidance of the Sex Instinct in Boys.

The impulses to this habit can be escaped by continuous occupation, which keeps one from spending more
time in bed and in sleeping than is necessary. Thoughts
about it can be banished from the mind by these occupations; for, so long as the subject is even in the imagination, it gnaws at one's vital powers. If one directs
his instincts towards the other sex, he meets with some
resistance; but if directed towards himself, they can be

gratified at any moment. The physical effect is extremely harmful, but the moral results are worse still. Here one crosses the bounds of nature, and desire rages without ceasing because it finds no real satisfaction. Teachers of grown adolescents have asked the question, as to whether it is well to allow boys to mingle with the opposite sex. If one or the other must be chosen, this course is by all means the better. In one instance he acts contrary to nature, but not here. Nature means him to be a man, as soon as he attains his majority, and perpetuate his species ; but the needs of our cultivated state sometimes make it impossible for him to educate his children.[1] Herein he sins against the social order. Thus it is best—yes, it is his duty—to wait until he is in a position to be married. In so doing, he acts not only like a good man, but also like a good citizen.

The adolescent should learn early to have a proper respect for the other sex, to earn their esteem by his uncorrupt activity, and thus to press forward to the noble prize of a happy marriage.

112. A second distinction which the adolescent begins to make about the time he enters society consists in
Society and Education. *the knowledge of class distinctions and the inequality of men.* As a child he must not be allowed to notice these things. He should not even be permitted to give orders to servants. If he sees that his parents give them orders, he can always be told, " We give them bread, and that is why they obey us;

---

[1] Cf. Section 26.

you do not do so, and therefore they are not obliged to obey you." Children know nothing about this difference, if parents themselves do not tell them of it. The youth should be shown that this inequality of men is an arrangement which has arisen because one person has attempted to get the advantage of another. The consciousness of the equality of man within civic inequality can gradually be awakened.

113. The youth must be accustomed to estimate himself absolutely, and not according to others. A high estimation of others in that which does not constitute the worth of man is vanity. The youth must also be taught to have conscientiousness in all things, and must strive not only to appear, but to be. Habituate him to see to it that, whenever he has once adopted a resolution, it does not become a vain one. Much rather should one make no resolution and leave the thing in doubt. Teach him to be contented with external circumstances and patient in labor (*sustine et abstine*), and teach him moderation in pleasures. When one does not desire pleasures merely, but will also be patient in work, he becomes a useful member of the community, and protects himself against *ennui*.

Various Applications of the Moral Law.

The youth should also be exhorted to joyousness and good-humor. Light-heartedness naturally results from a conscience without reproach. Recommend an equality of mood to him. By practice one can always succeed in making himself an agreeable member of society.

One must accustom himself to look upon many things

as duty. An action should be of value to me, not because it accords with my inclinations, but because I fulfil my duty in performing it.

Love for others, and afterwards cosmopolitan sentiments, should be developed. In our soul there is something which causes us to be interested (*a*) in ourselves, (*b*) in those with whom we have been brought up, and (*c*) in the *summum bonum*. Children must be made familiar with this interest, that they may warm their souls with it. They should rejoice over the good of the world, even if it is not to the advantage of their fatherland or to their own profit.

The child must be so trained as to attach only a mediocre value to the enjoyment of the pleasures of life. The childish fear of death will then disappear. Young men should be shown that enjoyment does not give that which it promises.

It is necessary, finally, to call his attention to the necessity of ordering his own accounts daily, so that at the end of life he may be able to compute its value.

SELECTIONS ON EDUCATION

FROM

KANT'S OTHER WRITINGS

SELECTIONS

I

PEDAGOGICAL FRAGMENTS[1]

1. SKILL is the first, but not the chief thing to be thought of. So is bread the first, but not the chief thing to be considered in marriage. The first thing is that which contains the necessary condition of the aim, but the aim itself is of absolute importance.

Aim.

2. Man must be disciplined because he is naturally wild, and taught because he is raw. Only in the order of nature is he good ; in the moral order he is bad. He must be developed into virtue. His education is not merely negative. He must feel restraint because he will be subject to civil restraint. Be brought up free? He must be drilled, trained (upright gait).

Discipline.

3. The child must be brought up free (that he allow others to be free). He must learn to endure the restraint to which freedom subjects itself for its own preservation (experience no subordination to his command). Thus he must be disciplined. This precedes instruction. Training must continue without interruption. He must learn to do without things

Training.

---

[1] I have numbered these Fragments to aid in facilitating reference to them and to let each Fragment stand out independently. Fragments 1 to 18 inclusive are Vogt's selection (*op. cit.*, pp. 115–118), chiefly from Erdmann's *Kant's Reflections on Anthropology.* Fragments 19 to 62 have been selected from Hartenstein, viii. pp. 609–644.

and to be cheerful about it. He must not be obliged to dissimulate, he must acquire immediate horror of lies, must learn so to respect the rights of men that they become an insurmountable wall for him. His instruction must be more negative. He must not learn religion before he knows morality. He must be refined, but not spoiled (pampered). He must learn to speak frankly, and must assume no false shame. Before adolescence he must not learn fine manners; thoroughness is the chief thing. Thus he is crude longer, but earlier useful and capable.

4. Both sexes must be educated and disciplined. Men need the former for society more than women do. It is worth while to examine the important opinion of Rousseau that the cultivation by education of the character of girls would have the greatest influence on the male sex and upon morals generally. At present girls are merely trained to good manners, but they are not educated to good morals and modes of thought: religion; honor, which is directed to that which others, what even one single person thinks.

The Sexes.

5. Until we shall have studied feminine nature better, it is best to leave the education of daughters to their mothers, and to let them off from books. It is not only natural, but proper to be polite, yielding, and mild towards beauty and youth, for it is honorable to be capable of being influenced by gentle impressions, and the roughness of gross force is hardly praiseworthy.

Girls.

6. Women are much more artistic, finer, and more regular when they resign themselves to the bent of their sex than are men; moreover, they have the intelligence to form this bent by reason. Thus, woman requires much less training and education, also less instruction, than man; and defects in her disposition would be less noticeable if she had more education, although a scheme for it which would agree with the destiny of her sex has not yet been invented. Her education is not instruction, but guidance. She must know men rather than books. Honor is her greatest virtue, domesticity her merit.

Woman.

7. Fathers are too indulgent towards their daughters, mothers towards their sons. Each must discipline his own sex.

8. It is a question how far education and instruction must be mechanical, and where cultivation must take place by means of concepts. Cultivation presupposes concepts. As speech is learned mechanically, so is arithmetic, *Learning.* also history, but still according to a plan formed by the understanding. Morality and religion must be treated logically.

9. Good and strong will. Mechanism must precede science (learning). Also in morals and religion? Too much discipline makes one narrow and kills proficiency. Politeness belongs, not to discipline, but to polish, and thus comes last.

10. It is not the sciences, but the public schools which polish. The sciences make one gentle and well-mannered, the universities polish, court-life makes one genteel and courteous. Rudeness comes from supposititious independence *Manners.* of all restraint for the sake of another. The coarse man believes that another's displeasure can do him no harm.

11. That man is good-hearted who is too good to do anything evil; so far as the heart is concerned, the good is considered only as sensuously or as physically good; but the same man can unhesitatingly do that which is morally bad. *Mere Good-heartedness.* A good-hearted man does not like to punish, he likes to do kindnesses; but perhaps he deceives and takes the part of a wretch who is in the wrong. It is very harmful to try to develop a good heart before a good character. The former is to be regarded as a small thing in comparison with the latter, but still it is not to be made contemptible.

12. First form character, then a good character. The former is done by practice in a firm intention in the espousal of certain maxims after reflection.

13. There must be a seed of every good thing in the character of men, otherwise no one can bring it out. Lacking that, analogous motives, honor, etc., are substituted. Parents are in the habit of looking out for the inclinations, for the talents and dexterity, perhaps for the disposition of their children, and not at all for their heart or character.

14. Character means that the person derives his rules of conduct from himself and from the dignity of humanity. Character is the common ruling principle in man in the use of his talents and attributes. Thus it is the nature of his will, and is good or bad. A man who acts without settled principles, with no uniformity, has no character. A man may have a good heart and yet no character, because he is dependent upon impulses and does not act according to maxims. Firmness and unity of principle are essential to character. Character is developed late and supports itself at last ; good-nature is lost with a happy heart and sociability, especially in the case of women,— and they have but little character anyway.

<small>Character.</small>

15. The more one presupposes that his own power will suffice him to realize what he desires the more practical is that desire. When I treat a man contemptuously, I can inspire him with no practical desire to appreciate my grounds of truth. When I treat any one as worthless, I can inspire him with no desire to do right.

16. When beds are well shaken up, they quickly spread themselves out again by their own elasticity. Old pillows retain impressions ; they are slow in resuming their former shape. This is the difference in the reception of strong impressions by young and by old people. The latter are sensitive to impressions, but lack elasticity. When the vital force begins to flow out again there is an agreeable languor present. One feels the preponderance of his vital forces ; but the old person feels their retardation, and the recovery is slow and hence unnoticeable. Old people do not need such emotions as hinder it.

<small>Impressions.</small>

17. Young people love that which is full of feeling because they are frivolous, and their impressions are so elastic as to disappear

quickly, and also because they do not as yet know the value of having control over one's own feelings and of not exposing them to the power of others.

18. Thinking people belong to a learned world which has uninterrupted continuity, even though several intervening centuries may have dreamed (slept). In this way the ancients belong to the modern learned or thinking world, the modern to the ancient,—that is, if they make use of the views of the old world. Thus we must honor the old learned world and be thankful to the ancients.

Unity of Learning.

---

19. Moral regeneration. That is useful (*mihi bonum*) which really or in imagination satisfies needs. The desires which are necessary to man, through his nature, are natural desires. The man who has no other desires, and in no greater degree, than those of natural necessity is a man of nature, and his ability to be satisfied with little is moderation of nature. The number of forms of knowledge and other perfections which the satisfaction of nature demands is the simplicity of nature. The man in whom the simplicity and the moderation of nature meet is the man of nature. He who could desire more than is naturally necessary is luxurious.

The Man of Nature.

20. The whole aim of the sciences is either *eruditio* (memory) or *speculatio* (reason). Both must result in making man more sensible (shrewder, wiser) in the position appropriate to human nature, and thus more easily contented. Taste, which is moral, makes one despise the science which does not improve him.

Science.

21. Young people have much feeling, but little taste.

22. Woman has fine taste in the choice of that which can affect man's feelings ; man has a blunt sense of this. Hence he pleases

most when he is the least concerned about pleasing. On the other hand, woman has sound taste in that which concerns her own feelings.

23. Man's honor consists in his own estimation of himself; woman's honor in the judgment of others. A man marries according to his own judgment; a woman does not marry against her parents' wishes. Woman meets injustice with tears, man with anger.

24. Novels make noble women fantastic and common women silly; they make noble men fantastic and common men lazy.

25. Rousseau's book serves to improve upon the ancients.

26. Because in civilized conditions there are so many unnatural desires, there also occasionally arises a motive for virtue; and because there is so much luxury in enjoyment and in knowledge, science arises. In the natural state one can be good without virtue and reasonable without science.

27. It is difficult to see whether man would be better off in the simple natural state than he is now: (1) because he has lost his

Nature and Happiness.

susceptibility to simple pleasure; (2) because he usually believes that the corruption which he sees in the civilized state also exists in the state of simplicity. Happiness without taste is based upon simplicity and the moderation of inclinations; happiness with taste is based upon the sensitive soul; calm. Hence one must be capable of happiness when alone, for then one is not annoyed by necessities. Rest after labor is more agreeable, and one should not pursue pleasure.

28. Rousseau proceeds synthetically, and begins with the natural man; I proceed analytically, and begin with the moral man.

The State of Nature.

However the heart of man may be constituted, our only question here is, whether the state of nature or of the civilized world develops more real sins and more facility to sin. The moral evil can be so muffled that only lack of greater purity, but never a positive vice, exhibits itself in actions (he is not necessarily vicious who is not holy) ; on the other hand, positive vice can be so developed as to become abhorrent. The simple man has little temptation to become vicious ; it is luxury alone which is very attractive, and when the taste for luxury is already very great, the respect for moral sensibility and for the understanding cannot restrain one.

29. Holy Scripture has more influence upon the improvement of the supernatural powers ; good moral education has more influence when everything is to follow nature. I grant that by means of the latter we can bring about no purifying holiness, but we *can* produce a moral goodness *coram foro humano*, and the latter is conducive to the former.

30. The threat of eternal punishment cannot be the immediate reason for morally good actions, but it can indeed be a powerful counterbalance for the incitement to evil that the immediate feeling of the moral be not outweighed. There is no such thing as an immediate inclination to morally evil actions, but there is to morally good actions.

31. Shame and modesty are two different things. The former is a betrayal of a secret by the natural movement of the blood ; the latter is a means of hiding a secret, for vanity's sake, likewise in the inclination of sex.

32. There is a great difference between conquering one's inclinations and rooting them out,—*i.e.*, acting in such a way as to lose them. Again, this is different from warding off inclinations,—*i.e.*, acting in such a way that one never acquires them. Old people need the former, young people the latter.

33. It requires a good deal of skill to prevent children from lying. For, as they have much to accomplish, and are much too weak to refuse to do as they are required or to es-   Lying.
cape punishment, they have much more incitement
to lie than old people ever have. This is especially true because, unlike old people, they can procure nothing for themselves, but everything depends upon the way they present a thing according to

the inclination which they observe in others. Thus they can only be punished for that which they cannot deny, and they should not be granted what they wish merely because of the reasons they advance.

34. When one is trying to develop morality, one should under no condition employ inducements which do not make the action morally good,—*i.e.*, punishment, reward, etc. Thus lying should be represented as *literally* vicious, as it indeed is, and it should not be included in any other moral category ; for example, that of duty towards others. One has no duties towards one's self, but one has absolute duties which are such in themselves—to act rightly. It is absurd that in our morality we seldom depend upon ourselves.

Moral Training.

35. In medicine we say that the physician is the servant of nature ; the same is true in ethics : keep the external evil at a distance, and nature will take the right path of her own accord. If a physician said that nature is corrupt, how could he improve her? Even so the moralist.

36. Man is not interested in the happiness or unhappiness of others until he himself is satisfied ; hence make him satisfied with little, and you will make kind men ; otherwise it is in vain. Universal brotherly love has something very noble and sublime about it, but it is chimerical. As long as one is himself so dependent upon things, he cannot sympathize with the happiness of others.

37. The simple man has a sense of right very early, but very late, or not at all, a concept of right. This sense must be much earlier developed than the concept. If he is taught first to develop according to rules, he will never feel. When the inclinations are once developed, it is difficult to imagine good or evil in other circumstances. Because I am now devoured by *ennui* unless I have continual pleasure, I imagine the same thing to be true of the Swiss cow-herd on the mountain, and he will not think of himself as a man who is satis-

Sense versus Concept Training.

fied and cannot desire anything more. One can hardly conceive that this lowliness is not filled with pain. On the other hand, even when other people are infected with imaginary evils, some cannot imagine how this idea could have been expected in their case. The aristocrat imagines that the evils of the disregard of vanished magnificence cannot oppress the citizen, and does not understand how he can accustom himself to count certain luxuries among his necessities.

38. Can anything be more perverted than to talk about the other world to children who have hardly begun life in this?

39. As fruit, when it is ripe, drops from the tree and falls to the ground in order to let its own seeds take root, so the man who comes of age separates himself from his parents, transplants himself, and becomes the root of a new race. Man must be independent that woman may depend entirely upon him.

40. It must be asked how far inner moral principles can bring a man. Perhaps they will bring him to the point where he is good, in the state of freedom, without great temptation. But when the injustice of others or the force of an illusion does him harm, this inner morality is not sufficiently powerful. He must have religion and encourage himself with the hope of the reward of a future life. Human nature is incapable of an immediate moral purity; but when its purity is worked upon in a supernatural manner, future rewards have no longer the character of motives.

41. The difference between false and true morality is this: that the former merely seeks correctives for evils, while the latter is concerned with preventing the existence of these evils.

42. It is unnatural that a man should spend the greatest part of his life in teaching a child how it shall live hereafter. Such private tutors as Jean Jacques are hence artificial. A child has but few services done for it ordinarily; as *Rousseau versus Schools.* soon as it gains a little strength, it of its own accord performs little useful actions of adults,—for example, in the case of country people and artisans,—and learns the rest gradually. Still,

it is fitting that a man should devote his life to teaching many others at the same time to live ; then the sacrifice of his own life is not to be counted. Hence schools are necessary, but to make them possible, Émile must be educated. It would be well if Rousseau had shown just how schools could arise from this. Country pastors can begin it with their own children and those of their neighbors.

43. I must read Rousseau until I am no longer distracted by the beauty of his style, and then I can estimate him reasonably. That great people shine only in the distance, and that a prince loses much in the presence of his valet, is because no man is great.

44. It is necessary to understand how the art and daintiness of the civilized constitution arise, and how in some regions of the world they are never met with (for example, where there are no domestic animals), in order to learn to distinguish that which is strange and accidental to nature from that which is essential to her. When one considers the happiness of the savages, it is not in order to return to the woods, but only in order to see what one has lost, while one has gained in other respects ; that one may not stick fast, with unnatural and unhappy inclinations, in the enjoyment and use of social luxury, and may remain a moral man of nature. Such an observation serves as a standard, for nature never makes a man a citizen, and his inclinations and efforts are all meant merely for the simple state of life. The chief object of most of the other creatures seems to be that they and their kind live ; when I assume this in the case of man, I must not despise the common savage.

The Simple State of Nature.

45. I can never convince another except through his own thoughts ; hence I must take for granted that he has a good and just understanding, otherwise it is vain to hope that he can be won over by my reasons. Likewise, I cannot move any one, in a moral sense, in any other way than through his own feelings ; hence I must take for granted that he has a certain goodness of heart, otherwise my description of

Mental Interaction.

vice will inspire him with no abhorrence, and my praise of virtue will never incline him towards it. But because it is possible that he have some morally just feelings, or because he can surmise that his feelings agree with those of the whole human race, that the evil in him is altogether evil, I must acknowledge to him the partial good which is in it, and represent to him as deceptive in itself the slippery resemblance between innocence and guilt.

46. It is said that the Christian shall not love temporal things. By this is understood that care must be taken very early to avoid the acquirement of such a love. But it is tempting God to nourish these inclinations and then to expect supernatural assistance in conquering them.

47. The first inequality is that of a man and a child, that of a man and a woman. The man regards it, in a manner, as an obligation, since he is strong and they are weak, not to sacrifice anything to them.

48. Every incorrect estimate of that which does not belong to nature's purpose destroys nature's beautiful harmony. By considering the arts and sciences so very important, one brings into contempt those people who do not possess them, and we are led into injustice, of which we would not be guilty if we regarded them more as our equals.

49. How many centuries passed before there was any real science, and how many nations there are in the world which will never have any ! We must not say that nature calls us to science because she has given us ability for it ; for, so far as the desire is concerned, it can merely be simulated.

50. Scholars think that everything is here on their account ; likewise the nobility. If one has travelled through desolate France, one can comfort himself in the Academy of Sciences or in high-toned companies ; so, when one has succeeded in freeing himself from all forms of begging in the Pontifical State, he can intoxicate

himself in Rome with the splendor of the churches and the antiquities.

51. Man may subtilize as much as he likes, he cannot force nature to lay down different laws. He must either work himself or others must work for him ; and this labor will rob others of their happiness in the ratio in which he tries to raise his above the average.

52. The evil effect of science upon men is principally this, that by far the greatest number of those who wish to display a knowledge of it accomplish no improvement at all of the understanding, but only a perversity of it, not to mention that it serves most of them as a tool of vanity.

53. Man's greatest concern is to know how he shall properly fill his place in the universe and correctly understand what he must be in order to be a man.

54. Youth must be taught to honor reason on moral as well as on logical grounds.

55. I am an investigator by inclination. I feel a great thirst for knowledge and an impatient eagerness to advance, also satisfaction at each progressive step. There was a time when I thought that all this could constitute the honor of humanity, and I despised the mob, which knows nothing about it. Rousseau set me straight. This dazzling excellence vanishes ; I learn to honor men, and would consider myself much less useful than common laborers if I did not believe that this consideration could give all the others a value, to establish the rights of humanity.

Rousseau's Influence.

56. The life of one who merely enjoys, without contemplation and without morals, seems to have no value.

57. In the civilized state man grows wise only very late, and one might well say, with Theophrastus, that it is a pity that he ceases to live just as he sees life opening.

58. In the metaphysical elements of æsthetics the various non-moral feelings are to be made use of; in the elements of moral metaphysics the various moral feelings of men, according to the differences in sex, age, education, and government, of races and climates, are to be employed.

59. One has reason not to refine his feelings too much, first, in order not to expose them to too much pain; second, in order to care for truer and more useful things. Moderation and simplicity require coarser feelings, and make one happy.

60. In the natural state no concept of God can arise, and the false one which one makes for himself is harmful. Hence the theory of natural religion can be true only where there is no science; therefore it cannot bind all men together.

61. It is best for us to be guided by the model of the ancients in all those things which appertain to fine or elevated feeling: in sculpture, architecture, poetry and eloquence, old customs and old constitutions. The ancients were The Ancients. closer to nature; between us and nature there is much that is frivolous, voluptuous, or slavishly corrupt. Ours is a century of beautiful trifles, of bagatelles, of noble chimeras.

62. Man has his own inclinations and a natural will which, in his actions, by means of his free choice, he follows and directs. There can be nothing more dreadful than that the actions of one man should be subject to the will of Free Action. another; hence no abhorrence can be more natural than that which a man has for slavery. And it is for this reason that a child cries and becomes embittered when he must do what others wish, when no one has taken the trouble to make it agreeable to him. He wants to be a man soon, so that he can do as he himself likes.

II

HUMAN PERFECTION AND PROGRESS

THAT Kant came to regard education as properly falling within
the bounds of ethics rather than within the realm of physical or

Pedagogy a
Branch of
Ethics.

natural science, and hence within theoretical philosophy, may be gathered from the following selections
from the Introduction to *The Metaphysical Elements
of Ethics*, Pt. II., Sections, 5, 8 (1797). In discussing those
ends which are also duties, he remarks about "Our Own Perfection," which is one of them :

The word *Perfection* is subject to many misconceptions. . . .
When it is said of the perfection belonging to man in general
(really to humanity) that it is in itself a duty to make this our

Perfection.

purpose, it must be understood as meaning that
which can be the *effect* of one's *action*, not that
which is a mere gift for which we must thank nature ; for otherwise it would not be a duty. It can therefore be nothing else than
culture of one's faculty (or natural capacity), in which the *understanding*, as the faculty of concepts, is consequently the highest of
those which refer to duties, but also at the same time of his *will*
(moral mode of thinking), to satisfy every duty in general. First,
it is his duty to elevate himself gradually out of the rawness of his
nature, out of animality more and more into humanity, through
which alone he is capable of setting purposes before himself ; to
supply his ignorance through instruction and to correct his errors,
and the technical-practical reason not only *recommends* this to him
as his ultimate purpose (of art), but the moral-practical reason

commands him absolutely to make this purpose his duty, in order to become worthy of the humanity which resides in him. Secondly, it is his duty to elevate the culture of his *will* up to the purest intention of virtue, where, namely, the *law* at once becomes the motive of his actions conformable to duty, and to obey it from a sense of duty which is inner moral-practical perfection.—Hartenstein, vii. p. 190.

Physical perfection,—that is, *cultivation of all faculties* in general, for the promotion of those purposes presented through the reason. That this is a duty, consequently an end in itself, and that its elaboration, without reference to the advantage which it yields us, does not rest upon a conditional (pragmatic), but an unconditional (moral) imperative, is shown by the following consideration. The power to set up before itself any end is the characteristic of humanity (distinguishing it from animality). With the end of humanity in our own person, there is therefore united the rational will, consequently the duty, to make ourselves through culture in general deserving of humanity, to provide the *power* for a realization of all possible ends, in so far as this power is to be found in man himself, or to further it,—that is, a duty to cultivate the raw capacities of his nature, as the means by which the animal first of all is elevated to man : consequently a duty in itself.

Self-
development
a Duty.

However, this duty is merely ethical,—that is, of wide obligation. How far one should go in cultivation (extension, or correction, of his faculty of understanding,—that is, in knowledge, or artistic ability) is prescribed by no rational principles ; the variety of circumstances, also, in which man can be placed renders very arbitrary the choice of the kind of employment for which he should cultivate his talent. Here, therefore, there is no law of reason for the actions, but only for the maxim thereof, which runs thus : "Cultivate the powers of thy mind and body into fitness for all purposes which can possibly come in thy way, uncertain as to which of them may some time be thine."—Hartenstein, vii. p. 195.

As late as 1798, towards the close of the "practical" or ethical period of his life, as some biographers characterize it, in discussing the conditions of human progress, Kant expressed the following view in *The Strife of the Faculties*, Section 10, Hartenstein, vii. pp. 406, 407.

In what order can progress towards the better be alone expected ?

The answer is, Not from the progress of things *from below upward* but *from above downward.*—To expect that one can succeed in educating not only good citizens, but also for the good capable of progressing and supporting itself, through the education of youth in domestic instruction and later in schools from the lowest to the highest in spiritual and moral culture, strengthened by the teachings of religion, is a plan which hardly promises the desired result. For, not only does the public insist that the expenses of the education of its youth should not fall upon it, but rather upon the state, while the state, on the other hand, has no money to pay salaries to thorough and enthusiastic teachers (as Büsching complains) because it needs all its funds for war ; but the whole machinery of this education has no continuity, if it is not projected according to a well-considered plan of the highest authority of the state, and according to its intentions, put into operation and uniformly maintained ; for this, indeed, it might be necessary that the state reform itself from time to time, and, trying evolution instead of revolution, continually advance towards the better. But since it is *men* who are to bring about this education, consequently such as have had to be educated for it themselves, in view of this weakness of human nature, under the uncertainty of the conditions which favor such an effect, the hope of its progress is only in a *wisdom from above* (which, when it is invisible to us, is called *Providence*), as a positive condition, but for that which can herein be expected and demanded of men, only negative wisdom is to be expected for the furtherance of this object : namely, that they see themselves obliged to let the greatest hindrance of the moral,—namely, war,—which always causes the moral to retrograde, . . . disappear in order to

Conditions of Progress.

opt a constitution which, by its very nature, without weakening self, founded upon real principles of right, can advance uninterruptedly towards the better.

In the *Anthropology*, etc. (1798), Hartenstein, vii. p. 653, in treating of "The Character of the Race," Kant presents this form of educational force in its natural, non-political aspect as follows :

The education of the human race in the *totality* of its species,— *i.e.*, taken *collectively* (*universorum*), not individually (*singulorum*), —where the multitude yields, not a system, but only a collected aggregate, with the struggle towards a civil constitution to be founded upon the principle of freedom, but at the same time upon the principle of lawful restraint in mind, man expects only from *Providence*,—*i.e.*, from a wisdom which is not *his*, but yet which is (through his own fault) the impotent *idea* of his own reason,—this education from above downward, I say, is wholesome, but harsh and severe, and is a very uncomfortable manipulation of nature which goes nearly to the length of destroying the whole race,—namely, the production of the *good* not intended by man, but a good which, once here, maintains itself, from the *evil* which is continually in internal disagreement with itself. Providence means that very wisdom which we notice with admiration in the preservation of the species of organized natural creatures which are continually laboring at the destruction of their own species and yet always protecting it, without, for that reason, assuming a higher principle in the provision for them than we do for the preservation of plants and animals.

Race Pedagogy.

16

III

LETTERS ON THE PHILANTHROPINUM
AT DESSAU

TO THE GENERAL PUBLIC[1]

THERE is no lack, in the civilized countries of Europe, of educational institutions, and of well-meant intentions on the part of

Present Education Bad. teachers to be useful in this matter; and yet it has been clearly proven that they were all spoiled at the outset; that, because everything in them is working in opposition to nature, the good to which nature has given the disposition is far from being drawn out of man, and that because we animal creatures are converted into men only by development, we would, in a short time, see entirely different men around us, if once that educational method were in full swing which is derived wisely from nature itself, and not slavishly copied after the old custom of rude and inexperienced ages.

But it is useless to expect this salvation of the human race to come from a gradual improvement of the schools. They must be

A Revolution in Schools Necessary. made over if anything good is to come from them, for they are defective in their original organization, and even the teachers must acquire a new cultivation. This can be brought about, not by a slow *reform*, but by a quick *revolution*. And for this nothing more is necessary than *a*

---

[1] This communication to the public in behalf of *The Philanthropinum*, dated March 27, 1777, appeared originally in the Königsberg newspaper, over Kant's initial. K. von Raumer, in 1843, in his *Geschichte der Pädagogik*, was the first historian of education to call attention to it by reprinting it in full.

school, radically rearranged according to the true method, directed by enlightened men, prompted not by selfish, but by noble zeal, and judged during its progress towards perfection by the attentive eyes of the connoisseurs of all countries, and also supported and furthered by the united contributions of all philanthropists until it attains completion.

Such a school is not only for those whom it educates, but also, which is infinitely more important, for those to whom it gives an opportunity to train themselves in gradually increasing numbers to be teachers, according to the true educational method,—a seed which, if tended

Training Teachers.

carefully, will produce in a short time a number of well-instructed teachers who will cover the whole country with good schools only.

The efforts of the general public of all countries should be first directed towards assisting such a model school, helping it in every way to reach that perfection whose sources it already contains. For to begin by copying its organization and plan in other countries, and retarding

Importance of a Model School.

it itself, which is to become the first complete example and nursery of good education, in its progress by lack of funds and other hindrances, is to sow seed before it is mature, and to reap weeds.

Now, such an educational institution is not merely a beautiful idea, but proves actively and visibly the feasibility of something which has long been desired. Surely it is a fact of our own age which, although overlooked by ordinary eyes, must be much more important, in the opinion of every enlightened observer who is interested in human welfare, than the brilliant nothingness on the ever-changing stage of the world at large, which does not advance the human race a hair's-breadth, even if it does not retard it.

Reputation, and especially the united voices of conscientious and astute connoisseurs in various countries, will already have made known to the readers of this paper the educational institute at Dessau (*The Philanthropinum*) as the only one which is characterized by these

The Institute at Dessau.

marks of excellence, not the least important of which is, that the very nature of its organization causes all the defects which may have attached to it at first to fall away naturally. The attacks against it which crop up here and there, and the occasional libels . . . about it are such ordinary tricks of fault-finding and of ancient usage defending itself on its dunghill that calm indifference on the part of this sort of people, who always look with malicious eyes upon everything which claims to be good and noble, would rather give rise to some suspicion of mediocrity in the good thing which is advancing.

An opportunity is now offered to render aid (which individually can be only small, but become powerful through numbers) to this institute which is devoted to humanity, and hence to the sympathy of every citizen. Were one to exert his inventive powers in order to think up some way in which a small contribution would help forward the greatest possible, most lasting, and most general good, he would settle on this one, since the seed of the good itself can be tended and cultivated in order that in time it may increase and perpetuate itself.

Aid solicited.

In accordance with these ideas and with the good opinion which we have of the number of right-thinking persons of our general public, we refer to the twenty-first issue of this newspaper, together with its supplement, and look forward to a large subscription from all gentlemen of the clerical and teaching classes, especially from parents, to whom nothing which will serve to improve their children's education can be indifferent; yes, even from those who, although they have no children of their own, yet as children had the advantage of an education, and for that reason will recognize their obligation to contribute their share, if not to the increase, yet at least to the education, of men.

Subscriptions to the monthly publication of the Institute of Dessau, entitled *Pedagogical Conversations*, are now being received at the rate of 2 Reichsthaler 10 Groschen in our money. But, since some increase may be demanded at the end of the year because of the as yet uncertain number of pages, it would perhaps be best (but this is left to individual discretion) to devote a ducat, in the way of subscription, to the furtherance of this work, whereupon the surplus would be refunded to every one who would

demand it. For the institute in question flatters itself that there
are many noble-minded people in all countries who would be glad
of such an opportunity to add, at this suggestion, a small voluntary
present to the amount of their subscription, as a contribution to
the support of the institute which is nearly perfect, but which
is not being helped as much as had been expected. For since,
as Herr O. C. R. Büsching says (*Wöchentl. Nachrichten*, J. 1776,
Nr. 16), the governments seem to have no money nowadays for
improvements in the schools, it will rest at last, if they are to be
made, with private persons of means, to promote by generous contribution such an important, common concern.

(Local subscriptions, for which receipts will be given, may be
handed to Prof. Kant from 10 A.M. to 1 P.M., or left at any time at
Kanter's bookstore.) K.

KANT'S LETTER TO THE COURT CHAPLAIN, WILHELM CRICHTON, IN KÖNIGSBERG

I venture unhesitatingly to promise myself the greatest and most
helpful interest, on the part of your Honor, for the support and
furtherance of an institution founded for the good of the world, as
soon as you are convinced of its usefulness. The Institute begun
by Basedow, and now under the entire direction of Herr Wolke,
has, in the hands of this tireless man, who was made for the
reform of the educational system, taken on a new form, as is
plainly to be seen from the recent reports of the Philanthropin,
which I have the honor to send you. Since the departure of several otherwise well-intentioned, but rather unpractical men, the
places are all filled with first-rate school-men who have combined
new and refined ideas with that which was useful in the old method
of teaching. The world feels keenly the necessity of improved
education nowadays, but the various attempts to improve it have
not succeeded. Those of F. von Salis and Bahrdt have been given
up. The Dessau Institute alone remains ; certainly simply because
it has Wolke at the head of it, Wolke, who is not to be deterred
by any obstacles, who is modest and indescribably energetic, who,

moreover, has the unusual disposition to be faithful without obstinacy to his plans, and under whose oversight the institution is bound to become, in time, the ancestress of all the good schools in the world, if only outside aid and encouragement are given it in the beginning.

From the enclosure your Honor will see that since the latest reports of the pedagogical undertaking have been sent to me for distribution, I am expected to encourage the public anew not only to continue its subscriptions, but to be favorable and benevolent in general to the Institute. I am heartily ready and willing to do it; but it seems to me that much more influence would be exerted if your Honor would be willing to espouse this cause and lend your hand and your pen to its furtherance. If you will allow me to give the Institute this hope, the result will be the greatest thanks and joyful acceptance of an offer so advantageous. I would then have the honor to wait upon you at any time convenient to yourself, and to give you the list of subscribers up to date, also, if there should be any other business necessary (which is not probable in this matter) which other more important matters would hinder your Honor from attending to, I would gladly undertake it.

Since I do not doubt that your Honor will be satisfied by the new and well-established arrangement of all that formerly failed to gain your full approval in the Institute, and since, under such conditions, I am sure of your sympathetic zeal for such an extensively useful institution, I am not afraid that my confidence will be taken in a wrong spirit.

I am, with the greatest respect,

Your Honor's most obedient Servant,

I. KANT.

[No date.]

IV

SELECTIONS ILLUSTRATING SOME TECHNICAL TERMS EMPLOYED IN THE LECTURE-NOTES

On the separation of *Discipline* from *Culture*, in the broader sense of the term, Kant laid considerable stress, and found great value in it even for theoretical philosophy, as may be seen in the following passage from the *Critique of Pure Reason* (1781), Hartenstein, iii. p. 475 :

The negative element of the instruction which merely serves to protect us from errors is more important than much positive teaching by which our knowledge could be increased. The *restraint* by which the continual inclination to depart from certain rules is limited and finally destroyed is called *discipline*. It is different from *culture*, which is supposed merely to furnish one form of dexterity without removing another already present. Hence to the *cultivation* of a talent which has already displayed an impulse to make itself apparent, discipline offers a negative,[1] culture and doctrine a positive contribution.

Discipline
versus Culture.

---

[1] I am well aware that people are accustomed, in the language of the schools, to employ *discipline* and *instruction* as synonymous terms. But there are so many instances in which the first expression, as training, is carefully distinguished from the second, as teaching, and the nature of things itself demands that we preserve the appropriate expressions for this difference, that I wish it might never be permissible to use that word in any other than a negative sense. [A note by Kant.]

To illustrate Kant's further use of the trinity of positive factors in educational activity, as these are picked out and named in Section 18, *b*, *c*, and *d*, and which served him repeatedly and in different connections as descriptive of human development as he regarded it, the following selections may be taken as typical :

We are *cultivated* highly by art and science. We are *civilized* to the point of being tiresome in all kinds of social politeness and propriety. But we are very far from being able to consider ourselves *moralized*. For the idea of morality belongs to culture ; but the use of this idea, which leads only to the imitation of custom in the love of honor and external respectability, constitutes mere civilizing.—*Idea of a Universal History from a Cosmopolitan Point of View* (1784), Hartenstein, iv. p. 152.

In the *Fundamental Principles of the Metaphysics of Morals* (1785), when treating of the scope of "imperatives" and of the various relations between "volition" and "obligation," Kant remarks,—

· · · Now, in order to make these appreciable, I believe that one would name them most suitably in their order, if one said they are either *rules* of skill, or *counsels* of prudence, or

Types of
Imperatives.

commands (*laws*) of morality. . . . One might call the first imperatives *technical* (belonging to art), the second *pragmatic*[1] (to welfare), the third *moral* (belonging to free behavior in general,—*i.e.*, to morals).—Hartenstein, iv. pp. 264, 265.

. . . Thus morality, and humanity, in so far as it is capable of morality, is that which alone has dignity. Skill and industry in labor have a market value ; wit, lively imagination, and moods

---

[1] It seems to me that this is the most exact meaning of the word pragmatic. For those *sanctions* are called pragmatic which are derived essentially, not from the rights of the states as necessary laws, but from *foresight* for the general welfare. A *history* is pragmatically compiled when it makes *wise*,—*i.e.*, teaches the world how it can look out for its interests better, or at least as well as antiquity did. [A note by Kant.]

fancy value ; truth in keeping promises, on the other hand, good-will founded on principles (not from instinct) have an intrinsic value.—Hartenstein, iv. p. 283.

Among the inhabitants of the earth, man is distinctly different from all other creatures on account of his possession of the three following capacities : *technical* (conscious, *mechanical*, for the handling of things) ; *pragmatic* (to use other men cleverly for his purposes) ; and *moral* (to act towards himself and others under laws according to the principle of freedom).—*Anthropology*, etc., Hartenstein, vii. p. 647.

The sum of Pragmatic Anthropology with reference to the destiny of man and the characteristics of his education is as follows : Man is destined by his reason to be in society with men and to *cultivate*, to *civilize*, and to *moralize* himself in it through art and sciences ; however great his animal propensity may be to yield passively to the attractions of indolent ease and of the well-being which he calls happiness, he must be active, in the conflict with the hindrances which beset him owing to the rawness of his nature, in making himself worthy of humanity. *[Cultivation, Civilization, Moralization.]*

Hence man must be *educated* for the good ; but he who is to educate him is again a man who is himself still raw and yet is to effect the very thing which he himself needs. Hence the continual deviation (of man) from his destiny with repeated returns to it.—*Ibid.*, p. 649.

V

MUSIC

SECTION 53. COMPARISON OF THE ÆSTHETIC VALUES OF THE FINE ARTS

Next to poetry, *when we have to do with charm and emotion of the mind*, I would place that art which approaches it most nearly and is most naturally connected with it,—namely, *music.*

Music and Emotion.

For although it does indeed speak through pure sensations without concepts, and consequently does not, like poetry, leave something for later reflection, yet it moves the mind in more ways and more intimately, although only temporarily ; but it is rather enjoyment than culture (the thought-play which is excited at the same time is only the effect of a mechanical association, as it were) ; and, judged by the reason, it has less value than any of the other fine arts. Hence, like every pleasure, it requires frequent variation, and cannot endure much repetition without engendering satiety. Its charm, which can be so generally communicated, seems to arise from the fact that every expression in the language has a tone appropriate to its meaning ; that this tone is more or less indicative of an emotion of the speaker, and also brings this forth in the hearer, who then in his turn excites the idea which is expressed in the language with such and such a tone ; and that, as modulation is, as it were, a universal language of the sensations, intelligible to every one, music uses it for itself alone in all its emphasis,—*i.e.*, as the language of the emotions,—and thus, according to the laws of association, communicates the æsthetical ideas which are naturally connected with it ; but that, because those æsthetic ideas are no concepts and definite thoughts, only the form of the combination of these sensations (harmony and melody) instead of the form of a language, serves by

250

means of their proportional pitch (which, since with tones it rests upon the relation of the number of vibrations of the air in the same time, so far as the tones are joined together simultaneously or consecutively, can be brought mathematically under certain rules) to express the æsthetic idea of a connected totality of an unnamable wealth of thought, according to a certain theme which produces the predominating emotion in the piece. Upon this mathematical form, although not represented by definite concepts, depends entirely the pleasure which unites the mere reflection upon such a number of simultaneous or consecutive sensations with this their play as a valid condition for every one of its beauty ; and it is the only thing according to which taste may appropriate a right to express in advance the judgment of all.

But mathematics has certainly not the least possible share in the charm and emotion which music produces ; it is merely the unavoidable condition (*conditio sine qua non*) of that proportion of the impressions, in their combination as well as in their change, whereby it is possible to combine them, and to prevent their destroying each other, making them to accord in a continuous moving and enlivening of the mind through the consonant emotions and thus to contribute to an agreeable self-enjoyment.

When, on the other hand, the value of the fine arts is estimated according to the culture which they procure for the mind, and when the increase of the faculties, which must come together in the judgment for knowledge, is taken as a standard, music takes the lowest place among the fine arts (as it takes, perhaps, the highest place among those prized for the pleasure they give), because it plays merely with sensations. In this regard the plastic arts far outstrip it ; for while they set the imagination into a free play, and which is one also adapted to the understanding, they at the same time incite an activity by producing something which serves the concepts of the understanding as a lasting and self-recommending means of combining themselves with sensibility, and thus, as it were, promote the urbanity of the higher powers of knowledge.—*Critique of Judgment* (1790), Hartenstein, v. pp. 338–340.

Music the Lowest Art.

VI

MEMORY

MEMORY is distinguished from merely reproductive imagination in that it is capable of *voluntarily* reproducing the former idea;

Memory *versus* Imagination.
hence the mind is not a mere play of the imagination. Fantasy—*i.e.*, creative imagination—must not intrude here, for the memory would thereby become *untrue.* The formal perfections of memory are : to *fix* something quickly in the memory, to *recall* it easily, and to *retain* it a long time. But these characteristics are seldom found together. When one believes he has something in his memory, but cannot bring it to consciousness, he says that he cannot *remember* it (not remember *himself ;* for that would be the same as making himself senseless). This endeavor, when continued, is very tiring for the head, and it is best to turn the attention for a while to other thoughts ; then the mind usually catches one of the associated ideas, which recalls the one sought.

To *fix* something in the memory *methodically* (*memoriæ mandare*) is called *memorizing* (not *studying*, as the ordinary man says of the

Methods of Memorizing.
preacher who merely learns by heart the sermon he expects to deliver later). This memorizing can be *mechanical*, or *ingenious*, or also *judicious.* The first of these is based upon mere frequent, literal repetition ; as, for example, in the learning of the multiplication table, where the learner must go through the whole series of words following one upon the other in the usual order, in order to reach what he is seeking ; for example, if the pupil is asked, How much is 3×7? he, beginning with 3×3, will probably arrive at 21 ; but if he is asked, How much is 7×3? he will not be able to remember so

soon, but will have to invert the numbers in order to place them in their accustomed order. When that which is learned is a solemn formula, in which no expression can be changed, but which, as we say, must be recited, people of the best memory fear to trust to it entirely (as though this very fear could confuse them), and hence consider it necessary to *read it off;* the most expert preachers do this, because the slightest change of the words would be ridiculous.

Ingenious memorizing is a method of stamping upon the memory certain ideas by association with allied ideas which in themselves (for the understanding) have no relation whatsoever to one another ; for example, the sounds of a language with entirely dissimilar pictures which are supposed to correspond to them : where one, in order to fix something in memory, burdens the latter with still more associations ; hence inconsistent as regular procedure of the imagination in the pairing off of that which cannot belong under one and the same concept, and at the same time contradiction between means and intention, since one is trying to lighten the labor of memory, but, as a matter of fact, one makes it more difficult still by the association, unnecessarily piled upon it, of very dissimilar ideas. That punsters seldom have a true memory (*ingeniosis non admodum fida est memoria*) is an observation which illustrates this phenomenon.

Judicious memorizing is no other than that of a table of the *division* of a system (for example, of Linné) into thoughts ; where, if one should have forgotten something, one can remember it by counting the members retained ; or of the *divisions* of a visualized whole (for example, of the provinces of a country on a map, which lie towards the north, west, etc.), because this demands understanding, and understanding, in its turn, comes to the help of imagination. The topic is a framework for general concepts, called *commonplaces*, which by division into classes, as when in a library one divides the books into cases with different labels, relieves the memory the most.

There is no *art of memory* (*ars mnemonica*) as a universal theory. Among the contrivances which particularly belong to it are mottoes in verses (*versus memoriales*) ; because rhythm contains a regular accent, which is greatly to the advantage of the mechanism of memory. We must not speak contemptuously of the wonderful men of memory, of Picus of Mirandola, Scaliger, Angelus Politian, Magliabecchi, etc., the polyhistors, who carried around in their heads as material for the sciences sufficient books to load one hundred camels, because they perhaps did not possess the necessary judgment to be able to select from all this knowledge that which could be most suitably employed ; for it is in itself merit enough to have gathered together in abundance the raw material, although other heads must come later to handle it with judgment (*tantum scimus, quantum memoria tenemus*). One of the ancients said, "The art of writing has destroyed memory (made it partly dispensable)." There is some truth in this ; for the ordinary man has the manifold things which are brought to him usually better arranged, to perform them in their order, and to recollect them ; just because memory is here mechanical, and no reasoning is added to it ; while, on the other hand, the learned man, through whose head many strange allied ideas go, forgets many of his errands or of his domestic affairs by distraction, because he has not grasped them with sufficient attention. But it is a great convenience, with a writing tablet in one's pocket, to be sure of finding, exactly, and with no trouble, whatever one has stowed away in the head, and the art of writing remains a glorious art, because, even though it were not employed in the communication to another of one's knowledge, it would still take the place of the broadest and truest memory, whose lack it can make good.

Forgetfulness (*obliviositas*), on the other hand, where the head, no matter how often it may be filled, is always empty, like a cask with holes bored in it, is a still greater evil. Sometimes this is undeserved, as in the case of old people, who can, it is true, remember the events of their younger years, but who always forget that which has just taken place. But still it is sometimes the result of habitual distraction, which principally attacks novel-readers. For, since in this kind of

Marginal note: Mnemonics.

Marginal note: The Evil of Forgetfulness.

reading the intention is only to amuse one's self for the moment, knowing it is mere fiction, the reader is entirely free to compose according to her [!] own imagination, which naturally distracts, and makes *absent-mindedness* (lack of attention to the present) habitual ; thus the memory is unavoidably weakened. This exercise in the art of killing time, and making one's self useless for the world, and then mourning over the shortness of life, is, aside from the fantastic frame of mind which it causes, one of the most hostile kinds of attack upon memory.—*Anthropology*, etc., Hartenstein, vii. pp. 497–501.

VII

PHYSICAL GEOGRAPHY

As, at the beginning of my academic instruction, I recognized the fact that a great carelessness on the part of the student body con-

Educational Value of Geography.

sists principally in their learning early to *reason speciously*, without possessing sufficient historical knowledge which could take the place of *experience*, I decided to reduce the history of the present condition of the earth, or geography in its broadest meaning, to an agreeable and easy summary of that which could prepare them for practical reasoning, and serve to arouse a desire to extend the knowledge thus begun. I called a discipline of this sort, from that part of it to which my attention was particularly directed, physical geography. Since then I have gradually enlarged this outline, and now I think to gain time by curtailing that division which has to do with the physical curiosities of the earth, in order to elaborate my exposition of its other parts, which are of more general utility. So this discipline will be a *physical-moral* and *political* geography, wherein *first* the curiosities of *nature* throughout her three kingdoms will be indicated, but with a selection of those, among innumerable others, which appeal particularly to the universal desire for knowledge, by reason of the charm of their rarity, or of the influence which they have upon the states through commerce and trade. This part, which also contains the natural relation of all countries and seas, and the reason of their connection, is the real foundation of all history, without which it would hardly be different from fairy-stories. The *second* division regards *man* according to the multiplicity of his natural characteristics and according to the difference in that which he considers moral, throughout the whole earth ; a very important and equally attractive study, without which it is difficult to form general judgments of man, and in which the comparison between themselves and with the moral condition of former times lays a huge map of the human race before our eyes. *Finally*, that which can be considered as a result of the interaction of both the above-mentioned forces—namely, the condition of the *states* and nations on the earth—will be considered, not so much as it rests upon the chance causes of the undertaking and the fate of individual men, as, for example, the succession of kings, conquests, or state intrigues, but rather in its relation to that which is more permanent, and which includes the distant foundations of all these,—namely, the situation of their countries, their products, customs, industries, commerce, and population. Even the rejuvenation, if I may call it such, of a science of such extensive views, on a smaller scale, is of great value, for in that way alone is unity of knowledge, without which all learning is fragmentary, acquired. And in a social century like the present one, may I not reckon the supply which a great diversity of agreeable and instructive knowledge of easy comprehensibility offers for the support of social intercourse among the advantages which it is no degradation for science to have in mind? At least it cannot be pleasant for a learned man to be often in the embarrassing position in which the orator Isocrates found himself, who, when once he was urged to say something at a social gathering, was obliged to answer, "What I know is not suitable, and what is suitable I do not know."—*Announcement of the Arrangement of his Lectures for the Winter Semester*, 1765–1766, Hartenstein, ii. pp. 320, 321.

VIII

KNOWLEDGE AND LOGICAL METHODS

KANT's psychological conception of knowledge, in so far as it can be a matter of concern for pedagogy, is derivable, not so readily from his systematic treatises comprising the Critical Philosophy, as from some of his minor writings, of which the following selection, being the closing paragraph of Section 8 of the Introduction to his *Logic*, which treats of "The Logical Perfection of Knowledge according to Quality," is a fairly clear specimen.—Hartenstein, viii. p. 65.

As regards the objective content of our knowledge in general, we may think of it in terms of the following gradations :

Degrees of
Knowledge.

The *first* degree of knowledge is : merely to have an idea.

The *second :* to have an idea consciously, or to perceive (*percipere*).

The *third :* to know (*noscere*) something, or to have an idea of something in comparison with other things, according to *identity* as well as to *difference*.

The *fourth :* to know something *consciously,—i.e., apprehend (cognoscere).* Animals *know* objects, but they do not *apprehend* them.

The *fifth :* to *understand* (*intelligere*) something,—*i.e.*, to apprehend or *conceive through the understanding by means of concepts*. This is very different from *comprehending*. One can conceive a great deal, although one cannot comprehend it for example, a *perpetuum mobile*, whose impossibility is shown in mechanics.

The *sixth :* to apprehend something through the reason, or understand (*perspicere*). We accomplish this in few things, and

258

our cognitions decrease in number the more we wish to complete their content.

Finally, the *seventh :* to comprehend (*comprehendere*) something,— *i.e.*, apprehend it through the reason or *a priori* in that degree which is sufficient for our purpose. For all our comprehending is only *relative,—i.e.*, sufficient for a certain purpose ; *absolutely* we comprehend nothing at all. Nothing more can be comprehended than what the mathematician demonstrates ; for example, that all the lines in a circle are proportional. And yet he does not comprehend how it happens that such a simple figure has these characteristics. The field of understanding, or [its faculty] the understanding, is hence in general much greater than the field of comprehending, or [its faculty] the reason.

LOGICAL METHODS

How heavily Kant's general treatment of the pedagogy of instruction was indebted to his borrowings from logic may readily be seen in the following portions from his *Logic* (Hartenstein, viii. pp. 133, 141–143), being the

General Methodology of Logic

SECTION 94

Manner and Method

All knowledge and its totality must conform to a rule. (Irregularity is irrationality.) But this rule is either that of manner (free) or that of method (constrained).

SECTION 95

Form of Science. Method

Knowledge, as science, must be arranged after a method. For science is a totality of knowledge as system and not merely as aggregate. It demands, therefore, a knowledge which is systematic, consequently arranged according to well-considered rules.

Section 96

Methodology.   Its Object and Purpose

As the elements of logic contain the elements and conditions of the completeness of knowledge, so, on the contrary, the general methodology, as the other part of logic, has to treat of the form of a science in general, or of the manner of bringing together the manifold of knowledge to make a science.

Section 114

Different Divisions of Method

As to that which particularly concerns *method* in the elaboration and treatment of scientific knowledge, there are various chief sorts, which we can indicate here according to the following division.

Section 115

1. Scientific or Popular Method

The *scientific* or *scholastic* method differs from the *popular* in that the former originates in fundamental or elementary propositions, while the latter is derived from the *usual* and the interesting. The scientific method aims at thoroughness, and hence puts aside all that is heterogeneous ; the popular method has *entertainment* in view.

NOTE.—These two methods thus differ in *kind*, and not in mere exposition ; popularity in method is consequently something different from popularity in exposition.

Section 116

2. Systematic or Fragmentary Method

The systematic method is opposed to the *fragmentary* or *rhapsodical*. When one has thought according to a method, and has then expressed this method in his exposition, and the transition from one proposition to another is plainly indicated, he has handled knowledge systematically.   On the other hand, if one has indeed thought according to a method, but has not arranged his exposition methodically, such a method must be called *rhapsodical*.

NOTE.—The *systematic* exposition is opposed to the *fragmentary*, as the *methodical* is to the *tumultuous*. The methodical thinks,—that is to say, can give a systematic, or a fragmentary exposition. The externally fragmentary exposition, which is in itself methodical, is *aphoristic*.

SECTION 117

3. Analytic or Synthetic Method

The *analytic* method is opposed to the *synthetic*. The former begins with the conditioned and the established, and proceeds to the principles (*a principiatis ad principia*), while the latter proceeds from the principles to their consequences, or from the simple to the complex. The former might be called *regressive*, the latter *progressive*.

NOTE.—The analytic method is also called the method of *discovery*. For the purpose of popularity the analytic method is the better adapted, while the synthetic method is better suited for the purpose of the scientific and systematic treatment of knowledge.

SECTION 118

4. Syllogistic.—Tabular Method

The *syllogistic* method is that one, according to which a science is expounded in a chain of syllogisms.

That method is called *tabular*, according to which a complete structure is presented in its entire connection.

SECTION 119

5. Acroamatic or Erotematic Method

The method is *acroamatic*, so far as one teaches alone ; *erotematic*, so far as he also asks questions. The latter method may be again divided into *dialogistic*, or *Socratic*, and *catechetical*, according as the questions are directed to the *understanding* or merely to the *memory*.

Note.—One can teach erotematically only by means of the *Socratic dialogue*, in which both parties must question and answer; so that it seems as though the pupil were also teacher. That is to say, the Socratic dialogue teaches through questions, by teaching the pupil to know his own rational principles and sharpening his attention to them. With the ordinary *catechism* one cannot teach, but only ask questions about that which one has taught acroamatically. Hence the catechetical method is good only for empirical and historical knowledge, while the dialogistic is adapted to rational knowledge.

SECTION 120

Meditation

By meditation we understand reflection, or methodical thinking. Meditation must accompany all reading and learning; and for this it is necessary that one *first of all* institute preliminary investigations, and *then* arrange his thoughts in order, or combine them according to a method.

IX

THE PEDAGOGY OF PHILOSOPHY

In all instruction of youth there is this difficulty, that one is obliged to anticipate the years with insight, and, without awaiting the maturity of the understanding, is supposed to impart such knowledge as, in the natural order of things, could be grasped only by a practised and tried reason. Hence arise the eternal prejudices of the schools, which are more stubborn and frequently more absurd than ordinary prejudices, and the precocious volubility of young thinkers, which is blinder than any other form of self-conceit, and more incurable than ignorance. However, this difficulty is not altogether to be avoided, for in the age of a very ornate civil constitution the finer insights belong to the means of progress, and become necessities which, from their nature, can be really reckoned only as ornaments of life, and, as it were, as the unnecessary-beautiful. At the same time, it is possible to make public instruction conform better to nature in this respect also, if not to make them agree entirely. For, since the natural progress of human knowledge is this, that the understanding is first developed by arriving, through experience, at intuitive judgments, and, through these, at concepts, that thereupon these concepts are recognized in relation to their grounds and results by reason, and finally in a well-arranged whole by means of science, so instruction must go the same way. Hence a teacher is expected to make of his hearer first an *intelligent*, then a *reasonable*, and finally a *learned* man. Such a procedure has this advantage, that, although the pupil may never reach the last stage, as usually happens, yet he has profited by the instruction, and has become more resourceful, and wiser, for life, if not for the school.

Conditions for teaching Philosophy.

263

If this method is reversed, the pupil snaps up a kind of reason before his understanding is developed, and he wears borrowed science, which is only, as it were, stuck on to him, and not grown on, whereby his mental ability remains as unfruitful as ever, and at the same time has become much more corrupt by the illusion of wisdom. This is the reason why one often meets learned men (real students) who give evidence of little understanding, and it is the reason why the universities send more insipid men out into the world than any other class of the general public.

Hence the rule for the conduct of instruction is as follows : to first mature the understanding and accelerate its growth by exer-

Method of teaching Philosophy.

cising the pupil in judgments of experience and making him attentive to that which the compared impressions of his senses can teach him. He should not make a bold leap from these judgments or concepts to the higher and more distant ones, but rather reach them by the natural and beaten foot-path of the lower concepts, which lead him further by degrees ; but all according to that intellectual ability which the previous exercise has necessarily produced in him, and not according to that which the teacher observes in himself, or thinks he observes, and which he also falsely presupposes in the case of his hearer. In short, he is to learn, not *thoughts*, but *thinking ;* he is to be *guided*, not *carried*, if he is to be able to *walk* alone in the future.

Such a method demands the very nature of philosophy itself. But, since this is really an occupation for maturity alone, it is no wonder that difficulties arise when one tries to accommodate it to unskilled youthful ability. The youth released from school instruction was accustomed to *learn*. Now he thinks he will *learn philosophy ;* but that is impossible, for he must now *learn to philosophize*. I will explain my meaning more clearly. All the sciences which one can *learn*, in the real sense of the term, can be divided into two kinds : the *historical* and the *mathematical*. To the first belong, aside from history, strictly speaking, natural history, philology, positive law, etc. But now, since in everything historical, personal experience or external testimony, but in every-

thing mathematical, the obviousness of concepts and the infallibility
of demonstration, go to make up that which is indeed given, and
hence on hand, and, as it were, only to be picked up, it follows
that it is possible to learn in both,—*i.e.*, to impress either upon the
memory or upon the understanding that which can be laid before
us as an already complete discipline. Hence, in order to *learn*
philosophy too, there must necessarily be one at hand. One would
have to be able to produce a book, and to say, "See, here is wisdom and reliable insight; learn to understand and grasp it; build
upon it in the future, then you are philosophers." Now, until some
one shows me such a book of philosophy, to which I can refer,—as,
for example, to Polybius, to explain a circumstance of history, or
to Euclid, to explain a proposition in geometry,—I beg to be allowed
to say that the confidence of the general public is abused when,
instead of extending the intellectual ability of the youth confided
to one's care, and developing them to a future more mature *personal* insight, one circumvents it with an alleged already complete
philosophy, contrived for the benefit of others; wherefrom results
a false show of science, which only in a certain place, and among
certain people, passes for real coin, but which everywhere else is
in bad repute. The peculiar method of instruction in philosophy
is *zetetic*, as some ancients called it (from ζητεῖν),—*i.e.*, *seeking,*—
and becomes only in more practised reason, in various connections,
dogmatic,—*i.e.*, *decided.* The philosophical author whom one
selects as the basis of a course of instruction should be regarded,
not as the model of judgment, but only as an occasion to judge of
him, yes, even against him; and the method of reflecting *for himself*, and coming to conclusions, is the thing, facility in which the
pupil is really seeking, and which alone can be useful to him; and
the different forms of knowledge which he may thereby gain are
to be regarded as accidental results, for whose rich abundance he
has only to plant the fruitful roots in himself. . . .

If we compare with this the usual procedure, which differs from
it so greatly, much can be understood which seems strange. As,
for example, why there is no kind of learning in handicraft,
wherein so many *masters* are found, as in philosophy; and, since

many of those who have learned history, jurisprudence, mathematics, etc., say themselves that they have not, however, yet learned enough to teach these subjects, why, on the

Philosophy differs from other Subjects.

other hand, there is seldom one who does not seriously imagine that, besides his other occupation, it would be quite possible for him to give lectures on logic, ethics, etc., if he cared to trouble himself with such trifles. The reason is that in the former sciences there is a common standard, but in the latter each person has his own. None the less, one can plainly see that it is very unnatural for philosophy to be a bread-earning art, since it is contrary to its very nature to have to conform to the illusion of demand and to the law of fashion, and that necessity, in whose power philosophy is still, can force it to press itself into the form of common approval. . . .

Logic.—Of this science there are really two kinds. The first kind is a criticism and guidance of the healthy understanding, as,

Two Kinds of Logic : General and Special.

on the one hand, it approaches coarse concepts and ignorance, and, on the other, science and learning. It is the logic of this kind which should be presupposed in the beginning of all academic instruction in philosophy ; the quarantine, as it were (provided I am permitted to express myself thus), which must be passed by the student who wishes to go from the land of prejudice and error into the realm of clear reason and science. The second kind of logic is the criticism and guidance of *specific scholarship*, and can never be treated other than according to the sciences whose organon it should be, in order that the proceeding which has been used in the application may become more uniform, and that the nature of the discipline, together with the means of its improvement, may be understood. In such a manner I shall add at the end of metaphysics a consideration of its own peculiar method, as an organon of this science, which would not be in its right place at the beginning, because it is impossible to make the rules clear in the absence of examples by means of which they can be shown *in concreto*. The teacher must, to be sure, be master of the organon from the beginning before he lectures upon the science, in order to guide himself by it, but he must never lecture on it to the student other than at the very end of the course. The criticism and guidance of the entire world-wisdom as a totality, this complete logic, thus has its place in instruction only at the end of all philosophy, since the then acquired acquaintance with it and the history of human opinions alone make it possible to present considerations on the origin of its insights, as well as of its errors, and to project the exact outlines, according to which such a structure of reason is to be erected permanently and uniformly.

I will lecture on the logic of the first kind, using the manual of Professor Meier ; since he has in mind the limits of my present purposes, and at the same time gives opportunity to include, along with the culture of the finer and scholarly reason, the training of the common but active and sound understanding, the former for the reflective, the latter for the active and civic life. At the same time, in connection with the *criticism* of *reason*, the very close relation of the contents gives opportunity to glance briefly at the *criticism* of *taste*,—that is, *æsthetics*,—the rules of one always serving to illustrate the rules of the other, and their contrasts are but means of comprehending both better.—*Announcement of the Arrangement of his Lectures for the Winter Semester*, 1765–1766, Hartenstein, ii. pp. 313–316, 318.

X

THE ACQUISITION OF CHARACTER

THE man who is conscious of having a character, according to his manner of thought, does not have it from nature's hand, but must always have *acquired* it. We can also assume that its foundation, like a kind of regeneration, a certain solemnity of the vow which he makes to himself, makes it and the time when this change in him took place ever memorable, like a new epoch. Training, examples, and instruction cannot possibly accomplish this firmness and perseverance in principles *gradually*, but only, as it were, by an explosion following all at once upon the satiety of the wavering condition of instinct. Perhaps there will be but few who have attempted this revolution before their thirtieth year, and still fewer who are firmly grounded before their fortieth. To try to become a better man by piecemeal is a vain attempt ; for one impression fades away while one is working on another ; but the foundation of a character is absolute unity of the inner principle of the conduct of life. It is also said that *poets* have no character ; for example, they offend their best friends rather than give up a witty jest ; or that character is not to be found among courtiers, who have to accommodate themselves to all sorts of forms ; and that firmness of character is an uncertain thing among the clergy, who pay court to the Lord of Heaven, but at the same time, and in the same frame of mind, to the lords of the earth ; that thus to have an inner (moral) character is, and will always be, only a pious wish. But perhaps the *philosophers* are to blame for this, in that they have never yet set this concept by itself in a sufficiently clear light, and have tried to represent virtue only in fragments,

(Margin note: Character and Individual Experience.)

268

but never in its whole beautiful form, and to make it interesting for all men.

In a word, to have made truthfulness in the inmost recesses of one's acknowledgment to one's self and at the same time in one's behavior towards others, one's highest maxim, is a man's sole proof of the consciousness of having a character ; and since this is the minimum which can be demanded of a rational man, but at the same time the maximum of inner worth (of human dignity), he must, in order to be a man of principles (to have a definite character), be capable of the most common human reason, and hence superior to the greatest talent, in point of dignity.—*Anthropology*, etc., Hartenstein, vii. pp. 616, 617.

XI

METHOD IN MORAL INSTRUCTION

THAT pedagogy and ethics were almost synonymous terms for Kant, at least in their more empirical aspects, appears strongly in **Ethics and Pedagogy Synonymous.** the following group of selections. Irrespective of the ultimate foundations of ethics, the establishment of any moral laws stood before him incomplete without a treatment of the problem of how these laws can be set into the experience of the individual. This attitude of mind comes out clearly in his critical and technical writings, where one would be least apt to look for it; whereas the *Lecture-Notes* scarce reflect this pedagogic moralism which agitated Kant in his philosophical moods. Indeed, the problem of moral education can be looked upon as the link connecting the Critical Philosophy with the pedagogical interests which seemed to antedate the development of that philosophy.

I

The following selections practically comprise the second part of the *Critique of Practical Reason* (1788), being the "Methodology of pure practical reason," and find their place here in view of the observation made above, and especially in view of the central position which they occupy in the development of the Critical system:

. . . By this methodology is understood the manner in which **Practical Ethics.** one can procure for the laws of pure practical reason *access* into the human mind and *influence* upon its maxims,—that is, make the objectively practical reason also *subjectively* practical.

270

Now, it is clear that those determining principles of the will which alone make the maxims really moral and give them a moral value—namely, the direct idea of the law and the objectively necessary obedience of it as duty—must be conceived of as the real motives of actions ; be-

Motives of Action.

cause otherwise *legality* of actions would, it is true, be accomplished, but not *morality* of intentions. But it must appear less clear to every one—indeed, at first sight totally improbable—that even subjectively that representation of pure virtue could have *more power* over the human mind, and be a much stronger motive in accomplishing that very legality of actions, and in producing stronger decisions to prefer the law from regard for it, to any other consideration, than all the allurements which arise from delusive ideas of pleasure and of all that which we reckon as happiness, or even than all threats of pain and evils. However, this is really the case, and were not human nature thus constituted, no manner of representing the law by means of digressions and recommendations would ever produce morality of intentions. It would be mere hypocrisy. . . .

To be sure, it cannot be denied that, in order to lead either an as yet unformed, or even a demoralized, character into the path of the morally good, some preparatory guidance is required to lure it to its own advantage or to frighten it through fear of injury ; but as soon as this mechanical work, this leading-string, has had some little

Preliminary Training in Morals Necessary.

effect, the pure moral motive must by all means be presented to the mind, which, not only because it is the only thing which founds a character (practical consequent mode of thought according to unchangeable maxims), but also because it teaches man to feel his own dignity, gives the mind a power, unsuspected even by himself, to tear himself loose from all sensuous adherence, in so far as it aims at governing, and to find ample recompense in the independence of his intelligible nature and of the greatness of soul, to which he sees himself destined, for the sacrifices which he makes. Thus we wish to prove by observations, such as any one can make, this characteristic of our mind, this susceptibility to a pure moral interest, and consequently the moving power of a pure idea of virtue, when it is properly brought home to the human heart, as the most powerful, and, when it comes to duration and punctuality in following moral maxims, as the only motive for the good. At the same time it must be remembered that, if these observations only prove the reality of such a feeling, but not a resulting moral improvement, this does no harm to the only method of making the objectively practical laws of pure reason subjectively practical by the mere pure force of the idea of duty, as though it were an empty fantasy. For, since this method has never been put into operation, experience cannot show anything of its results one can only demand proofs of the susceptibility to such motives which I will now briefly indicate, and afterwards sketch in a few words the method of the foundation and cultivation of genuine moral characters.

When one observes the course of conversation in mixed companies, consisting not only of scholars and subtle reasoners, but also of business men, and of women, one notices that, besides telling stories and joking, another form of entertainment finds a place,—namely, argument; for the first, if it is to be new and interesting, is soon exhausted, while the second easily becomes insipid. Now, in all argument there is nothing which more arouses the participation of people who are usually easily bored by all subtle discussion, and which brings about more liveliness in the company, than that about the *moral value* of this or that action, by which the character of any person is to be made out. Those to whom everything subtle and speculative in theoretical questions is usually dry and tiresome soon join in when it is a question of deciding the moral content of a related good or bad action, and they are as exact, as speculative, as subtle in thinking out everything which could reduce, or even throw suspicion upon the purity of intention and consequently the degree of virtue in it, as no one would expect from them in the case of any other object of speculation.

I do not know why the educators of youth have not long since made use of this inclination of reason to enter with pleasure upon

[margin note] A Device from Daily Life.

even the most subtle examination of suggested practical questions, and why, after having laid a purely moral catechism at the foundation, they have not searched the biographies of ancient and modern times with the intention of getting illustrations of the duties laid down, on which, principally by the comparison of similar actions under different circumstances, they might exercise the judgment of their pupils in noting their greater or less moral significance. In this way they would find that even early youth, otherwise as yet immature for all speculation, soon becomes very sharp-sighted, and not a little interested as it feels the progress of its judgment ; but the principal thing is that it can be hoped with confidence that the frequent exercise in knowing good conduct and in applauding it, and in noticing even the slightest deviation from it with regret or contempt, even if done up to this point only as a play of judgment in which children can vie with each other, will yet leave behind a lasting impression of esteem, on the one hand, and abhorrence, on the other, which, through the mere habit of frequently regarding such actions as worthy of praise or blame, would make a good foundation for uprightness in the future course of life. Only, I would spare them examples of so-called *noble* (extra-meritorious) actions, with which our sentimental writings are so lavish, and would refer everything to duty and to the value which a man can and must give himself in his own eyes through the consciousness of not having transgressed it, because that which runs out into empty wishes and longings for unattainable perfection produces mere novel heroes who, while they pride themselves upon their feeling for the transcendentally great, free themselves thereby from the observance of their common and ordinary responsibility, which then seems to them unimportant.

. . . We will first point out the criterion of pure virtue by means of an example, and, supposing that it be submitted to a ten-year-old boy for his judgment, we will see whether he would necessarily be obliged to judge as he does without being led to it by the teacher. Let some one relate the story of an honest man whom one is trying to persuade to join the slanderers of an innocent and helpless person (as, for example, Anne Boleyn upon the accusation of Henry VIII. of England). He is offered rewards,—

Illustration of Method in developing the Idea of Duty. that is, valuable presents or high rank ; he refuses them. This will call forth mere praise and approval in the mind of the hearer, because it is gain. Now he is threatened with loss. Among these slanderers are his best friends, who now withdraw their friendship, near relatives who threaten to disown him (he is poor), powerful persons who can persecute and wound him in every place and circumstance, a reigning prince who threatens him with loss of freedom, yes, of life itself. Now, that his cup of suffering may be full, in order to make him feel deeply, one may represent his family, threatened with the most extreme distress and poverty, as *begging him to yield*, and him, although honest, yet with feelings not firm and unresponsive either to pity or to his own need, at a moment in which he wishes never to have seen this day which exposes him to such unspeakable pain, yet remaining true to his principle of uprightness, without wavering and without doubting : my youthful hearer is led by steps from mere approval to admiration, from there to amazement, finally to the greatest reverence and a lively wish to be such a man himself (although not, to be sure. in his condition). . . . Thus morality must have the more power over the human heart the more purely it is presented. From this it follows that if the law of morals and the image of holiness and virtues are to exercise any influence at all upon our minds, they can exercise it only in so far as they are laid to heart pure, unmixed with any ideas of well-being, as a motive, because they show themselves most splendidly in suffering.

To call attention to this method is more necessary than ever in our age, when it is hoped to have more effect upon the mind with

The Pedagogy of his Age Morally Weak. soft, melting feelings, or lofty, swelling pretensions which weaken, rather than strengthen, the heart, than by means of the plain and serious idea of duty more suitable to human imperfection and to progress in the good. It is completely contrary to the end in mind to set honorable, magnanimous, and deserving actions before children for their model, with the intention of attracting them to such actions by inspiring them with enthusiasm. For, since they are still so backward in the observation of the commonest duty, and even in the correct judgment of it, this amounts merely to making dreamers of them betimes. But even among instructed and experienced men this supposed motive has, if not a detrimental, at least no genuine moral effect upon the heart, which, however, is what it was desired to accomplish.

All *feelings* must accomplish their effect in that moment when they are most lively and before they subside, especially those which are to produce unusual effort, or they do nothing ; for the heart naturally returns to its usual moderate action, and then falls into the debility which characterized it previously, because something was used merely to excite, but not to strengthen it. *Principles* must be based on concepts ; on any other foundation can arise only spasmodic efforts, which can give the individual no moral worth, nor even create self-confidence, without which the consciousness of his moral disposition and of such a character, the highest good in man, cannot exist at all. . . .

Principles versus Feelings.

The method then proceeds as follows. . . . Now, there is no doubt that this practice and the consciousness of a culture thus arising, of our reason judging merely of the practical, must gradually produce a certain interest even in the law of reason, and consequently in morally good actions. For we finally come to love that the consideration of which makes us feel the extended employment of our cognitive powers, which is especially promoted by that wherein we find moral justification ; since the reason can be contented only in such an order of things wherein, by its own power, it is able to determine *a priori*, according to principles, what should happen. An observer of nature also comes to prefer those objects which at first were objectionable to him, when he discovers the great finality in their organization, and so his reason is charmed in contemplating it. . . .

The Psychological Basis of the Method.

But this exercise of the judgment, which makes us feel our own cognitive powers, is not yet true interest in the actions and their

morality. It merely shows that man likes to amuse himself with such a criticism, and it gives to virtue, or the mode of think-
The True Aim in Moral Teaching. ing according to moral laws, a form of beauty which is admired, but is not on that account sought after (*laudatur et alget*) ; as everything a consideration of which produces subjectively a consciousness of the harmony of our powers of representation, and whereby we feel our entire cognitive powers (understanding and imagination) strengthened, produces a satisfaction which may be communicated to others, while the existence of the object remains indifferent to us because it is regarded only as the occasion of becoming conscious of the endowment of the talents in us which are elevated above animal nature. Now, however, the *second* exercise begins its work,—namely, to make observable the purity of will in a living exposition of the moral disposition by examples, first only as its negative perfection, in so far as in an action done from duty no motives of inclination have any determining influence ; whereby the pupil is kept attentive to the consciousness of his *freedom ;* and although this renunciation causes pain in the beginning, yet, by releasing that pupil from the constraint of even real needs, a freedom from the manifold discontent in which all these needs involve him is announced, and the mind is prepared for the reception of contentment from other sources. Thus the heart is freed and lightened of a burden which is always secretly oppressing it, when by pure moral decisions, examples of which are cited, an inner power, otherwise not known to him, is disclosed to man, *the inner freedom* to release himself from the violent importunity of the inclinations to such a degree that none, not even the dearest, shall have any influence at all upon a decision for which we are now to use our reason. . . . Upon this [respect for ourselves], when it is well grounded, when man fears nothing so much as to find himself, upon self-examination, contemptible and worthless in his own eyes, can every good moral disposition be grafted ; because this is the best, yes, the only guard to keep at a distance from the mind the pressure of ignoble and destructive impulses.

I have wished only to point out the most general maxims of the methodology of moral cultivation and exercise. Since the diversity of duties requires special determination for each variety, and hence would be such a prolix affair, I shall be excused if, in a work like this, which is only preparatory, I content myself with these outlines.—Hartenstein, v. pp. 157–167.

II

In discussing "The Indwelling of the Bad Principles along with the Good ; or, The Radical Evil in Human Nature," in the first part of the philosophical theory of religion (1792), Kant observes :

. . . The moral culture of man must begin, not with the improvement of his morals, but with the transformation of his mode of thought and with the founding of a character ; although usually one proceeds differently, and fights singly against vices, but leaves their common root undisturbed. Now, even the most narrow-minded *Moral Culture Dependent on Mental Processes.* man is capable of the impression of all the greater respect for a dutiful action the more he withdraws from it in his thoughts other motives which could, through self-love, influence the maxim of the action ; and even children are capable of detecting even the slightest trace of a mixture of impure motives ; for then the action loses at once, in their eyes, all moral value. This capacity for good is cultivated incomparably, and gradually goes over into the mode of thought, by citing the *example* even of good men, and letting one's moral pupils judge the impurity of many maxims from the real motives of their actions ; so that *duty*, for duty's own sake, begins to gain noticeable weight in their hearts. But to teach children to *admire* virtuous actions, however much sacrifice they may have cost, is not the right disposition for the mind of the pupil to get towards the morally good. For however virtuous one may be, yet all the good which he can ever do is only duty ; but to do one's duty is nothing more than to do that which is in the usual moral order, consequently does not deserve to be admired. This admiration is rather a lowering of our feeling for duty, just as though it were something extraordinary and meritorious to obey it.—Hartenstein, vi. pp. 142, 143.

III

SECTION 97

Kant's interest in the problem of moral instruction continued with increasing vigor and clearness, as may be seen in the following selection from his last great work on ethical philosophy, being the major portion of the first section of the second part, " Ethical Methodology," of the *Metaphysical Elements of Ethics* (1797), Hartenstein, vii. pp. 289–297 :

Ethical Didactics

SECTION 49

That virtue must be acquired (is not innate) lies in the very nature of its concept, without there being any necessity to refer to anthropological knowledge derived from experience. For the moral faculty of men would not be virtue were it not produced by the *strength* of the resolution in the conflict with such powerful opposing inclinations. It is the product of pure practical reason, in so far as the latter, in the consciousness of its superiority, gains through freedom the upper hand over those inclinations.

Virtue is not Innate.

That virtue can and must be *taught* follows naturally from the fact that it is not innate ; thus the theory of virtue is a *doctrine*. But because power to carry out the rules is not acquired by means of the simple theory as to how one shall conduct himself in order to conform to the idea of virtue, the Stoics thought that virtue could not be *taught* by mere representation of duty, by admonitions, but that it must be culti-

Virtue a Product of Teaching.

vated, trained by attempts to withstand man's inner enemy (ascetically) ; that one *cannot* do at once everything he *wishes* to do, if he has not previously tried and trained his powers, to do which a *resolution* must be at once and fully made ; because otherwise the mind (*animus*), by capitulation to vice, in the hope of quitting it gradually, would be impure and vicious in itself, and therefore could produce no virtue (as virtue rests upon one single principle).

Section 50

As to the doctrinal method (for every scientific theory must be *methodical*, otherwise the exposition would be *tumultuous*), it must also not be *fragmentary*, but *systematic*, if the theory of virtue is to represent a *science*. However, the exposition may be either *acroamatic*, since all those to whom it is addressed are mere hearers, or *erotematic*, where the teacher asks his pupils questions about that which he wishes to teach them ; and, again, this erotematic method is either *dialogistical*, as when he puts questions to their *reason*, or *catechetical*, as when he merely puts questions to their *memory*. For when one examines the reason of another, it can be done in no other than a dialogistic way,—*i.e.*, when teacher and pupil *both* ask and answer questions. By questioning, the teacher guides his pupil's train of thought, in that he merely develops the disposition to certain concepts which it already contains, by means of cited instances (he is the midwife of his pupil's thoughts) ; the pupil, who thus becomes aware of the fact that he is able to think for himself, brings it about, by his counter-questions (about obscurity, or the doubt which opposes the granted principles), that the *teacher* himself, according to the *docendo discimus*, *learns* how best to question. (For it is a demand which concerns logic, and one not yet sufficiently taken to heart : that it furnish rules as to how one shall *seek* appropriately,—*i.e.*, not always merely for *determining*, but also for *preliminary* judgments (*judicia prævia*), which will be suggestive ; a theory which can serve even the mathematician as a cue to discoveries and which is often utilized by him.)

Methods of teaching Virtue.

Section 51

The first and most nêcessary *doctrinal* instrument of the theory of virtue for the raw pupil is a moral *catechism*. This must pre-
cede the religious catechism, and cannot be woven into the teachings of religion as a mere interpolation, but must be taught by itself, and as an independent whole ; for the transition from the theory of virtue to religion can be made only through purely moral principles, because otherwise religious creeds would be impure. Hence precisely the greatest and most worthy theologians have hesitated to draw up a catechism for that theory of religion required by state laws, and to vouch for it ; yet one would believe that this were the least which one were justified in expecting from the great treasure-house of their learning.

A Moral Catechism Most Important.

On the other hand, a *moral* catechism, as a foundation of the duties of virtue, meets with no such scruples or difficulties, be-
cause it can be developed from common human understanding (so far as its content is concerned) and must be adapted to the didactic rules of primary instruction (so far as the form is concerned). But the *Socratic-dialogistic* method does not vouchsafe the formal principle of such instruction for this purpose ; because the pupil does not know how to question ; the teacher is the only questioner. But the answer which he methodically entices from the pupil's reason must be couched and preserved, hence confided to his memory, in decided, not easily altered, expressions ; in which particular the *catechetical* method differs as well from the acroamatic (wherein the teacher speaks alone) as from the dialogistic (wherein both parties question and answer).

It is strictly Pedagogical.

Section 52.

The *experimental* (technical) means for the formation of virtue is the *good example*[1] in the teacher himself (to be of exemplary guid-

---

[1] *Beispiel* (example), a German word, which is usually employed synonymously with *Exempel* (example), is not really of the

ance) and the *warning* example in others ; for imitation is, in the yet uncultivated man, the first effort of will towards the adoption of maxims which he subsequently makes for him- self. The contracting of habits is the foundation of a persistent inclination without any maxims at all, by the frequent satisfaction of the inclination ; and it is a mechanism of the disposition rather than a principle of the mode of thinking, whereby *forgetting* becomes subsequently more difficult than *learning*. But as to the force of the *example* (be it for good or evil) which may be offered to our natural bent for imitation or for warning, that which others give us cannot found maxims of virtue. For these maxims consist precisely in the subjective autonomy of the practical reason of each individual ; therefore the law, and not the behavior of other men, must be our guiding principle. Hence the educator will not say to his demoral- ized pupil, "See the example that good (orderly, industrious) boy gives you !" for that would only cause him to hate the good boy, because he places *him* in a disadvantageous light. The good ex- ample (the exemplary conduct) is not to serve as a pattern, but only as a proof of the practicableness of that which duty demands ; thus it is not the comparison with some other man (as he is), but with the idea (of humanity) of what he should be, hence with the law, which must supply the teacher the never-failing standard of his instruction.

Ethical Value of the Teacher's Example.

---

same significance. To take an *Exempel* from something, and to cite a *Beispiel* in explanation of an expression, are two totally different concepts. An *Exempel* is a particular case of a *practical* rule, in so far as the latter represents the practicability or imprac- ticability of an action. A *Beispiel*, on the other hand, is only the particular (*concretum*), represented as contained in the general ac- cording to concepts (*abstractum*), and is hence only the theoretical representation of a concept. [A note by Kant].

Note

Fragment of a Moral Catechism

The teacher puts questions to his pupil's reason about that which he wishes to teach him, and when the pupil does not know how to answer the question, the teacher suggests the answer to him (guiding his reason).

Teacher.—What is your greatest, yes, your whole desire in life?

Pupil—(is silent).

Teacher.—That you may always have everything you wish for. What is such a condition called?

Pupil—(is silent).

Teacher.—It is called happiness (perpetual prosperity, joyous life, complete contentment with one's condition). Now, if you held in your hand all the happiness (which is possible in the world), would you keep it all for yourself, or would you divide it with your fellow-men?

Pupil.—I would divide it; make others happy and contented too.

Teacher.—That shows that you have a pretty good *heart;* but let us see whether you have a good *understanding* too. Would you provide a lazy man with soft pillows, so that he might spend his life in sweet idleness, or keep a drunkard supplied with wine and whatever else is necessary for intoxication, or give a cheat an agreeable form and manners with which to outwit others, or the violent man boldness and a strong fist, that he be able to overpower others? These are means which every one desires in order to be happy in his own way.

Pupil.—No, not that.

Teacher.—So you see that if you had all the happiness in your hand, and had the best intentions in the world, you would not hand it over to every one who wished to seize it, without consideration, but you would first try to find out how worthy of happiness each one was. But you would not hesitate first to supply yourself with everything you thought essential to your own happiness?

Pupil.—Yes. [No?]

Teacher.—But would it not occur to you to ask yourself whether you deserve to be happy or not?

Pupil.—To be sure.

Teacher.—That in you which strives for happiness is *inclination ;* but that which limits your inclination to the condition that you first be worthy of that happiness is your *reason*, and that through your reason you can limit and overcome your inclination, that is the freedom of your will. Now, for knowing how to go about having your share of happiness and yet not being unworthy of it, you have the rule and the instructions solely in your *reason ;* that is the same as saying that it is not necessary to learn this rule of your conduct from experience, or from other people ; your own reason teaches and enjoins upon you what you have to do. For example, when it happens that you can gain a great advantage for yourself or for your friends by a well-planned falsehood, and yet not harm any one else, what does your reason say to that?

Pupil.—I must not lie, no matter how great the advantage might be for me and my friend. Lying is base and makes a man unworthy to be happy. This is an unconditioned necessity through a command, or a prohibition, of reason, which I must obey ; in the face of which all my inclinations must be silent.

Teacher.—What do we call this necessity which is laid directly upon us by reason, to act according to its law?

Pupil.—It is called *duty.*

Teacher.—Hence the observance of his duty is the universal and sole condition of man's worthiness to be happy, and the two are one and the same thing. But even when we are conscious of such a good and active intention, through which we consider ourselves worthy (at least not unworthy) to be happy, can we found on this the firm hope of being happy?

Pupil.—No, not upon that alone ; for it is not always in our power to secure it, and the course of nature is not of itself directed according to merit, but the happiness of life (our well-being generally) depends upon circumstances which are by no means under man's control. So our happiness remains only a wish without ever becoming a hope, unless some other power is added to it.

Teacher.—Is reason justified in accepting such a power, which distributes happiness according to man's merits and shortcomings, controls all nature, and rules the world with the highest wisdon —*i.e.*, in believing in God?

Pupil.—Yes; for we see in the works of nature, which we can judge, such diffused and deep wisdom as we can explain to ourselves in no other way than as the unspeakably great art of a World-Creator, from whom, then, in that which concerns the moral order, in which the greatest ornament of the world consists, we are justified in expecting an equally wise rule,—namely, that when we do not make ourselves *unworthy of happiness*, which we do by not fulfilling our duty, we may hope to come in for our share of it.

In this catechism, which must be carried out through all the articles of virtue and of vice, the greatest attention must be directed to founding the law of duty, not upon the advantages or disadvantages which man will reap from its observance, but purely upon moral principle; and that these advantages or disadvantages be mentioned only incidentally, as in themselves dispensable additions, but which serve the palate of the naturally weak as mere vehicles. The *shamefulness*, not the *harmfulness* of vice (for the doer himself) must be ever prominently represented. For when the dignity of virtue in actions is not elevated above all else, the idea of duty itself disappears and dissolves into mere pragmatic precepts; for then man's nobility disappears from his own consciousness, and he is corruptible and for sale at the price which seductive inclinations offer him. Now, when this is developed wisely and at the proper time, from man's own reason according to the differences in age, in sex, and in social status, still there is something which must form the conclusion, which stirs the soul deeply, and sets man in a place where he cannot but regard himself with the greatest admiration for his own innate dispositions, the impression of which never disappears. Thus when, at the close of his instruction, his duties are once more summarized (recapitulated) in their order, when, in the case of each of them, he is reminded that all the evils, hardships, and sufferings of life, even the threat of death which may come to him

The Aim of the Catechism.

just because of his obedience to duty, cannot rob him of the consciousness that he is superior to and master of them all, the question arises at once : What is it within you which believes itself able to combat all the powers of nature in and around you, and to conquer them when they oppose your moral principles? When this question, whose solution entirely transcends the power of speculative reason, and which yet arises of itself, is laid to heart, the incomprehensibility in this self-knowledge must give the soul an exaltation which excites it the more strongly to the observance of its duties the more it is attacked.

In this catechetical moral instruction it would be of great value to moral education to raise some casuistic questions at each analysis of duty, and to let the assembled children test their understanding, how each one would think to solve the ensnaring problem given him. Not only because this is a culture of the *reason* best suited to the ability of an uninformed person (because reason can decide much easier in questions as to what duty is than in regard to speculative questions), and hence the most feasible way of sharpening the understanding of youth generally, but especially because it is man's nature to love that in the study of which he has acquired systematic knowledge (in which he is now well posted), and thus the pupil is, by such exercises as these, drawn unconsciously into the interest of morality.

Value of Casuistry.

But it is of the greatest importance in education not to mix the moral catechism with the religious catechism (to amalgamate them), much less to let the former follow the latter ; but rather always to make the former very clear, with the greatest industry and minuteness of detail. For, without this, religion will result in nothing but hypocrisy, making one acknowledge one's duties from fear, and pretend to sympathize with that which is not in one's heart.

XII

MORAL INSTRUCTION AND META-PHYSICS

In addition to the selections in the preceding group, the following from *The Metaphysics of Morals* (1797) clearly show Kant's conception of the independence of ethical principles of all anthropological considerations, and, in turn, the dependence of a true pedagogy of morals upon the constructions of a guiding metaphysics.

The counterpart of a metaphysics of morals, as the other portion of the division of practical philosophy in general, would be moral anthropology, which would contain only the subjective conditions, the favorable as well as the unfavorable, of the *realization* of the laws of the first part, in human nature, the creation, extension, and strengthening of moral principles (in the education of the school and public instruction), and other similar teachings and rules which are based on experience, and which are indispensable, but which absolutely must not be premised before metaphysics, or be mixed with it ; for otherwise one runs the danger of producing false, or at least indulgent moral laws, which represent as unattainable that which is not attained simply because the law is not intuited and set forth in its purity (in which also its strength consists), or entirely counterfeit or impure motives are employed for that which in itself is conformable to duty and good, and which leaves remaining no secure moral principles ; neither as a guide for criticism nor as a discipline of the mind in the pursuit of duty, whose rule must absolutely be given *a priori* only through pure reason.—Introduction, Hartenstein, vii. p. 14.

Moral Anthropology.

. . . All instruction in morals in lecture-halls, from the pulpit, and in popular books becomes ridiculous when it is dressed out with metaphysical odds and ends. But it is therefore not useless, much less ridiculous, to trace the basic principles of ethical theory in metaphysics ; for one must, as a philosopher, arrive at the principle of the concept of duty ; for otherwise neither certainty nor clearness for ethical theory is to be expected. To depend in this case upon a certain *feeling*, which is called *moral*, because of the effect expected from it, can indeed satisfy the popular teacher very well ; inasmuch as he desires, as a touchstone of moral duty, to reflect upon the problem : If every one in every case made your maxim a universal law, how could this maxim be consistent with itself? . . .

Metaphysics versus Popular Modes of Thought.

But, indeed, no moral principle is based, as is commonly supposed, on any *feeling*, but such a principle is really nothing else than the obscurely thought metaphysics which resides in the rational capacity of every man, as the teacher can easily assure himself who attempts to catechize *socratically* his pupil on the imperative of duty and its application to the moral judgment of his actions. Its exposition (the technique) need not always be metaphysical nor the language necessarily scholastic, if he does not wish to train his pupil to be a philosopher. But the *thought* must extend back to the elements of metaphysics, without which we are to expect no certainty and purity, yea, not even a motive power in ethical theory.

If one deviates from this principle . . . ethical theory becomes corrupted in its source, both in schools and lecture-halls, etc. However disgusting *metaphysics* may be to those supposed teachers of philosophy who speak *oracularly*, or like geniuses, about the theory of duty, yet for those who thus usurp the authority of a teacher it is an indispensable duty to carry their ethical principles back to it, and first of all to go to school on its benches.—Preface to Pt. II., Hartenstein, vii. pp. 178, 179.

XIII

CONSCIENCE

Conscience was to Kant a psychological token of the validity of his distinction between phenomenon and noumenon, between mechanism and freedom, between nature and reason. His further characterization of this faculty, which will throw light upon its treatment in the *Lecture-Notes*, is found in the following selections :

With this agree perfectly the judicial expressions of that wonderful power in us which we call conscience. . . . There are instances where men, from their early childhood, even with a bringing-up which was profitable to others, show wickedness so early, and continue to develop thus to maturity, that they are considered born rascals and, so far as their mode of thought is concerned, quite incorrigible ; but at the same time they are judged for that which they do or leave undone, their offences are censured as guilt, yes, they (the children) themselves regard these reproofs as well founded, as though they, in spite of the hopeless natural characteristics of mind attributed to them, were just as responsible as any other person. This could not occur if we did not presuppose that everything which arises from their choice (as, without doubt, every intentionally executed action does) is based upon a free causality, which from early youth expresses its character in its manifestations (the actions). . . . —*Critique of Practical Reason* (1788), Hartenstein, v. pp. 102, 104.

Conscience is not an acquisition, and there is no obligation to acquire it ; but every man, as an ethical being, has it originally in himself. To be bound in duty to conscience is as much as saying,

288

to have the duty to recognize duties. Conscience . . . is an unfailing fact, not an obligation and duty. . . . A lack of conscientiousness is not lack of conscience, but an inclination not to respect its judgments.—*The Metaphysical Elements of Ethics*, Introduction (1797), Hartenstein, vii. p. 204.

. . . The consciousness of an *inner tribunal* in man ("before which his thoughts accuse or justify one another") is *conscience*. . . .

This original intellectual and (since it is the idea of duty) moral capacity, called *conscience*, has this peculiarity, that although its business is a business of a man with himself, he is obliged by his reason to look upon it as carried on at the command *of another person*. For the transaction is here the conduct of a *law-case* (*causa*) before a judge. . . .

. . . So must conscience be thought of as the subjective principle of a responsibility for one's deeds before God, which has to be fulfilled.—*Ibid.*, vii. pp. 245, 246.

19

XIV

METHOD IN ÆSTHETIC INSTRUC-
TION

METHODOLOGY OF TASTE

THE division of a critique into elements and methodology, which precedes science, cannot be applied to the critique of taste, be-

A True Pedagogy of Æsthetics Impossible.

cause there is not, and cannot be, a science of the beautiful, and the judgment of taste is not determinable by principles. For what pertains to the scientific in every art which aims at *truth* in the exposition of its object, is, indeed, the indispensable condition (*conditio sine qua non*) of fine art, but not art itself. There is, therefore, for fine art only a *manner* (*modus*), not a *method of instruction* (*methodus*). The master must show the pupil what he should make and how he should make it ; and the universal rules, to which he finally reduces his method, can serve to recall upon occasion its chief moments rather than dictate them to the pupil. But then herewith reference must be made to a certain ideal, which art must have in mind, although it may never completely attain it in practice. Only by awakening the imagination of the pupil to conformity with a given concept, through the observed insufficiency of the expression for the idea, which the concept itself does not attain, because the idea is æsthetic, and by sharp criticism, can it be prevented that the examples which are placed before him be regarded by him forthwith as archetypes and even as models for imitation subjected to no yet higher norm and to his own criticism ; and so that genius be choked, and also with it the freedom of the imagination itself in its conformity to law, without which no fine art, yea, not even a taste rightly judging it, is possible.[1] . . .

. . . The true propædeutic for the founding of taste is the development of moral ideals and the culture of the moral feelings ; since only when sensibility is brought into agreement with this can genuine taste take on a definite unchangeable form.—*Critique of Judgment* (1790), Hartenstein, v. pp. 366–368.

---

[1] The omitted paragraph will be found translated in the Introduction, p. 88, in connection with intellectual education.

INDEX

INDEX

THE END